Eyewitnesses at Nuremberg

Eyewitnesses at Nuremberg

Hilary Gaskin

'I keep saying to myself, "This is history. You're living history."'
(court-room guard to Priscilla Belcher, Nuremberg, 1946)

ARMS AND
ARMOUR

To Jon Bate and in memory of Ron Chapman

First published
in Great Britain in 1990
by Arms and Armour Press, Villiers House,
41–47 Strand, London WC2N 5JE.

Distributed in the USA
by Sterling Publishing Co. Inc., 387 Park
Avenue South, New York, NY 10016–8810.

Distributed in Australia
by Capricorn Link (Australia) Pty. Ltd,
P.O. Box 665, Lane Cove, New South Wales
2066, Australia.

British Library Cataloguing in Publication Data
Gaskin, Hilary
Eyewitnesses at Nuremberg.
1. West Germany. Nuremberg. German
War Criminals. Trials, history
341.69
ISBN 1-85409-058-5

Designed and edited by DAG Publications Ltd.
Designed by David Gibbons; edited by Michael
Boxall; layout by Anthony A. Evans; typeset
by Saxon Printing Ltd, Derby; camerawork by M&E
Reproductions, North Fambridge, Essex;
printed and bound in Great Britain by
Butler & Tanner Ltd, Frome and London.

*Jacket illustration: Paul Graven (black helmet, flanked by
two 'snowdrops') visits the court-room to check on the
guards.*

THE
SCARBOROUGH
PUBLIC LIBRARY
BOARD

Contents

Acknowledgments

Many people have given unstinting help towards the preparation of this book. Firstly I must thank its twenty-four participants, who welcomed me to their homes, racked their memories on my behalf, and entered into unflagging correspondence afterwards over details that remained to be cleared up. Without these people there would be no book, and it is for them to judge whether I have managed to produce something that does justice to their experience.

Others have helped along the way with contacts, suggestions and advice. Among these, I am particularly indebted to Christopher Ridgway, Jonathan Steinberg, Drexel Sprecher, the staffs of Reuters, the Public Record Office and the Imperial War Museum, in particular the Department of Sound Records, Mark Jones, Tony Trebble and Gwyniver Jones of the BBC, Lieutenant-Colonel George Truell, Lieutenant-Colonel R.A. Costain, Priscilla Jones, John Harding, Frank Gillard, Robert Flach, Fritz Hellendal, Neal Ascherson, Richard Luckett, Jay Winter, Cathrin Boerckel, Edward Moss and Bradley Smith.

I am indebted to this book's participants (particularly Eddie Worth, Associated Press) for permission to reproduce photographs in their possession. 'The Nuremberg Trial, 1946' by Dame Laura Knight is reproduced by permission of the Imperial War Museum.

Lastly I should like to thank my husband, whose judgement, advice and constant encouragement have sustained me throughout.

The participants in this book

Roger Barrett, officer in charge of documents

Priscilla Belcher, visitor to the trial

Hume Boggis-Rolfe, visitor to the trial

Brady Bryson, lawyer

Mary Burns, secretary

Anna Cameron (née Reagan), secretary

Ron Chapman, clerk

Patrick Cooper, airman stationed in Nuremberg

Sylvia, Countess De La Warr (formerly Lady Maxwell-Fyfe), visitor to the trial

Paul Graven, prison guard officer

Whitney Harris, lawyer

Daniel Margolies, lawyer

Seaghan Maynes, journalist

Bernard Meltzer, lawyer

John Pine, visitor to the trial

Dorothy Reilly (née Owens), secretary

Alfred Steer, administrative head, language division

Joseph Stone, lawyer, Subsequent Proceedings

Annabel Stover (née Grover), secretary

Jean Tull (née Tuck), secretary

Peter Uiberall, interpreter

Leonard ('Andy') Wheeler, lawyer

Yvette, Lady Wilberforce (née Lenoan), visitor to the trial

Eddie Worth, photographer

The defendants: a court-room guide

These biographies of the defendants and the diagram that follows them are taken from a handout given to all visitors to the court-room. The wording of the handout is reproduced in a form as close as possible to the original, save that obvious errors have been corrected.

GOERING, Hermann Wilhelm
Successor designated to Hitler, Sept. 1939
Member of the Reichstag, 1928–
President of Prussian State Council, 1933–
President of the Reichstag, 1933–
Prime Minister of Prussia and Commander-in-Chief of the Prussian Police, 1933–
Reich Minister for Air, 1933–
Commander-in-Chief of the Luftwaffe, 1935–
Trustee for the Four Year Plan, October 1936–
Reichsmarschall, 1940
Chairman of Ministerial Defence Council
Reich Hunting and Forest Master
SS General
SA General

HESS, Rudolf
Deputy Führer for all Party affairs until 1941
Successor Designate II of the Führer, 1939–41

RIBBENTROP, Joachim von
Party Delegate for Questions of Foreign Policy
Reich Foreign Minister, Feb. 1938–
Member of Secret Cabinet Council
Member of Reichstag
SS Brigadier-General

ROSENBERG, Alfred
Reichsleiter for Ideology and Foreign Policy, 1933–
Reich Minister for the Occupied Eastern Territories, 1941–
Member of the Reichstag
SA General
Publisher of NS monthly periodical
Born 1893, Reval; of German Baltic extraction; studied architecture; did not participate in fighting in 1914–18; in 1918 in Paris; rumoured to have been a spy; continued studies in Munich; joined Nazi Party; first editor of *Völkischer Beobachter* 1921; participated in 1923 putsch; since then always one of the most prominent Nazi leaders; 1933 Hitler's private envoy in London; 1941 Reich Minister for Occupied Eastern Territories; has been the official Party 'philosopher'; his book *Mythos des 20. Jahrhunderts* ranks in party literature second to Hitler's *Mein Kampf*; was also responsible for the introduction of the crudest form of anti-Semitism into Germany and the Nazi Party.

FRANK, Hans
Governor-General of Poland, 1939–

Reich Minister without Portfolio
Member of the Reichstag
SS General
Chief of Party Lawyers Organization,
  1933–42
President of International Chamber of
  Law and Academy of German Law,
  1933–42
Born 1900; father was a barrister and
  struck off register for corruption;
  studied law; one of leading Party
  lawyers before 1933; in 1933
  Bavarian Minister of Justice; until
  summer 1942 leader of NRSB, and
  head of Party law division
  succeeded by Thierach; 1939–45
  Governor-General of Poland.

KALTENBRUNNER, Ernst
Chief of Reich Security Department,
  Jan. 1934
Chief of Criminal Police, Div. V,
  Reichsicherheitshauptamt 1941–
Member of the Reichstag
General of the Police
SS General
Born 1903, Ried (Austria); elementary
  school; law studies in Graz; 1926
  Dr; 1933 Gauradner [sic] and legal
  adviser to the SS, in Austria; 1933–
  4 commander of SS-Standarte 37
  and later of the whole SS, in
  Austria; 1934 took part in Dollfuss
  putsch and was imprisoned in
  Wollersdorf detention camp for 4½
  months; later 1 year in prison;
  March 1938 Commander of SS-
  Abschnitt Ostmark; Staatssekretär
  for security in the Seyss-Inquart
  government; SS-Brigadeführer;
  1941 Lieutenant-General of Police;
  Jan. 1943 Chief of RSHA; 1944 War
  Merit Cross with Swords; Jan. 1945
  reported Chief of Amt V.

FRICK, Wilhelm
Reichsleiter
Head of Nazi Parliamentary Group in
  Reichstag, Reich Minister of
  Interior, 1933 Member Ministerial
  Council, 1939–43

Reich Protector in Bohemia and
  Moravia Aug. 1943–
Member of Secret Cabinet Council
SS General
Born 1887, Alsenz, Pfalz; father a
  teacher; law studies at Göttingen,
  Berlin, Heidelberg universities;
  since 1900 in state administrative
  service; 1904–24 with Munich
  Police; no war service; after 1919
  early sympathizer with Nazi Party;
  helped 'Feme' murderers (Freikorps
  members) to escape capture; took
  part in 1923 putsch; 1930–1
  Minister in Thuringian (first
  German Nazi) government, in
  charge of education; 30 Jan. 1933
  Reich Minister of the Interior; 1939
  member of the Ministerial Defence
  Council; succeeded by Himmler
  Aug. 1943; since then Reich
  Protector.

STREICHER, Julius
Gauleiter of Franconia, 1933–6
Editor of *Der Stürmer*; notorious
  anti-Semite; member of the
  Reichstag; schoolmaster by
  profession; honorary leader of SA

KEITEL, Wilhelm
Field Marshal and Chief of
  Oberkommando der Wehrmacht
Born 1882, Helmscherode
  (Braunschweig); 1901 Fahnrich;
  1914–18 Adjutant and staff
  appointments; 1919 member of a
  Freikorps; 1920–5 military school
  and regimental appointments; 1925
  Reichswehr Ministry; 1929 head of
  Army Organization Dept.; 1931
  Oberst; 1934 General-Major; 1935
  Wehrmachtamt; 1938 appointed as
  above; Nov. 1938 Generaloberst;
  July 1940 General-feldmarschall;
  1940 Knight's Cross; conducted
  French armistice negotiations at
  Compiègne; one of the pro-Hitler
  generals.

FUNK, Walther, Dr

Vice-President of the Reich Chamber
of Culture
Secretary of State in Propaganda
Ministry, 1933–7
Reich Minister of Economics, 1937
President of the Reichsbank, 1939
Member of the Ministerial Defence
Council
Born 1890, Trakennen (Ostpreussen);
studied law, economics,
philosophy, literature, music at
Berlin and Leipzig; 1912 journalist;
1916 on staff of *Berliner
Börsenzeitung*; 1921–30 chief
editor of same; joined Nazis and
became economic adviser to Hitler;
1932 Mdr.; 1933 Press Chief of the
Reich Government and
Staatssekretär in Ministry of
Propaganda; helped Goebbels in
creating Chamber of Culture; Nov.
1937 succeeded Schacht as Reich
Minister of Economics; 1939
succeeded Schacht also in
presidency of Reichsbank; unlike
most other Nazi leaders, was not a
failure before starting his Party
career; had no economic
programme of his own, but was
largely an opportunist; most of the
war-important responsibilities of
his Ministry were given to Speer in
1944; since then, may have lost his
seat on the Ministerium;
directorships included
Golddiskentbank, Continentale Ol,
AG.

SCHACHT, Hjalmar
Reich Minister of Economics 1933–6
Commissioner of Four Year Plan,
1936
Reich Minister without Portfolio,
1936–9
President of the Reichsbank until
1939
Born 1877, Tingleff (Schleswig); was a
journalist in Berlin; joined the staff
of a propaganda office of the
German export industry; 1903 head
of economic archives of the

Dresdnerbank; 1908 Deputy
Director of same bank; 1914–18
financial adviser of the Banking
Section of the German General
Govt. in Belgium; 1916 having left
the Dresdnerbank joined the staff of
the Nationalbank für Deutschland;
1918 joined the Democratic Party;
Nov. 1923 was appointed Currency
Commissioner and President of the
Reichsbank; 1930 came into
contact with Hitler and made
financial resources available to him;
was again President of the
Reichsbank under Hitler and in
1936 became Economic Director of
the Third Reich; was first
commissioner of the Four Year
Plan, but succeeded by Goering in
1936, thus losing the position as
Minister of Economics; Nov. 1937
reinstated as Minister of
Economics; Jan. 1939 removed
from Presidency of Reichsbank;
1943 was reported to have been
expelled from the Nazi Party; his
arrest was reported in autumn 1944,
but he was subsequently supposed
to have been released; in Jan. 1945
he was again said to be in prison in
Berlin.

DOENITZ, Karl
Commander-in-Chief Navy
Commander-in-Chief U-Boats
Chancellor, May 1945
Born 1891, Grunar (near Berlin);
1910 joined Navy; 1914 transferred
to Naval Air Arm; became flight-
observer, later seaplane squadron
leader; 1916–18 U-Boat Service;
taken prisoner; 1919 taken over by
new German Navy; 1929
commanded cruiser *Emden*; 1932
on staff of the Naval Station North
Sea; 1935 Kapitän zur See and Cdr.
of U-Boats; 1939 Konteradmiral;
1940 Vice-Admiral; 1942 Admiral;
1943 Gross-Admiral; since Jan. 1943
command as above; April 1940

Knight's Cross; April 1943 Oak
Leaves to the Knight's Cross.

SCHIRACH, Baldur von
Chief of Reich Youth, 1932
Gauleiter, Vienna
Member of the Reichstag, 1932
Reichsstadthalter of Vienna
Reich Defence Commissioner
Hitler Youth Leader, 1932
President of Friends of the German
  Academy
Born 1907, Weimar; son of theatrical
  director; was educated at Weimar
  and there heard Hitler speak; 1925
  joined the NSDAP while studying
  at Munich University; 1927
  appointed leader of NS, Students'
  Union; 1932 became a member of
  the Reichstag and National Leader
  of the German Youth; May 1933
  was named Leader of the Youth of
  the German Reich; wrote verses,
  songs and books for the Movement

SAUCKEL, Fritz
Gauleiter of Thüringen 1927
Reichsstaatshalter of Thüringen, 1933
Plenipotentiary-General for
  Manpower, March 1942
Reich Defence Commissioner

SPEER, Albert
Reichsleiter
Head of Party Technical Affairs Office
Building Inspector for Party Rallies,
  1933
Building Inspector for Berlin, 1937
Reich Minister for Armament and
  War Production, Feb. 1943
Plenipotentiary for Building, Electric
  and Water Power
Chief Ruhr War Damage Repair
  Commission
Chief of Organization Todt, Feb. 1942
President Reich Research Council

PAPEN, Franz von
Vice-Chancellor, 1933–4
Ambassador to Austria, 1934–8

Ambassador to Turkey, to 1944
Born 1879

JODL, Alfred
Chief of Staff (Operational)
High Command of the Wehrmacht,
  1942

NEURATH, Constantin von
Reich Minister of Foreign Affairs,
  1932–8
President of Secret Cabinet Council,
  1938
Reich Protector of Bohemia and
  Moravia, 1939–41
Member of the Reichstag
SS General, 1943
Member of the Academy for German
  Law

SEYSS-INQUART, Dr Arthur
Reich Minister of Interior and
  Security, 1938–9
Reichsstaathalter Ostmark, 1939–40
Reich Commissioner for Occupied
  Netherlands, 1940
Reich Minister without Portfolio,
  1940
SS General
President of the German Academy

RAEDER, Erich
Admiral Inspector of German Navy,
  1943
Commander-in-Chief of German
  Navy, 1928–43

FRITZSCHE, Hans
Ministerialdirektor, Reich Ministry of
  Propaganda
Bevollmächtigter für die Politische
  Gestaltung des grossdeutschen
  Rundfunks (Plenipotentiary for the
  political supervision of
  broadcasting in Greater Germany)
Head of broadcasting division in
  Propaganda Ministry

Floor-plan of the court-room

1 Goering
2 Hess
3 Ribbentrop
4 Keitel
5 Rosenberg
6 Frank
7 Frick
8 Streicher
9 Funk
10 Schacht
11 Doenitz
12 Raeder
13 Von Schirach
14 Sauckel
15 Jodl
16 Von Papen
17 Seyss-Inquart
18 Speer
19 Von Neurath
20 Fritzsche
21 Interpreters
22 Defence
counsel
23 Marshal of the
Court
24 Witness-stand
25 Speaker's stand
26 Court recorders
27 Secretaries to
the court, etc.
28 Lt.-Col.
Volchkov,
Russian
alternate judge
29 Maj. Gen.
Nikitchenko,
Russian judge
30 Sir Norman
Birkett, British
alternate judge
31 Sir Geoffrey
Lawrence,
British judge
32 Atty. Gen.
Biddle,
American judge

33 Judge Parker,
American
alternate judge
34 Prof.
Donnedieu de
Vabres, French
judge
35 M. Falco,
French
alternate judge

36 Prosecutors'
desk
37 British
prosecutors
38 American
prosecutors
39 Russian
prosecutors
40 French
prosecutors

41 Seats for
distinguished
visitors

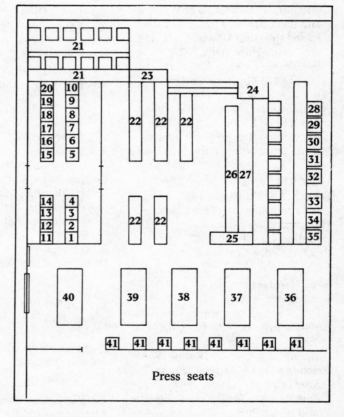

The Nuremberg Trial: defendants, convictions and sentences

Defendant	Count 1	Count 2	Count 3	Count 4	Sentence
Martin Bormann	not guilty	not charged	guilty	guilty	death
Karl Doenitz	not guilty	guilty	guilty	not charged	10 years
Hans Frank	not guilty	not charged	guilty	guilty	death
Wilhelm Frick	not guilty	guilty	guilty	guilty	death
Hans Fritzsche	not guilty	not charged	not guilty	not guilty	acquitted
Walther Funk	not guilty	guilty	guilty	guilty	life imprisonment
Hermann Goering	guilty	guilty	guilty	guilty	death
Rudolf Hess	guilty	guilty	not guilty	not guilty	life imprisonment
Alfred Jodl	guilty	guilty	guilty	guilty	death
Ernst Kaltenbrunner	not guilty	not charged	guilty	guilty	death
Willhelm Keitel	guilty	guilty	guilty	guilty	death
Erich Raeder	guilty	guilty	guilty	not charged	life imprisonment
Alfred Rosenberg	guilty	guilty	guilty	guilty	death
Fritz Sauckel	not guilty	not guilty	guilty	guilty	death
Hjalmar Schacht	not guilty	not guilty	not charged	not charged	acquitted
Arthur Seyss-Inquart	not guilty	guilty	guilty	guilty	death
Albert Speer	not guilty	not guilty	guilty	guilty	20 years
Julius Streicher	not guilty	not charged	not charged	guilty	death
Constantin von Neurath	guilty	guilty	guilty	guilty	15 years
Franz von Papen	not guilty	not guilty	not charged	not charged	acquitted
Baldur von Schirach	not guilty	not charged	not charged	guilty	20 years

Introduction

Eyewitnesses to a great event look at it through many different lenses. In 1203, when Constantinople fell during the Fourth Crusade, two eyewitnesses, Geoffroy de Villehardouin and Robert de Clari, left behind their accounts of what happened. Geoffroy de Villehardouin, a French nobleman and sometime Marshal of the province of Champagne, was a skilled statesman, diplomat and negotiator who, during his participation in the Fourth Crusade, was on familiar terms with many of its leading figures and involved in some of the decisions that they made. He had a lively desire to analyse and explain the events that he saw, and a high conception of his military, political and religious duty. Robert de Clari, by contrast, was an unlettered common soldier who followed his lord to the Holy Land, and who was much preoccupied by the details of army life, the excitement of battle and the dazzling sights that met him in Constantinople. This contrast in viewpoint is immensely enriching: the two eyewitnesses often noticed quite different things about the same event, and their accounts are both invaluable.

Seven hundred years later, just after the Second World War, the four victorious Allied powers, Britain, the United States, France and Russia, met in Nuremberg, in Germany, to try those Nazis whom they had designated major war criminals. Many of the leading figures in this momentous proceeding have published their diaries, memoirs and autobiographies; there is also, of course, a considerable volume of purely legal writing on the subject. But there were many people at that trial who found themselves there quite by chance, and who formed part of the enormous network of effort that was needed to ensure that everything ran smoothly. After it was over they went back to their old lives. The twenty-four people, both British and American, whose reminiscences form this book are people of that kind. With the exception of one or two lawyers in the group they have not written anything – or even, in some cases, spoken very much – about Nuremberg and their experiences there. They arrived at Nuremberg by varied routes, and contributed their skills to the running of the trial; in one or two cases they worked elsewhere in occupied Germany and attended the trial as visitors. The impressions that they took away with them are sometimes similar, sometimes widely different, and include many things not to be found in official histories of the trial. In this book they talk about the circumstances that brought them to Nuremberg, the work that they did there, their memories of the court-room, their life in Nuremberg, and their feelings about the whole experience and the part that it played in their lives.

The Nuremberg Trial of German Major War Criminals, also known as the International Military Tribunal, opened, after months of discussion and preparation, on Tuesday 20 November 1945, in the court-room of the Palace of Justice in Nuremberg. It was to last for nearly a year: the Tribunal announced the verdicts and sentences on Tuesday 1 October 1946. Present in the dock, and on trial for their lives, were Karl Doenitz, Supreme Commander of the German Navy; Hans Frank, Governor-General of Poland; Wilhelm Frick, Reich Minister of the Interior and Protector of Bohemia and Moravia; Hans Fritzsche, an official in the Reich Ministry of Propaganda; Walther Funk, President of the Reichsbank; Hermann Goering, Chairman of the Reich Council for National Defence and Commander of the Luftwaffe; Rudolf Hess, Deputy Leader of the Nazi Party; Alfred Jodl, Chief of the Wehrmacht Operations Staff; Wilhelm Keitel, Chief of Staff of the Wehrmacht; Constantin von Neurath, former Protector of Bohemia and Moravia and Minister without Portfolio; Franz von Papen, former Chancellor of Germany and Ambassador to Turkey; Erich Raeder, former Commander-in-Chief of the German Navy; Joachim von Ribbentrop, Foreign Minister; Alfred Rosenberg, Minister for the Occupied Eastern Territories; Fritz Sauckel, Plenipotentiary for Labour Mobilization; Hjalmar Schacht, former Minister of Economics and President of the Reichsbank; Baldur von Schirach, Reich Youth Leader; Arthur Seyss-Inquart, Reich Commissioner in the Netherlands; Albert Speer, Minister of Armaments and War Production; and Julius Streicher, former Gauleiter of Franconia and founder and editor of *Der Stürmer*, a rabidly anti-Semitic newspaper. Martin Bormann, head of the Party Chancellery, was tried and sentenced to death *in absentia*, and Robert Ley, Director of the Labour Front, hanged himself in his cell on 29 October, before the trial started. Ernst Kaltenbrunner, head of the Reich Security Office, was not present at the opening of the trial because he had suffered a stroke; he arrived later. Hitler had, of course, forestalled the trial by committing suicide, as had Heinrich Himmler, head of the SS, and Josef Goebbels, head of the Reich Ministry of Propaganda.

No event quite like the Nuremberg Trial had been known before. After the First World War there had been moves to put the Kaiser and various German officials and military leaders on trial, but the Allied nations encountered fierce German resistance against which they were unable to put through a coherent and determined plan of action, and when some trials of sorts eventually opened in Germany in 1921 (they were held by the Germans themselves) only a handful of the defendants received prison sentences (all of them short ones). Experience of this fiasco, however, helped to concentrate people's minds the next time the situation arose; and during the troubled inter-war years there had also been developments such as the Kellogg-Briand Pact of 1928, in which sixty-three nations (including Germany) renounced war as an instrument of national policy. Although events in the decade which followed might suggest that this pact was nothing more than a general declaration which signatory nations could (and did) break with impunity, it was there on paper and the Axis leaders could not claim to be ignorant of it.

The defendants at the Nuremberg Trial were each charged on one or more of four counts: count one, the Common Plan or Conspiracy; count two, Crimes against Peace (the planning and waging of aggressive war); count three, War Crimes (such as the shooting of prisoners of war); and count four, Crimes against Humanity (such as the persecution of the Jews and the destruction and exploitation of occupied countries). The Common Plan was defined in the opening Statement of Offence: 'All the defendants, with divers other persons, during a period of years preceding 8th May, 1945, participated as leaders, organisers, instigators or accomplices in the formulation or execution of a common plan or conspiracy to commit, or which involved the commission of, Crimes against Peace, War Crimes, and Crimes against Humanity ... and are individually responsible for their own acts and for all acts committed by any persons in the execution of such plan or conspiracy.' The Americans handled this count of Conspiracy, and also the prosecution of what had been designated criminal organizations, such as the SS. The British handled the second count, while the Russians and the French dealt with the third and fourth counts for Eastern and Western Europe respectively.

Goering was convicted on all four counts, as were von Ribbentrop, Keitel, Rosenberg and Jodl. With the exception of Goering, who committed suicide in his cell by swallowing a cyanide capsule a few hours before he was due to be executed, they were all hanged (see table on p. xii). Von Neurath was also found guilty on all four counts but, in recognition of the lesser severity of his crimes, was only sentenced to fifteen years' imprisonment. Kaltenbrunner, Frank, Frick, Streicher, Sauckel, Seyss-Inquart and the absent Bormann were found guilty on sufficient counts to be sentenced to death by hanging. Raeder was found guilty on all the counts on which he was charged and was sentenced to life imprisonment. Hess was found guilty on counts one and two but innocent on counts three and four, and Speer vice versa; Hess was sentenced to life imprisonment and Speer to twenty years. Funk, Doenitz and von Schirach were also found guilty on some counts and innocent on others, and were given sentences ranging from ten years to life imprisonment. Schacht, von Papen and Fritzsche were acquitted.

The defendants were prosecuted by teams of lawyers from the four Allied powers, and were given the chance to choose their own defence counsel. They hired German lawyers, including Nazis. There were eight judges: Francis Biddle (United States), Sir Geoffrey Lawrence (Britain), Professor Henri Donnedieu de Vabres (France) and Major-General I.T. Nikitchenko (Russia), and their alternates, Judge John Parker, Sir

Norman Birkett, Robert Falco and Lieutenant-Colonel A.F. Volchkov. The four chief prosecutors were Justice Robert Jackson (United States), Sir Hartley Shawcross (Britain), M. François de Menthon (France) and General Roman Rudenko (Russia). In practice, Sir Hartley Shawcross did not spend much time at the trial, on account of his duties at home as Attorney-General, and Sir David Maxwell-Fyfe shouldered much of the responsibility for directing the British team. The prosecution teams were backed up by four Allied delegations of researchers, interpreters, translators and clerical staff, who worked in offices in the court-house and were billeted in various requisitioned houses in and around Nuremberg. The Grand Hotel also plays an important part in many Nuremberg reminiscences: some of the lawyers stayed there, people ate there, and many were dependent on its Marble Room for much of their entertainment.

When the Allies occupied Germany, they divided it into four zones; Nuremberg, where the trial was held, was in the American zone. It is important to remember that while this trial of German Major War Criminals was being held, other smaller trials were going on all the time – and went on for years afterwards – in military courts in the other zones and in Japan, China and the Soviet Union. Then, after the main trial was over, General Telford Taylor succeeded Justice Jackson as head of the American team, new lawyers and judges came out to Nuremberg, and over the next two and a half years more people, including army leaders, industrialists and concentration camp doctors, were prosecuted in what were known as Subsequent Proceedings (see table on p.187). A powerful sense of the historical and legal momentousness of the trial is conveyed by the words spoken by Justice Jackson when he rose to open the case for the prosecution on 21 November 1945:

> The privilege of opening the first trial in history for crimes against the peace of the world imposes a grave responsibility. The wrongs which we seek to condemn and punish have been so calculated, so malignant and so devastating, that civilisation cannot tolerate their being ignored, because it cannot survive their being repeated. That four great nations, flushed with victory and stung with injury, stay the hands of vengeance and voluntarily submit their captive enemies to the judgment of the law, is one of the most significant tributes that Power ever has paid to Reason.

Jackson went on to stress the symbolic nature of the trial. What was being brought to account was not just the defendants but what they stood for:

> In the prisoners' dock sit twenty-odd broken men. Reproached by the humiliation of those they have led, almost as bitterly as by the desolation of those they have attacked, their personal capacity for evil is forever past. It is hard now to perceive in these miserable men as captives the power by which as Nazi leaders they once dominated much of the world and terrified most of it. Merely as individuals their fate is of little consequence to the world.
>
> What makes this inquest significant is that these prisoners represent sinister influences that will lurk in the world long after their bodies have returned to

dust. We will show them to be living symbols of racial hatreds, of terrorism and violence, and of the arrogance and cruelty of power. They are symbols of fierce nationalisms and of militarism, of intrigue and war-making which have embroiled Europe generation after generation, crushing its manhood, destroying its homes, and impoverishing its life.

Many of the reminiscences collected in this book develop the themes outlined here by Jackson: the broken nature of the men in the dock and the difficulty of conceiving of them as the ruthless driving force of the Nazi machine; the sense of the trial as an example for the future, an admonitory recording of perennial evils. Jackson's reference to 'the humiliation of those they have led' is also suggestive: the decision to hold the trial in Germany rather than in some neutral arena meant that the humiliated German people were an ambient presence throughout the proceedings. The participants in this book have much to say about the city and people of Nuremberg, as well as about the trial itself. Nuremberg, a stronghold of Nazism and site of Hitler's most potent rallies, then a victim of devastating Allied bombing, was as powerful a symbol as the court-room.

For several reasons, the selection of participants for a book like this has to be somewhat arbitrary. Many methods were used to find them, from consultation of documents to the following up of chance remarks, but I am aware that there remains a large number of ex-Nuremberg people whom even these methods could not reach. Several major problems are involved here. Firstly, the further one travels down the hierarchy, towards the jobs which did not capture the headlines, the more difficult it is to find people: lawyers and the like often appear in *Who's Who* and similar publications, while clerks tend to have been erased from the record. Secondly, although this was a military tribunal, it was staffed to a large extent by civilian personnel who were drafted in because of their various skills, who had a temporary military ranking, and who did not stay in the armed forces after the trial was over; consequently military records are of limited use in tracing them. Thirdly, people at the Nuremberg Trial – particularly if one travels down the hierarchy – tended to be young; the result of this, where women are concerned, is that many of them have changed their names in the intervening years.

These problems notwithstanding, the participants gathered together in this book represent a substantial cross-section of activity at Nuremberg. There are lawyers, interpreters, secretaries, a journalist, a clerk, a photographer, a guard, an airman, the wife of one of the British prosecutors, and various visitors who sat in the gallery. One or two of these people could be said to represent the context of the trial rather than the trial itself: Paul Graven guarded the prisoners, and Patrick Cooper was part of the army of occupation and was never inside the court-room; John Pine was a prosecutor at British trials elsewhere in Germany, and visited Nuremberg to see what the main trial was like; Hume Boggis-Rolfe, another visitor, worked for the Allied Control Commission in

Berlin, which effectively 'ran' Germany since defeat had caused its vital administrative structures to disintegrate. They and all the others illustrate the scale of the Allied effort in post-war Germany; Joseph Stone, a lawyer at the Subsequent Proceedings, is included to illustrate its continuance after the main trial was over. In their reminiscences the participants invoke a whole host of other characters of many nationalities, and remember the exhilaration of meeting and working with people from other countries; the Americans, in particular, often inadvertently point up the strikingly cosmopolitan nature of their own society in the process.

Various as the participants are in many ways, something which is common to all their narratives is their content of 'ordinariness': the accumulation of detail about the way they worked, travelled, ate, socialized, coped with often primitive facilities in a devastated city, and generally sought to achieve a routine and a normal life under conditions which could be anything but normal. To present only the exciting and dramatic incidents that they remember – the outbursts in the witness-box, the shooting at the Grand Hotel, the night of the executions – would be to distort both the actual nature of the trial, which was gradual, slow-paced and often tedious, and the picture of Nuremberg as they knew it. The variety in their accounts occasionally brings disparity. It should be remembered that memories can be fallible, that the passage of time can distort recollections and change perspectives, and that individual participants tended to have a necessarily partial perception of what was going on; a reader looking for an 'edited' history of the trial, with divergences and inaccuracies ironed out, will not find it in this book. What is contained in these pages becomes, in the end, a meditation on the way in which one event can be distilled through many different consciousnesses, seen through many different lenses. Ron Chapman, who was a very young corporal working as a clerk in the British administrative section, was exhilarated by the experience, and by the material comforts of life in the American zone; his mainly descriptive and anecdotal reminiscences are characterized by omnivorous powers of observation and recall. By contrast, Daniel Margolies' reminiscences, while not lacking in anecdotes, carry the stamp of a lawyer's mind: to a much greater extent than Ron Chapman he looked at Nuremberg through the lens of his work. Priscilla Belcher transmits a view of Nuremberg that was marked by a degree of personal suffering. Alfred Steer knew Germany well, having studied there during the 1930s, and was passionately opposed to Nazism. Peter Uiberall was a Jewish refugee returning to Europe. And so it goes on.

With a cross-section of memories goes a cross-section of attitudes. In the final chapter of this book, the participants reflect on the Nuremberg Trial itself and on war crimes trials today. There were many people at Nuremberg who found that what they saw and heard in the court-room and encountered in their daily lives gave them much to ponder over. All seem to be agreed on Goering's domination of the court-room, and on the extraordinary contrast between the charisma of evil in his case and its utter insignificance and banality as manifested in many of the other defendants. There were other contrasts to be observed. 'In that ruined city death and destruction are ever present. They had to come into the picture,' said Dame Laura Knight after completing her oil painting 'The Nuremberg Trial, 1946', in which a study of the defendants in the dock gradually merges, in the top left-hand corner of the canvas, into an image of the bombed city. The contrast between the order of the court-room and the chaos and rubble of Nuremberg – not to mention the rest of Germany, and Europe – caused many who were there to reflect painfully on war and its victims, and a sense of irremovable and troubling complexities runs like a thread through many of the reminiscences gathered here. Undoubtedly there were also people at Nuremberg who, for various reasons, did not reflect very deeply upon the trial and the issues which it raised. Any study seeking to give a full and rounded impression of Nuremberg must confront this difference head on. It may be tempting, but it is not productive, to take the view that because the Nuremberg Trial is an important and serious issue we should erase from the record the memories and views of those who never thought about it because they were just doing a job or concentrating on having a good time; in so doing, indeed, we may actually do a disservice to our assimilation of the lessons of Nuremberg. For it is only by acknowledging the fact that not everybody 'on our side' reflects upon a given event as we would like them to that we can find a way in to an understanding of the concept – a very resonant one in this context – of unreflective action on the other side, a concept which was documented and exposed with such shattering effect at Nuremberg.

Such contrasts are part of the enormous variety of Nuremberg experience which this book seeks to illustrate. The record of the trial has hitherto lacked a substantial body of views 'from the ranks' to set beside the views 'from the top' and the published histories, although many accounts of this type, on other subjects, have emerged from the two World Wars. The immense value and importance, to the historical record, of accounts like the following, the reason for gathering them together, lies in what they can teach us about ourselves and our relationship to history. The fact that so many ordinary people were drawn into the Nuremberg Trial, and lived through it in so many different ways, serves to remind us that a great historical event must not be regarded as something being played out on a stage by larger-than-life figures, in a time and a place quite separate from our own experience. The Nuremberg Trial involves us all, and the participants' involvement provides a clear illustration of this inescapable fact, regardless of whether they, or we, would choose to acknowledge the importance of the trial on an intellectual level. The following accounts, which are left largely to speak for themselves, come from a disparate group of people who found that they were eyewitnesses at Nuremberg. This book is their testimony.

1. Routes to Nuremberg

Alfred Steer, administrative head, language division
I had been in command of a number of small ships in the Western Pacific, and I had decommissioned the last one, USS *Roper*, APD20, in Mare Island, California and had been out of contact with the situation in the United States. A friend on the ship and I decided to go into business together, which involved getting a special type of surplus ship from the army, and I went to Washington to see if I could arrange a surplus deal. After I had been in Washington a few days I found that Moran Towing and Salvage Co. of New York City had snaggled off every one of these ships that I wanted, and there was no possibility of getting any of them. So I was feeling fairly low, and I walked round to the Mayflower Hotel, and got talking to a major in the bar. I was feeling sorry for myself, and having one drink after another. Somehow or other I mentioned that I could speak German, and he said, 'Why don't you go to Nuremberg?' I said, 'What the heck is at Nuremberg?' 'Well,' he said, 'They're going to have a big trial, and try all these Nazis.' 'You're kidding!', I said. 'No,' he said, 'it's true. There's some colonel over in the Pentagon who's recruiting people to go. Why don't you go and see him?' I thought, 'Well, by golly, I will!'

I had been an exchange student in Hitler's Germany in 1935-6, and I had conceived a violent opposition to Nazism. I could have been released from the navy before I went to Nuremberg – the navy had installed a points system to govern release dates, and it would have required another two months' service. But on the other hand I had this feeling that I wanted to be in at the death; I wanted to see the end of that thing. I hated it and everything it stood for. So I went to Nuremberg with that feeling.

The day after my drinking spree at the Mayflower I went to the Pentagon, and, sure enough, I found Colonel Dostert. And two days later the navy changed my orders and I flew to Nuremberg. I'd been in Nuremberg before the war, and as the plane circled over the city and I looked down, I got the shock of my life. I wasn't looking *at* the houses of Nuremberg, I was looking *into* the houses of Nuremberg. Every roof was gone. The only things standing were the walls, and not all of *them*, of course. It was the most incredible sight, and the first I had seen of the bombing in Europe. Of course, I then learned that every German city looked like that.

Whitney Harris, lawyer

During the war I served in the United States navy for four and a half years, and at the end of the war I was transferred to the OSS [Office of Strategic Services]. That was the forerunner of the CIA in the United States, and it was really our first major intelligence service. I was assigned to the investigation of war crimes in the European theatre. When I went to Europe I set up an office in England, right beside British Intelligence at St James, and there I received intelligence information which I submitted back to the United States. In the early summer of 1945, Mr Justice Jackson came to England and established preliminary headquarters at Mount Street, with a nucleus of his staff. His purpose was to meet with the representatives of the United Kingdom, France and Russia, in an effort to work out an agreement for the trial of the major war criminals. While these negotiations were going on, from time to time I would take documents which I thought would be of interest to the prosecution staff up to Mount Street. At that time, of course, the effort was to negotiate an agreement, and not much was being done with respect to obtaining evidence, so the evidence that I could provide was happily received, to say the least. Then I was invited to join the staff, and I went down to Nuremberg and stayed there until the end of the trial.

Roger Barrett, officer in charge of documents

I happened to get to Nuremberg because I had been called back from my position as an enlisted man to go to officer candidate school in the Judge Advocate General's department, and one of the men in the department had been a lieutenant to Justice Robert Jackson, who had said to him, 'If you find any young, hard-working, clean-cut trial lawyers, bring 'em along!' I had my orders to report to somewhere overseas, but I got a call from the Secretary of War's office saying 'Go to London.' We went to a building in Mount Street and started working on preparation for the trial.

Seaghan Maynes, journalist

When the war broke out I was a correspondent on a newspaper in Belfast, in Northern Ireland. I came over to London, to Fleet Street, and joined the Press Association, which is the domestic news agency for Britain. After a year or so I switched over to Reuters. We all knew that D-Day was coming up, and I was very anxious to get into the action. I was then assigned to General Patton's Third American Army, for the invasion of Europe. We went through Normandy, all the 'battles of the hedgerows' and so on. Patton was such a tremendous character, there was a great news value to him. He was also an extremely good general. I travelled with his tanks down to southern France, and then up to the Czech border. So I saw much killing and bombing, and then I saw the concentration camps.

Usually, with the tank columns, we'd travel with reconnaissance units, and we'd hit the camps before anyone else, really, had been in. I remember on one occasion going in, and the inmates were literally crawling around on the ground, crying for food. In my trench-coat pocket I had some army rations, which included sugar cubes. I threw one to one of these poor creatures, and he grabbed it, and about four or five others rushed on top of him, and were trying to get their fingers into his mouth to take the sugar out. On another occasion I was walking over a piece of ground in the camp, and it was very soft, sagging, and I later discovered that this was a pit where bodies had been buried, and I'd walked over the whole lot. The German guards were often caught before they could escape, and they were often killed by the inmates. At Buchenwald, which was one of the camps I went to, they had caught one of the commandants and hung him on the barbed wire. This is the sort of thing we'd see as we were going in. We entered these camps absolutely 'raw' to what had happened in them, though we'd heard all sorts of reports; the bodies, and the awful condition of the people in the camps, were a surprise to some of us. But you do get hardened to it. After all the battles in Normandy, with the bodies of children, soldiers, civilians ... after a month or so you do become accustomed to it and you don't think there's anything terribly strange in the headless body lying across the road. And in the camps one did get accustomed to death and starvation and brutality.

There were a lot of phoney stories written about the camps. The reality was bad enough, but often some correspondents were inclined to exaggerate. For instance, I was in Buchenwald when we were told that there were human skins down in the medical unit. There was a Czech doctor there, and sure enough there was a book bound with human skin, with tattoos on it. But the odd thing was that the doctor, who was Jewish and an inmate of the camp, showed us two stomachs preserved in glass jars: the stomach of an inmate, all shrunken, and the stomach of a guard, with some fat on it. It struck me as odd that the Germans should have allowed the stomach of a guard to be stuck into a glass jar for exhibition in this doctor's surgery. Also, why did the doctor have the skins? Presumably whoever wanted them should have taken them. There are some odd little stories arising out of these well-publicized events. At one camp we went into, within half an hour there were typewriters going in one of the buildings, and there were inmates, chaps who didn't seem to have been ill-treated at all, sitting typing out press releases and handing out press statements about what had happened to the inmates. And we'd just entered the damn place! So there was a degree of organization there.

Mauthausen was a bad camp. That was where they killed British paratroopers: they used to make them carry rocks up from the bottom of a quarry, throw them over the edge, and then go down and do the same thing again; and eventually they were shot. There was a young British paratroop officer with us, who must have been about twenty-two, whose job was to find out as much as he could about what had happened to the British paratroopers in Mauthausen, and I had to stop him flogging one of the guards, a very elderly man, who wasn't answering the questions as well as the young chap thought he should. I felt he was *unable* to give any information – he was an elderly chap who looked as though he had been employed in the cook-house rather than the extermination squad. I thought it was a bit odd that his hands were tied to the bars of a window, and he was being flogged – a pretty poor example of trying to get information out of a suspect. These little things stick in your mind, things that should not have been, that caused you to think about humanity, brutality, and so on.

I finished the war in Czechoslovakia. When peace broke out, I was assigned to Berlin and Hamburg in the British zone to cover the post-war developments. The Germans were completely subdued, battered, and also very hungry. Little war crimes trials of local people began. Then, when the Nuremberg thing was set up, I was assigned to go down there and report on it.

Daniel Margolies, lawyer

I was drafted into the army. They passed the draft, I think, in 40 or thereabouts, and I was one of the first people drafted. At that time I was an attorney in the office of price administration. Mr Nixon, who later became President, was one of the people working for me. I was rather older than the average recruit, about thirty-four years old. We were drafting people who were about nineteen or twenty. They sent me to Fort Sill, in Oklahoma, where I got my basic training in the artillery. Fort Sill is in a rather desert-type country. Sitting Bull, I believe, was round there – anyway, I saw a lot of Indians. They really wanted me to be a truck-driver: in the artillery you have a cannon attached to a truck and you drive the truck. Anyway, I was a very unsuccessful truck-driver.

I had been working in the United States Senate for the Committee on Labor for a number of years, and when the OSS was organized they set up a section on labour, because the trades union movement had connections with seamen's unions and so on, who moved around the world and picked up a certain amount of information, and information was what the OSS was presumably interested in: although we were an organization that went in for sabotage and so on, we were supposed to get information. And I had been counsel for a committee of the Senate Labor Committee, and my name came to the attention of someone in OSS who was in charge of the labour section, which was part of Secret Intelligence. So they sent a telegram to Fort Sill, saying could they get hold of me for OSS? Now, normally you couldn't be released from basic training till the end of it, and it was never quite clear to me whether the response from Fort Sill, which was that they could have me whenever they wanted me, was complimentary or not. So I was released before the end of my basic training, and sent off to work on Labor Secret Intelligence. I was with OSS, then, until the end of the war, serving in London and then on the continent. When the war in Europe ended I was somewhere in Germany, on a mission. I was in charge of secret agents, and I moved about a bit.

Justice Jackson, who was on the Supreme Court, selected General Donovan, head of the OSS, to be on his staff; Mr Donovan, for reasons that I've never known exactly, picked me to work on this staff; and I never had a chance to ask him why because he resigned shortly before the trial opened. Meantime, in June 1945, I'd gotten my orders to proceed to Paris. They had a preliminary group that was being organized, to examine documents, and I guess they thought that with my experience as an investigator and the fact that I worked ... I don't know *why* they picked me, since I never met Mr Donovan after that to see how I had been selected. But they assigned six young ladies to me – they had been Germans, they were refugees, and they had been recruited somewhere or other. We met in Paris and left for Frankfurt – the war in Europe was over by this time. The files of the OKW [Oberkommando der Wehrmacht] were in Frankfurt, and we went through those files to select documents for the trial. At this point it was August. We completed our work in a few weeks, and then went on to Nuremberg, which was then being prepared for the trial because the court-house had been damaged and had to be repaired. And then, of course, they had to arrange accommodation for the attorneys and the staff that were coming in. The Grand Hotel had been hit by a bomb, and it was not all that grand – I mean, it had a big hole in the middle and you had to walk on planks to get from one part to another. We also took over private homes from people. Meantime, the files of Weltemburg had been located and brought to Nuremberg, and I worked on those files for a while. So I was in what you might call the documentary section at that time, although I didn't know I was.

The main body of attorneys with Mr Jackson had not yet arrived. They were in Washington and then later in London, busily negotiating the terms of the indictment – who would be indicted, and what the indictments would say, and matters of that sort – and deciding how the American staff would be structured. They did in fact set up a documen-tary section and another section which interrogated prisoners. I was originally in the documentary section, but we were very short of people who knew German, to read, speak or understand, and I was familiar with the language compared with a lot of other people, therefore I was taken out of the documentary section and placed in the interrogation section. By this time the lawyers had turned up – they came from London, finally, and started working and preparing for the case. I think this was now September when they arrived, bringing with them, I'm glad to say, my wife, who had been an attorney at the Embassy in London working on the Blockade Commission. She was an outstanding attorney – she was editor-in-chief of the *Law Review* of Wisconsin Law School, the first woman Stirling Fellow at Yale Law School – and she was still operating under her maiden name, although we had got married in London. Mrs Shipley, who was in charge of visas at the State Department, made it her business to keep husbands and wives from being in the same theatre of war, so we waited: I knew I was going to London, and she got herself transferred to the Embassy in London, and we got married there. Then we were separated, because I was sent on the continent. I left her to the buzz bombs – and it was much safer on the continent, I must say, in spite of my battle stars! But she was one of the leading lawyers of her generation, and so they brought her to Nuremberg, not knowing that her husband was there. At that time the US military authorities in Germany forbade wives to join their husbands, and Mr Jackson applied the same rule to attorneys on the staff at Nuremberg. So she arrived as Harriet Zetterberg, and I was Lieutenant Margolies – I had by this time become an officer. We were put up in the same hotel room in the Grand Hotel, as Miss Zetterberg and Lieutenant Margolies.

Anna Cameron, secretary
In December 1941, at the bombing of Pearl Harbor, I was working at the Treasury Department, the Bureau of Internal Revenue, which collected alcohol and tobacco taxes. By January 1942 I thought this was a very unexciting place to be, so I asked to be transferred to the War Production Board. I went to work for the Combined Resources Committee – it was America and England combining their resources. They were trying to unify the nuts and bolts that went into different parts of machinery, because we had to co-ordinate the tanks and the planes and the guns so that both English and Americans could use them and repair them. I enjoyed that. I was working for a man called Marshall J. Dodge, Jr, and half the time he'd be in England, and half the time he'd be in the United States. Then in 1944 he said to me, 'You know, you would really enjoy living and working in England.' I said, 'I can't imagine how people get to work there, with the shortages and everything,' but he said, 'The bus lines are better there than they are in the United States. People are doing very well. You'd like it.' I couldn't go as part of the War Production Board, because they had no American women workers overseas, so I went to the American Red Cross, the War Department, the OSS, which was a precursor of the CIA. And what do you know – by October of 1944 they hired me, and I told them I wanted to go to Europe, and I was in training until January of 1945. Then I was assigned to London. We went overseas on the *Aquitania*, and all of the personnel on the ship were British. One of the rules was that nobody was ever going to help the women who got on that ship. If you couldn't take care of yourself, if you couldn't get yourself on to that ship and get your luggage on to that ship, nobody was going to help you. There were ten women and ten thousand soldiers, and the general said, 'The soldiers are the most important people in this world, not you women. We can always get a stenographer to do what you're doing.' So you should have seen us trying to get our luggage up the gangplank! We had to help each other. And the fellows all stood by; they had been told not to lift a finger to help us. They clapped every time one of us got to the top of the steps!

We were told that we would not have a submarine escort, because the *Aquitania* could go faster than any submarine. But we had a marine guard on our door all the time – ten thousand men and ten women. We had two meals a day, breakfast at ten and dinner at four, and that was it. We landed in Glasgow, and some officers from the British army got on the train with us and escorted us to London. We moved into a billet, which was for all kinds of young women who were from out of the city. It was very primitive – no bathtubs – so I never had a real bath in six months. But I lived. It was fine; I liked it. Towards the end of the war – this was January to about April 1945 – there was still a raid every now and then, but nothing serious. I finally moved to a house with a few other women, and we lived right across the street from the police station that handled the case of Jack the Ripper! I really was impressed with the British police – they were so polite and nice. I remember one night one of them came over and said, 'Lady, this is a purple alert, and you must put all of your lights out.' And I remember going down to the basement and pulling the shades and everything, and I'd just gotten *Time* magazine from the PX [Post Exchange]. So I sat on the floor and read *Time* magazine from end to end. But nothing happened, and then next morning everything was fine.

There was VE Day, which was very wonderful: everybody celebrating, everybody so happy. And then about July we were told that we were going to be dismissed and we were to go home. But I applied to go to work for the War Department, because I thought it would be interesting. September the 3rd, 1945, my thirtieth birthday, was the day the war officially ended. We went to the airport in London, and I took my first aeroplane ride, from London to Nuremberg. Oh, I was shocked when I landed. It was a pile of rubble. Almost nothing was standing except the court-house, the Grand Hotel, the Faber pencil factory and the stadium. In the old city the church was still standing, and the wall, and the moat was still there. I was depressed for two weeks. It really troubled me, to think how awful war is. There's got to be a better way – even today I think that. All wars are unnecessary, but they go on, I don't know how to stop them. To see the people... they were so devastated. Everywhere you looked, on the roads, people would have their belongings in baby-carriages, handcarts, wheelbarrows, pushing them down the road, trying to go home, trying to *find* a home. And yet, people *looked* reasonably decent. A lot of the German girls used to go out with the American soldiers, and they would wear skirts made out of khaki army blankets, but they would put red embroidery round the edges. The thing that troubled me was sitting in the Grand Hotel and eating, and seeing those people outside looking in. I didn't enjoy my food as much as I usually do. But I didn't know what to do, you know? I mean, they'd been our enemies and they would have killed me, six months ago. But that didn't really enter my mind; I just had the usual human commiseration for a fellow-human in trouble. I think we all felt that way.

Peter Uiberall, interpreter

I was born in Vienna, the son of an Austrian businessman who had most of his family in the United States: three brothers, uncles, cousins and so on. He was a sort of stay-behind – he had not gone to the States prior to World War One, and then came World War One, and he was a non-commissioned officer in the Austrian army. When the war was over it was a little difficult; he started his business over again. And so it came that he was the last of his family who was still in Vienna. This turned out to be a great advantage for all of us, because as soon as Hitler marched into Austria on the 11th of March, 1938, our relatives in the United States tried to find out what they had to do. They signed the various affidavits of support, which we, thank God, did not really need, but they were necessary in order to obtain a visa to the United States. And by the 4th of April, which was pretty fast, I was called by the United States Consulate to let me know that these documents had arrived, and that whenever I had a passport I should come and present myself to obtain the visa. I had been in the United States before, on a visit to my family in 1933, which was probably one of the reasons why the US Consulate was so fast in getting me the visa – they had my file, and they knew all about me. So I had a little knowledge of English, and an accent even worse than it is now! Others had to wait much longer. I had some difficulties getting the passport – there was a great deal of intentional procrastination. There was now a Nazi administration in Austria, and people were just sitting on these passports, because they had no reason to be nice to the people who wanted to leave, especially the Jews. I was Jewish; my wife (my late first wife) was not. She was descended from many generations of Austrian army officers.

In order to receive permission to leave the country, you had to present to the authorities various documents to the effect that you did not owe any taxes. If you had lived in different districts of Vienna over recent years, you had to go to every one of these districts in order to get a certificate. I had to go to several, and it took me quite some time. I finally got all the documents, and the passport didn't come back. Nothing happened. Then somebody told me, 'I know somebody who can help you get your passport. You go into such and such a street' – which happened to be one block from where my parents lived – 'and there is a garage. You go in there, and on the left is a little room, where Mr So and So is. You tell him what you want, and he will help you get your passport. It's 200 schillings' – which wasn't really exorbitant, considering what it meant. So I went to the garage, and in the room was a very nice middle-aged man. I was introducing myself, when all of a sudden I saw, hanging on the wall, a police uniform. He was in civilian clothes. He saw my expression of consternation, and said, 'Don't worry. I'm a driver for the police, and this is why I can help you get your passport. All I do is, I go into the office where the passports are stacked, at a time when there's nobody there, I look for your passport, and I put it on top of the stack. You will get it in the mail.' And he said, 'If you have any questions about it, look at this wall.' The wall was covered in postcards addressed to him, from outside Austria, and saying simply, 'Best regards and thanks.' They were his credentials. All of these people had obtained their passports with his help. They were not false passports – it was just getting them out of the clutches of the Gestapo or whoever was holding them back. I said, 'Why are you doing this?' He said, 'My daughter has a Jewish husband, and they had to get out. In this way I can help them.' I found out many years later that his name was the same as that of a niece of Adolf Hitler, and it is entirely possible – this is just my guess – that because of this he was able to do such things without getting into too much trouble. But I was very grateful to the man, and I sent him a postcard from Zurich when I finally made it.

We went by train. We had our passports, and we had the equivalent of four dollars, which was all we were allowed to take out. A distant relative of my wife's was in the Nazi Party. He was not a Jew-baiter or anything like that; he was a former army officer who was a German Nationalist, as so many were. I'm not apologizing for him – I didn't like the guy, except that he came to the station with us and got us into the train safely. We took the long train ride from Vienna to the Swiss border, where the border controls came in, and I was wondering ... There was one thing wrong with my passport, I had found: it was stamped on a Sunday. There was a very nice man at the office who did overtime, in order to help people, and stamped a lot of passports on a Sunday. I was scared that the guards might take exception to that, but they did not. They took my wife into a separate compartment, with a woman officer, and she had to undress, and they searched her, because they could not figure out why in the world a non-Jewish woman should want to leave their Nazi paradise. But we got through, and we got to Zurich. Here the train waited for two hours before going on to Basle and then Paris. Everybody left the train, but we didn't. The cleaning-woman came in and swept the compartment; we still sat there. Finally, the Swiss conductor came in and said, 'What are you doing? Why don't you get off?' I said, 'We are just transit passengers, emigrating to the United States, and we don't have a Swiss visa.' He said, 'This is Switzerland, not Germany! Go out and walk around, but don't miss your train.' So we got out and walked around, and even spent some twenty-five cents of our four dollars on ice-cream, which was wonderful in freedom!

A lot of things had happened before we left, in Vienna. Friends of mine were arrested. I myself was working under a Nazi commissar who had taken over my father's business. I was in a very peculiar position, because I was an employee of the firm; my father had been thrown out as the owner, and this commissar, a graduate of a business school, had been put in charge. *He* ordered *me* to continue my work, which was foreign correspondence in English and French, because there were some assets that he thought he would get in from the British and the French, who were smart enough never to send anything! It was the Nazi commissar, I must say, who called me in one day and said, 'I see from the records that you were in America, and I see you were making speeches.' I said, 'I was invited by the Carnegie Endowment to talk to American students about international relations.' I had published a literary magazine in Vienna. 'It is reported in the Gestapo file on you that you said some unfriendly things about the National Socialist movement. I understand you have applied for a visa to the United States.' I said, 'Yes, we have most of our family there.' And he said, 'Let me tell you something. When that visa comes up, don't hesitate. Go!' And I'm grateful to the man. Of course he served his own purpose, because everything that my father had built up in his life was under his control and became the property of the Nazis. At the same time, I appreciate his honesty.

I had a very interesting conversation with him once, alone in the office. He called me in and said, 'I see you went to the Hochschule für Welthandel', of which he was a graduate. 'Did you know Professor So and So?' You know how it is when you talk to somebody who has had the same teachers, and all of a sudden, a man from the opposite end of the spectrum is one with whom you can establish some kind of contact. He had made a remark that all Jewish businessmen were crooks. I said, 'Mr Schauerhuber, how could you make a statement like that? My father has never done anything dishonest in his whole life, at least not to my knowledge – certainly not as a businessman.' He said, 'The Führer says so, and the Führer is always right.' So I said, 'Mr Schauerhuber, I want to make a suggestion to you. You examine the books over the past fifteen years, and see if you find *anything* that was dishonest – a violation of customs regulations, or money transference regulations. And if you find that everything is all right, you must promise me, on your word of honour, that nothing will happen to my father.' And he did – he kept his word. A whole troop of Nazi auditors swarmed all over the place, and one day he called me in and said, 'I see there has been a transfer of $5,000 to the United States – how come?' And I could show him that two years earlier my father had borrowed $5,000 from one of his brothers in New York, and I had gone to the Austrian National Bank and received a certificate to the effect that this money had come in, and we were therefore authorized to buy the foreign currency to pay it back with. My father had transferred no money out of the country – we arrived in this country poor as church mice, because he had not violated a single rule of the Austrian government or any other government. Don't get me wrong – I'm not defending a Nazi commissar. But this was a personal experience that was very interesting to me. He eventually got into trouble, I understand, and was sent to a concentration camp, so he was probably not a very good Nazi in the first place.

It was very difficult for me, when I came here as an immigrant in 1938, to make people in the United States understand what was going on over there. Thank God I had an aunt who was a businesswoman in New York, who believed me. And whenever I asked her to make out an affidavit, she did, and she saved quite a number of people, whole families. She didn't have much economic strength, but she had the will and the reputation, and the American authorities accepted her affidavits. Most of the Jews over there were not so lucky. I had an aunt, a cousin and her husband and little girl who were taken from Vienna to concentration camps and perished there. I had one schoolmate who was taken to Buchenwald, but he had an American connection, and he was let out of Buchenwald after a year, when his visa to the United States came up.

There was a time in the beginning when the Nazis were still very careful about not offending the United States too much. It didn't last long. But in 1939 and 1940 it was still possible for some people who had demonstrable ways of getting to the United States to get out, even a very few whom the Nazis had in some kind of confinement. But after that, of course, there was no such chance. The worst year in the round-up of Jewish people was 1942.

When I got to America I eventually went into the army, the infantry. I got in very late, in 1944. The army had not called me up because I was too old for them, over twenty-seven. I was working on a farm, as a labourer, and that was also an exclusion point. But when our citizenship papers came along, in June 1944, my wife signed up for the Women's Army Corps and I went to the draft board and said, 'Here I am. I want to get in.' I was given various tests, and they discovered that I knew German and had some knowledge of French, and that I had a fairly good ear for signals. The interviewing officer then said, 'This is interesting. Under all other circumstances we would send you into intelligence, but we have just received orders that everything that is upright and warm goes into the infantry.' So I was sent to an infantry camp in the south, and so was my wife. Our camps were in Georgia, about a hundred miles apart; we could not even see each other on weekends because a camp pass covered only fifty miles.

As I got through basic training, my platoon officer called me and said, 'You know, your score on the initial test was good, and you could apply for officer candidate school.' I said, 'Are you kidding, sir?' I was thirty-three years old. He said, 'Yes, of course! If *I* could do it, you can do it!' I applied, and I got to the infantry school in Fort Benning, Georgia, where I was enrolled in an officer candidate course, one of several ways of getting an infantry commission. They called me 'Pop' in the platoon, because I was much older than everybody else. I got through by the skin of my teeth. It was a fabulous experience for me, as a thirty-three-year-old man: the training and all that was wonderful. I became a second lieutenant in the infantry, and on graduation day my wife, who by that time was a corporal in the Women's Army Corps, came down. Then I was sent to an infantry training camp to train others in the technique of mortar fire. My problem in infantry school had been, I thought, my accent. I asked one of the psychologist officers who interview you in the course. He said, 'Do you have a problem, lieutenant?' I said, 'Yes, my accent. If I take American troops into combat' – which I did not have to, thank God – 'they might resent a foreigner.' 'If *you* don't worry, nobody else is going to worry about that.' So I found myself in Camp Joseph T. Robinson in Arkansas, teaching the technique of mortar fire to recruits, having just learned it myself a few weeks earlier. We were out in the field, with an easel and all the displays set up, and I had done my first hour, and I was waiting for the first reaction. One little fellow came up to me and said, 'Loo-tenant, where you from?' I was hedging. I said, 'Well, my home state is New Jersey.' I had come in from New Jersey. 'No, I don't mean that. Where you from sort of originally, like?' I said, 'I understand what you mean, yes. I was born and raised in Vienna, Austria.' 'Austria – that's Europe, ain't it?' 'Yes, that's Europe.' 'Europe – that's probably where we're gonna go, ain't it?' 'Yes, probably.' So he turned round and shouted, 'Hey, you guys! Listen to this! We got us a loo-tenant who's from Europe! Isn't that great?' And I never had any problem. My platoon was proud of their lieutenant who was originally from Europe, where they were going to go. But it was late in the war, and they were spared it.

Before the end of that tour of duty, I was informed that I was selected to go to the Pacific theatre. By that time the war was over; it was late August 1945, after the atomic bombs had been dropped. I had taken so long to train. On the day I got my second lieutenant's bar, Hitler committed suicide; no connection between the two, I assure you! Then there was the unfortunate task of finding the remains of service personnel all over the world, and identifying them and bringing them home. It was called 'graves registration'. I was to go to the Pacific theatre and serve in this. But my wife had gone to Germany already, and was stationed near Frankfurt, in an office that prepared material for the Nuremberg Trial. In the same office there were some American lieutenants who were angry because they'd gone through the war and now they couldn't go home, because their native tongue was German and they were still needed. There was a points system for release from active duty, and one day one of them said, 'We have enough points now. Can't we go home?' The officer in charge said, 'No, because there isn't a single army officer left in the States who speaks German and who could replace you.' So my wife piped up and said, 'That is not true, sir! My husband speaks German, as his native tongue, and he's just been assigned to graves registration in the Pacific!' So when I went on leave to New York, where my parents lived, I found a letter from the army instructing me to report to Washington D.C., some room in the outer ring of the Pentagon. When I turned up at the office the man I was supposed to report to wasn't there, but they told me, 'This is probably in connection with the war crimes trials, and there is a Colonel Dostert down the hall, who is getting people ready to go overseas.' I reported to him, and he asked, 'Do you speak German?' I said, 'Yes, sir, it's my native tongue, I had some years at the University of Vienna.' 'OK', he said. 'In the next room there is a desk. You go in there and sit down, and I'll send you people, and you can test them for their German.' And that's how I started. A few days later, along with many others, I was put on a plane and flown to Frankfurt; then we travelled by road to Nuremberg.

I arrived in Nuremberg on the 24th of October 1945. It was an incredible situation. I was billeted in the Grand Hotel, and I was one of the people whose room was on the other side of the hole down its middle, which was covered by planks. When I went into my room, the first thing I saw was a pair of shoes upside down at about eye height. I looked further down, there were legs, and there was a man standing on his head. He turned out to be a very nice gentleman, Professor Bogoslowski, who had a Russian language school in Boston, Massachussetts. I was assigned as his room-mate. After a few days Colonel Dostert arrived, and he put a whole bunch of his immediate staff, including me, into a house.

John Pine, visitor

In 1939, before the war, I was a solicitor, one of the solicitors of the Great Western Railway. I was there because my father was *the* solicitor to the Great Western Railway company. I was also in the Inns of Court Regiment. It was a regiment that was formed before the First War, being made up of professional people; it then proceeded to fight as a regiment, and so there were 600 professional people in the ranks, and so on and so forth. They had terrible casualties as soon as they went into battle – about 350 – and they realized that it wasn't a terribly good way of using officer-producing people. On the 3rd of September, 1939, I was mobilized. We were in fact mobilizing at our headquarters, in 10, Stone Buildings in London, at 11 o'clock on the 3rd of September, and we all listened to Chamberlain's speech as the clock chimed eleven, and realized that we were at war. And immediately the sirens went, and we all rushed down into the cellars and put our gas-masks on! After about twenty minutes of this we thought, 'Well, *this* isn't good enough!', and took our gas-masks off and put our heads out of the window, and gave it up as a bad job.

I was commissioned in May 1940, and became an instructor in tank gunnery – about which I felt that I knew nothing at all! – and then a staff captain in the Legal Services. Then I was approached and asked if I would like to go into one of two things: one was the Enemy Property branch of the army, and the other was the Legal Division of the Control Commission. And I chose the Control Commission. On the 8th of June 1945 we flew over in an old Dakota to Detmold, and then on to the first headquarters of the Control Commission – or it may have been the headquarters of the Legal Division of the Control Commission – at Lübeck. It was then that I started prosecuting, and going to the various military government courts, and working there.

Andy Wheeler, lawyer

A close friend was responsible for getting me there. He called all the lawyers that he knew in the American Law Institute and other places, to send us over for this trial. I went over with a group of others on July 4th, 1945, stopping on the way in London. In the Northumberland Hotel, the man who was going to assist me walked in and said good afternoon, then he looked up and said, 'My God, it's Andy Wheeler!' It was Frank Wallis, my partner at home in my law firm!

Bernard Meltzer, lawyer

The State Department had borrowed me from the navy, in the spring of 1945, for work on the drafting of the UN Charter in San Francisco. When

I was there, wondering about my next navy assignment, Frank Shea, whom I'd known in Washington during the New Deal, telephoned me and asked if I'd like to go to Nuremberg. The prospect seemed exciting and challenging. I said 'Sure.' And that's how my assignment there came about.

Ron Chapman, clerk

When the war broke out I was only fourteen. I was at Cambridge County High School for Boys, up Hills Road, and I joined the Air Training Corps – I think we were all air-minded and wanting to be Spitfire pilots in those days. I did actually volunteer for the RAF, and I got quite a long way, and then they decided my eyesight wasn't good enough and would let me down. I was a little bit disappointed, and I think more as a fall-back than anything else I joined the army. In August 1943, when I was seventeen years and eight months, knowing I was going to be called up at eighteen, I volunteered, much to my parents' disgust, as in those days they did not want you to go until it was really necessary. I was sent to Bovington camp in Dorset, which was the home of the tank corps, and also Lulworth Cove where the gunnery school was.

But there were so many people at that time, in 1943 ... it was a time when things were going quite well for us in the Middle East, and a lot of young people were coming into the forces. And there was a great clamour to get into the 'glamorous' regiments, and very few out of the hordes actually made it. So I never went into the actual tank corps, but I was posted to Aldershot, the Service Corps, and I was to take up clerical work, because I'd done a bit of clerical work in the army before. I was sent to Aldershot to learn, of all things, typing, considered very sissy in those days, on old tin typewriters. And I'll always remember, at Aldershot, just after we'd started this typing instruction, there was one lad there who was a bricklayer, and who was all thumbs and fingers, *terribly* frustrated with this typing. It was a hot afternoon, and we were in these Nissen huts, and the windows were open, and he got so frustrated with the machine, and typing out the letters, that he picked the typewriter up, and stood up, and flung it straight out the window in his frustration! The typewriter went sailing across the room. He just couldn't stand it any more, you know, everything snapped. Hot weather. So the sergeant calmly looked up and went out to fetch it back, and we expected to see him come back with an armful of pieces. He came back with it in one piece, and plonked it on the table, and said, 'Right – carry on.' It was most amazing, but they were very 'utility' and made to withstand all sorts of punishment.

I got on quite well there, and so a few of us were then chosen to go to London, for a crash intensive shorthand-typing course. We were billeted in Mecklenburg Square, off Gray's Inn Road. The houses had been damaged in the bombing and were being propped up with those long poles. Each day we had to march up to a polytechnic, that wasn't being used as such, off the Liverpool Road. In fourteen weeks we had to learn eighty words a minute shorthand. We also had one period a day of general army administration and organization, clerical work involving an army brigade. Whilst we were there the doodlebugs, the V-1s, started. Being in London, you really got close. We literally lived in the shelters. One of the bombs dropped on the Royal Free Hospital, which was in Gray's Inn Road just at the back of where we were living. It was about six o'clock in the evening, in broad daylight. We all went down and helped. Luckily it fell on an empty ward, but some of the nurses were quite badly injured by flying glass.

After that course I was posted to what they called the Psychological Warfare Consolidation Team. It consisted of a mixture of Canadians, most of whom were French-speaking, and civilians who were attached to the Army Cinematograph Section, and who wore a uniform but didn't have a rank. They were civilians in uniform. And there were a number of intelligence officers. It was a most amazing assortment really. All it was really meant to do was follow in the path of the troops, and to keep the locals – French, Belgian, Dutch and so on – up to date with what was happening. There was a lot of panic, a lot of uncertainty, a lot going on, and they were listening to British radio, German radio, their own radio, and there was confusion, and we tried to bring the local people films of what was actually happening. There was also intelligence: going around, talking to people, trying to pick up any stories, about Germans who were still around, perhaps, as fifth columnists, about how the local people had been treated, and so on. So it was quite a mixture. But we were attached to SHAEF, the Supreme Headquarters of the Allied Expeditionary Force, which was Eisenhower's headquarters, and we did wear on our shoulders the SHAEF badge: it was a flaming sword on a black background (which was the tyranny of the Nazis), and overhead were the colours of the rainbow, which was supposed to be the coming of the liberation and the awakening of the new world.

We were in Belgium when the war finished. It was a nice evening, and I remember one of our officers bringing out a bottle of cognac and inviting us all to have a drink, which was very unusual, and he said that the armistice had been signed. And from then on, you gradually got the Belgian prisoners returning home, as the prisoner-of-war camps were overrun. You'd be in the village on a particular night and you'd hear the village band coming up the street, and everyone would rush out, saying, 'A prisoner-of-war has returned!' Every time one came they got the whole village band out, and he was chaired through the streets followed by the whole village. Nearly every night, from then on, you'd see one or two come back.

Then we went to Holland, to The Hague. We were following up – the British consolidation teams were going through the countries as they were being liberated. So we were close to Paris, then close to Brussels, then close to Amsterdam, although at that time The Hague was the seat of the Dutch government. They had only just been liberated, at The Hague, and there were street parties every night, with orange bulbs put in the trees – the trees were all lit up, quite an amazing sight. Holland, I should say, was the people [sic] most relieved to be liberated, because they had, if anything, suffered more than the French and the Belgians.

In The Hague we learned that the warfare consolidation teams were going to be disbanded. We had gone through France and Belgium more or less as a unit, the whole time, but now we were going to be disbanded, and gradually people got posted away from the unit, until there were only a few of us left. Five of us were given travelling forms, and we said cheerio to the rest – quite emotional, really, because we'd been together quite a long time. And we got postings to Nuremberg, which at that time we didn't know a lot about because the trial hadn't quite started, and it wasn't very public, what was going to happen at the trial – we just knew we were going to Germany, Nuremberg.

It was a really frightening experience arriving in Nuremberg. It had not long before suffered a 1,000-plane bombing raid, so when we got out of the train the platform was literally just a piece of paving. It was cold, there was snow on the ground, it was two o'clock in the morning, we'd been travelling for hours, we were dishevelled, dirty, and we went to the American transport office on the station. We didn't know where we were to go, and *they* didn't know where we were to go. We were posted to the BWCE, which was the British War Crimes Executive, but these American policemen didn't know anything about it. So they suggested we went to a transit building in Nuremberg for the night, and then sorted it out next day. They took us in a jeep to a three-storeyed brick building in the centre of Nuremberg. It was absolutely crammed with American police – not a bed spare. We finished up sleeping in the corridor, on a blanket. We just flopped out – we were very tired. The next day a truck took us to Zirndorf, a village about nine miles away, and we were billeted in a gymnasium.

Mary Burns, secretary

At the end of World War Two, I was stationed in London, as part of the OSS. Because of our laws, the OSS was disbanded within sixty days of the end of the European theatre, so you had a choice of either going home or finding something else to do. I made an application to one place, and through that application the word got through that Justice Jackson was coming to London, and that he had no staff, and a number of people from OSS in a position similar to my own – in that we weren't eager to get home, as a lot of the married people were – applied. I was interviewed by an aide to Justice Jackson, and transferred to his staff in London. I remained in London during the summer, and subsequently went to Nuremberg. I was working indirectly for Justice Jackson. He had brought a secretary from the Supreme Court, and there were other military types in London who were loaned, so to speak, to him as aides. He was given a small office on Mount Street, and I was in position, so I maintained that office because I just happened to be there. My position evolved into part of Jackson's personal staff, and once we got on the road his son, Bill Jackson, who was a lieutenant in the navy and a graduate lawyer, was loaned to his father at his father's request. There were four of us on his staff, in London and Nuremberg.

Brady Bryson, lawyer
I was in the United States Navy, as a reserve officer. I didn't get into the service until fairly late. America came in in late 1941, and at that time I was twenty-seven years old, married, with two children. America was calling up young unmarried people first. But the time came when people of my generation began to consider military service, and I would say this happened to me in 1943. I was a young practising lawyer in Philadelphia at that time. I was enrolled in the navy as a beginning officer, an ensign, and was given a course of indoctrination. Then I was sent to a communications school at Harvard University, where I was to learn naval communications, with the prospect of being a deck officer with a communications responsibility. At the end of that instruction, I was surprised to find myself ordered to Boulder, Colorado, where the navy was conducting a language school. I discovered from my orders that I was to study Russian, in the Rocky Mountains, which was a surprise, but not an unwelcome one. So I went out to the University of Colorado, and studied Russian there for six months or so, quite uncertain as to how the navy expected to use my skill, if I acquired any, in the Russian language. I was then sent to Washington, where I was assigned to intelligence and communications work for the navy, which did involve the use of the Russian language. After some months of this, in the spring of 1945, it appeared that the European phase of the war was coming to a close, and I was approached by the navy and asked if I would go to Europe and serve as a liaison officer between the American and the Russian legal staffs, because of my familiarity with the Russian language, which at that time, I guess, was a pretty scarce commodity. They wanted to determine whether it would be acceptable to me, because obviously they didn't want to send me if I didn't want to go, particularly near the end of the war.

So I made my way to Nuremberg. It was an interesting experience for me, because prior to the war there really had been no commercial transatlantic air service. You just couldn't go abroad on an aeroplane. During the war, long-range air flights and equipment were developed, and a lot of experience was gained. By the end of it the army was operating a transport service from the United States to Paris. So I got to go abroad for the first time, on an aeroplane. At that time I guess I was thirty, and it was an exciting thing to do, although today quite boring! We left from Washington. I had orders from the navy, an interesting set of orders for a young naval officer. They authorized me to have upon request any top-priority air travel that I needed, to any place in the world outside the continental limits of the United States. So I was sort of turned loose on the foreign world with my travel documents.

The trip over was in that old workhorse of an American plane that was used so much in those days for military transport – a B48, or something like that. It had bucket seats along each side. There was no service, of course, and each of us had been warned to bring a sandwich or something if we expected to eat anything. The people on the plane were a mixed lot: there were military of various kinds, certain civilians. There was another lawyer on the plane who was going to Nuremberg, and we of course got friendly because of our common destination. There was an actress from France, who had been doing a tour in South America and had then come to the United States, and in some fashion had been provided with transportation back to Paris on this military plane. So we enjoyed the trip; they were interesting people, particularly to me.

We landed in Paris, at Orly airport; as I recall, it took us twenty-four hours from Washington to Paris, with only two brief stops. I went into Paris on a bus. I had the address of a billeting office in Paris, and I went there and showed my credentials. I think the billeting officer was not familiar with navy rankings and didn't realize how junior I was, so I was put up in a hotel. I think I spent a week in Paris, not for any particular reason except that I had some expectation that other people going to Nuremberg would show up. I was just looking for travel companions. Finally there turned up at the hotel a British army officer, a captain I think. We got friendly, and it turned out that he had a thought of going down to Nuremberg: he seemed to be footloose in much the same fashion as I was. He had access to a jeep, so finally he said, 'Why don't we take the jeep and drive to Nuremberg?' That appealed to me. He did the driving – we didn't have a driver – and we set out. When I arrived in Nuremberg, I checked in at the Grand Hotel and got settled, and looked up Telford Taylor, as I had been advised to do.

I didn't know Telford at that time; I don't think I had encountered him in my legal experience. I went to see him, and ... nothing that I say here is intended to be in the slightest way critical of anybody that I encountered; we were all doing different things, and had our minds occupied with what we were responsible for. He was pleasant, but I didn't find him particularly communicative. He told me that a Colonel Robert Storey was, *de facto* if not officially, the chief of staff there, and that perhaps I should go see Robert Storey. Taylor did say that if he could be of any assistance at any time, to come to see him. And so I walked out, a little puzzled to have been given this assignment and sent that far away, and nobody seemed to expect me or quite understand what it was I was going to do, as I described it. I began to wonder whether there really *was* any need for a person with a legal background and some knowledge of the Russian language to serve as a connecting link between the American and Russian legal staffs. The longer I stayed, the stronger this suspicion became.

I was assigned to a billet, and this billeting officer knew very well the ranks of navy personnel, so I was assigned a bunk in a stack of bunks, in a room with a lot of army non-commissioned officers. But nobody asked me to leave the Grand Hotel, so I thought, 'Well, the thing to do is just to stay here until someone suggests that I leave.' I had caught on quickly how post-war military life worked! So I settled down quickly at the

Grand Hotel, and occasionally dropped by this other place to see if there were any messages for me or anything of that sort.

Priscilla Belcher, visitor

I was with the American Red Cross, an army hospital recreation worker. I had been in England for over a year, then they closed the hospital down and I was assigned to Germany, to Nuremberg. It was a large hospital which had been an SS hospital at Ansbach, on the outskirts of Nuremberg, and it served over 20,000 Americans who were stationed in and around the area. It was a beautiful hospital, very well planned. It had red crosses on the roof, and there had been an anti-aircraft gun and radar in the central tower, until some British airmen came along and put a bomb through the window and blew the tower up.

I had seen the damage that had been done in England, but I honestly wasn't quite prepared for the severe damage that I saw in Germany. When I got there, in May, it was a hot day and we drove into town; we drove through piles of rubble, and it still smelt, and people were trying to clear things up. I smoked a cigarette, and the driver stopped the car to go into some office, and we were surrounded by kids and men, and I realized that they were after the butt of my cigarette when I had finished it. It was sort of overwhelming – if I threw it out, there'd be murder. It was my first introduction to the city.

Annabel Stover, secretary

I was in England during the war. I left Washington on my birthday, which is the 5th of June, and arrived in England on D-Day, and I spent about a year and a half working for the intelligence group out at Bletchley Park. I was attached to the American Embassy, and worked for General Telford Taylor as a secretary.

I was in England during the buzz bombs, and both the V-1s and V-2s, and of course I never mentioned that in any of my letters home; I don't know if my parents ever realized how close I was to them. I was staying in Knightsbridge Mansions, across from Harrods' department store, and one of the first things I remember was the ack-ack batteries set up in Hyde Park. All of a sudden these ack-acks started off, and I ran to the window to look out, and there was a plane with a light on, coming down. I thought, 'Well, if this dummy doesn't know enough to turn off his lights so these people can shoot at him, why, he *ought* to get hit!' And it was a V-1, with no pilot on board: it was just the flash from the plane that kept it flying. I only stayed in a bomb shelter one night, and it was so crowded and so dirty that I thought, 'If I'm going to get killed I'm going to get killed upstairs, not down here.' But then I was moved out to Bedford, and I would only come in to London to work at the embassy maybe one or two days a week. I was out at Bletchley for the rest of the time, intercepting the German messages.

After the war I stayed on for a period of time, and then General Taylor came back through London, and said he had been hired by Justice

Jackson to go to the Nuremberg War Crimes Trial, to be one of the assistant chief prosecutors, and would I like to go on over to Nuremberg? I had some reservations about going over there, but I decided that I would go.

Jean Tull, secretary

During the war I was a temporary civil servant at the Foreign Office, in the Psychological Warfare Section, and then after the liberation of Paris I went to work at SHAEF Main. There was SHAEF Rear, in London, SHAEF Main, in Paris, and SHAEF Forward, which I think was in Rheims. I was working for the deputy director of the intelligence section. The head of the section was an American, and when the war ended he offered us all jobs at Nuremberg. I was involved in the preparation of two cases, that of Schacht, in the main trial, and that of an air force officer named Milch, in the Subsequent Proceedings.

Yvette Wilberforce, visitor

I am French, and when the war broke out I was reading law at the Faculty of Law at Rennes, at which my father was a professor. He later became Dean after he had come back from prison camp. During the First World War all his friends were mobilized, but he had tuberculosis and was sent to a sanatorium instead, and he always had a hang-up about that; so when he could feel that there was another war coming he arranged to be in the Military Justice, with the rank of captain. So he went away to the war and was captured on the Maginot Line. I went on doing my studies at the Faculty of Law throughout the war.

This was occupied France, of course. We did our best – we helped prisoners escape, and so on. Once we had two escaped prisoners in our garden, and that was when posters were put on the walls, saying that anyone who was caught helping prisoners to escape was liable to be shot. My mother and I were out shopping, and we stopped and read one of these posters, and my mother said, 'Oh look! Who would do such a thing?' 'Yes indeed, who would?' said I, and we went on our way. And we had two prisoners! It was very awkward, because the houses on either side were requisitioned by Germans, and their dogs were barking a lot more than usual those two nights that we had them. Our house was not requisitioned because my brother had diphtheria quite early in the occupation, and they put a little board on our front door saying, 'Diphtheria – no member of the Wehrmacht is allowed in this house.' Fine! We kept it for two years, and we changed the pins every now and then. We dressed the men in my father's fishing clothes, and took them to the train to the free zone, separately: one of them with me, talking animatedly, and the other with one of my brothers. I was very scared. It was this business of being shot. One *was* shot. We heard it. We were near the public park, where there was a very large sunken area – the beautiful planning of the previous century. People could even play football in it. That was where they took people to be shot, and they took them past our house. Germans had something that nobody who has not heard it can understand: they wore very heavy, noisy boots. It was part of their feeling of power, that they would march with a great clanging noise at every step. They marched in step a lot, and made this awful noise which made our hearts stop. They sang a lot also, when they marched, and they marched their prisoners at a brisk pace. Very often, at six o'clock in the morning, we heard a detachment of them walking past very fast, and we knew, so we were waiting ... I was hoping my mother wasn't awake, and of course she always was. And then after a while we heard the shots. We remained in bed, cold and upset, and tried not to meet each other's eyes at breakfast.

I am almost a Doctor of Law; I just didn't finish my thesis, although I started it. When the occupation of Berlin began, they needed lawyers. My father had just become, from Dean of the Faculty of Law, a judge of the Supreme Court, and at the same time as his appointment he was asked if he wouldn't mind doing a stint of six months at the Legal Directorate in Berlin, which was denazifying German law and putting into form of law any decisions of the other organs of the government of Germany. It was on a quadripartite basis, and we were the French; I worked there as the French secretary. As my father was a judge of the Supreme Court, and so were the French judges at the Nuremberg Trial, Monsieur Donnedieu de Vabres and Monsieur Falco, we were invited to visit them in Nuremberg and attend the trial. My father went first, and later on I went with his assistant, Professor Monier of the Faculty of Law at Paris.

Dorothy Reilly, secretary
I was working at the Department of Justice, in the so-called War Division, during the war years. Judge Biddle's resignation was honoured by President Truman, and he was appointed to be the principal judge at the Nuremberg Trials. He could choose anyone he wished to be a member of his staff, so he started with the lawyers. One was Captain Adrian Fisher, who was still in uniform, and then there was Mr James Rowe – he was on a ship in the Pacific, but he resigned from the navy and joined the tribunal staff. He then chose Herbert Wechsler, who was an excellent administrator, his right-hand Justice in the War Division, and a Chicago lawyer named Quincy Wright. Judge Biddle then turned to staff appointments. He had a secretary named Mary Johnson, who was on the verge of retirement, and he thought that, since the trials were not supposed to last more than three months, it would be a great cap to her career. Her husband had no objection to her going off, so she accepted. Then there was Grace Maddox, who had worked in the department for many years in the Solicitor General's office. There was another girl named Pauline Burke, who was supposed to be the fourth member, but Pauline was reluctant to leave her husband and child, so I was invited in her stead. I had an interview with Judge Biddle and he accepted my application. Another lady, who worked in the Anti-Trust Division Library for many years, Louise Resweber, joined us, and that made four.

We went through the FBI check, and informed our parents. We were to leave from New York, in early October, on the *Queen Elizabeth*, which was still fitted as a troop ship. We landed at Southampton, but there was an immediate change of plan, and instead of going to London we got on an aeroplane and went to Paris. We were there about three days, then we headed for Berlin, to be there on the date that the indictment was being presented. We were billeted in a suburb of Berlin. After the presentation of the indictment, the judges went into conference, a so-called executive session; they wanted daily copy on their minutes. Grace and I both took shorthand. It went all right, but neither of us spoke French, and Judge Biddle occasionally would lapse into French with his French colleagues. So it soon became apparent that they would have to arrange for court reporters. Two weeks later we went to Nuremberg. The Tribunal staff – in other words the four ladies – were billeted in a guest-house on Hebelstrasse. Grace and I, Mary and Lou, and Jenny Bean who had been Judge Parker's secretary for a long time, spread out in this great house; there was almost no furniture. Ultimately, since we had so much space, four or five of the court reporters were billeted with us. The lower floor had a beautiful room with an enormous bar, and at the rear of the house were a swimming-pool and tennis-courts, none of which was used at this time. It must have been lovely in its day. The judges occupied the main house next door.

Then people had to inspect the chambers that had been prepared for the judges. The main part of the Palace of Justice was not damaged very much, but this whole section was, and what they had done was build a kind of Bridge of Sighs between this repaired section of the Palace and the court-room. Some of the staff raised great questions as to why the chambers for the judges weren't more workable. There were boards on the floor, no rugs, rough-hewn desks, and so on. At any rate most of the problems were settled.

The first thing I remember was taking a tour of the Palace of Justice. The windows of Judge Biddle's chambers overlooked the exercise yard of the prison, and although we weren't, of course, free to go into his chambers every day, when he was out we used to watch. The gaol itself, to my recollection, seemed to be in a kind of semicircle, and the exercise yard was in the middle. Mr Rowe was asked to go down to Salzburg, to check out in person the health of the elder Krupp, and came back with the news that it would be impossible to put him on trial. I recall taking the memorandum on that.

Hume Boggis-Rolfe, visitor
I joined the army in 1939. I served in the intelligence corps, and was involved in the North African campaign. I was sent to Carthage and Marrakesh, when Churchill was recovering from illness. Then I was posted back to England at the beginning of May 1944, with a view to doing a job at SHAEF. I was told to form a unit for tactical and strategic intelligence-gathering in France, when we landed. But before I'd finished

recruiting, the scheme came to nothing: Montgomery vetoed it, on the grounds that there would never have been time to interrogate people in the way proposed, marshal information and so on, while the army was on the move. You could collect tactical information in that situation, but not economic or intelligence information, which involved a much more long-term process. So instead I was sent to work as an instructor at the British Army Control Commission School in Worthing. We commandeered five of the largest hotels, and I lectured, in the Pier Pavilion among other places, on the German intelligence services and the paramilitary organizations. The course as a whole was set up to teach members of the army how to disband the German army and how to deal with the civilian population. Then, in about May 1945, I was appointed to the Control Commission in Berlin. I arrived in August, and it was from there that I visited the Nuremberg Trial, in November of that year.

Patrick Cooper, airman
I went into the American forces in 1945, and went through my basic training. By the time I'd finished training the hostilities were over, and so I never actually got into combat. We had been trained for the invasion of Japan, and we were terrified, because we knew what that was probably going to entail – they were telling us. Nobody expected the Japanese to surrender – it was against their religion – and so we expected the bloodiest possible battle in the invasion of Japan, with enormous casualties. So when they dropped the atomic bomb, I and a great many other young soldiers just threw our hats in the air – I mean, we were delighted. We were totally ignorant of the implications of that thing, and we weren't looking that far ahead; all we thought about at the time was that we were going to be spared this horrific prospect of invading the Japanese islands.

In due course, instead of being sent to Japan I was sent to Germany, in the army of occupation. I arrived in Germany in late 1945, but I was moved around a bit and then finally, in the very early part of 1946, I fetched up in a little town just outside Nuremberg. The main war crimes trials had been going on for a little while when I arrived.

Eddie Worth, photographer
I worked for the Associated Press. It's the largest photo- and news-gathering organization in the world, and it has an office in every capital city in the world. I only started as a motorcyclist. My father was a lawyer's clerk, and wanted me to go into the law. I belonged to a motorcycle club, and one day the club got a letter from British Movietone News saying they were thinking of hiring motorcyclists to pick up films and rush them to Kay's film studios in north London, so that they could have film of big events on the same evening. Nobody else in the club wanted to do it, but I said, 'I'll have a go at that,' and lo and behold I got five pounds for an afternoon's work! I didn't earn that much in a month, nearly, in the office I was in. So that was my downfall! I took the work on permanently, and

then I joined AP as a motorcyclist. At first, two or three times a week, I used to take a package down to Southampton and put it on a liner to America – it was called the American Mail. There was no one flying the Atlantic, and no wire photos, so the only way to get the stuff to America was to put it on a boat. Sometimes, to beat the opposition, we'd find out that there was a ship leaving Ireland. They used to stay outside Queenstown, and I used to fly out there with a package, get on the tender, and go out to the ship. This way we'd beat the opposition by a couple of days. It was a very cut-throat business, mainly because of AP, who were newcomers to England. There *were* lots of agencies in England, but they were sleepy old jobs, and our firm really shook them up.

When the war was first declared I was a British war correspondent and spent my time on the south coast waiting for the invasion. I had a hut on the top of Shakespeare Cliff, from which I used to watch. On a clear day I could even see Calais town hall clock. Then, when it looked as if there wasn't going to be much of an invasion, I came back and did several jobs, with convoys and things like that. When the Americans came into the war, since I was working for an American company I was turned into an American war correspondent. They had an American still pool, with the photographers in one hat and all the different armies in another hat, and from this lottery I came out with the Canadian armies. I had a choice of uniforms, and so I took the best of everything: I had British battledress trousers, because they had more pockets than any of the others, and I had very nice Canadian field boots, and an American tin hat which covered my ears better than any of the others.

Then I was sent down to Cranbury Park, just outside Southampton, to get ready for the Normandy invasion. I went to France on a cargo vessel. When it got light it was the biggest surprise of my life: there were so many ships in the Channel and round the beaches that it looked as though, if you'd been a good jumper, you could have jumped from England to France! Half-way across there were big monitors firing shells, and there were battleships, and cruisers, and destroyers, and landing craft. We got into our landing craft and made a dash for the shore. I think the fellow who was driving it was nervous – there were certainly a lot of shells whizzing everywhere – and we landed half-way up the beach. When the ramp came down we didn't even get our feet wet!

We drove up into Normandy. Being with the Canadians, it was a very interesting front: we went all along the coast, through all the channel ports and all the rocket sites – V-1s and V-2s. Then I went to Holland. I was in Antwerp for the opening of the River Scheldt – the ships could now go right up it for the chase through Germany. The Jerries knew about it, and started sending V-1s and V-2s over. I had gone to the hotel, because they said the ceremony of opening the port was going to be postponed until the next day; and I was just leaning over the table to sign the register when there was what sounded like the most awful clap of thunder, and then another one. The hotel's revolving doors went whizzing past me down the hall, and I put the pen down and thought,

'Right, this is not for me.' So I went outside, and there was the most appalling sight. A V-2 rocket had landed on the town square, at midday, with everybody out shopping. All I could see were piles of bodies. It had blown the square clear in the middle and they'd all landed up against walls and things, two or three high. A terrible thing. I took pictures of it all and I thought, 'They'll never be published.' We sent them up, and they censored just the tops – where there would be a name above a hotel, or something like that – just to show the terrorism of the Germans. They were published all round the world. I was really surprised. Letters of congratulation came back from New York, you know: 'V-2 – wonderful show!', and that sort of thing. But it was pretty rough, one of the worst sights I've ever seen. I remember one of them was a very pretty little ATS girl, down on the ground, flat – it had blown her down and killed her. She was a lovely little thing. That affected me, actually. With soldiers, you expect it, but little girls ... But usually, in situations like that, you were just getting on with the job. You didn't even notice them. You'd think, 'This is a good story, or a bad story,' and things like that. I've been on convoys, and during the night you'd hear a boom, because they used to torpedo the stragglers – they didn't come near us because we were so heavily protected. The speed of the convoy was the speed of the slowest ship, but these were terrible old steamers and they would get engine failure or something, and then you'd just have to leave the poor devils. You were sorry for them, but you still had a job to do.

I was one of the first people into Belsen. I only got in there because I was changing over from the Canadians: the war was developing very fast, and they wanted me to change from the Canadian coastal section, where everything had finished, and join the British. I found myself in the middle of Celle, starving as usual and looking for the British PR outfit. I was directed to the military government headquarters, where they were having a very nice meal. We'd nearly finished when in came a fellow, as white as a sheet. He said, 'I've just seen a terrible sight – there's a camp down the road, with thousands of people dying!' He didn't know I was a war correspondent; I pricked up my ears, put down my knife and fork and legged it outside. And down the road was Belsen.

When I was there the Germans were still in command, because we only had a handful of fellows – I mean, we couldn't have run the thing. They had been feeding them by boiling up potatoes still in their hessian sacks, not washed, or anything. Then they would trundle barrows around, and heave a sack through the window of each hut, and the inmates would scramble for them. Some of them were so weak that when we went in there we had a job to tell the living from the dead. Skeletons, they were. The only other photographer who went in with me was a fellow from British Movietone News, who was rather rotund, unfortunately. He looked slightly out of place among all these poor starving things. The inmates nearly all had typhus, so the main job was to get enough medics in there, and DDT, and things like that. On the first occasion I went in like a lamb to the slaughter; the next time I went in I was stopped at the gate, and a fellow with a great big puffer of DDT put it down my neck and up my trouser legs, because the whole place was swarming with lice. The smell was the worst: you couldn't get it out of your nostrils for days.

After that I came back to Britain and waited for things to subside; and one day we got a message from our parent office in New York, saying would I go and see the start of the Nuremberg Trial? They told me to give it a day or two, so I packed a weekend bag, and lo and behold I came back ten months later – a typical assignment with AP!

It was a nightmare journey to Nuremberg. Europe was in absolute ruins, especially Germany, and the only train was a military train, which had no glass in the windows. On the way, refugees were getting in the windows, trying to get a lift in the right direction, and every now and then a great big American sergeant, slightly inebriated, would come rushing down the train shouting, 'Alles raus! Alles raus!' All these poor devils would hop out again, and of course as soon as he had gone they would hop in again! When we arrived at Nuremberg an American truck was waiting for us, and it took us out to Stein, which was just outside Nuremberg, and dumped us at a lovely castle which was owned by Faber, the pencil king. There were French, British, Americans and Russians in this place, and of course I was with the Americans.

My bedroom was about the size of a cricket pitch, with a lovely painted ceiling – over my bed was a painting of a girl skating on the ice, wearing furs and things. The meals were absolutely unbelievable, especially as I'd been half-starved throughout the war. You name it, they put it on for us. We really enjoyed ourselves, especially the Russians, who'd never seen food like it in their lives. They used to have on the tables tureens full of boiled eggs and things like that, and the Russians would come down in the morning, take a pint glass and crack as many eggs into it as they could, and then go down the table pouring in Heinz tomato sauce and all these things that they'd never seen before – and that was just for starters! Then they'd *really* get down to it. We were being looked after by an old German soldier from the First World War, and we came back one day and noticed that there were no Russians around, and asked him what was going on. He told us that some very nasty-looking gentlemen, with red bands round their hats, had come in. Obviously some of these Russians had been talking about the tremendous time they were having – there was a grand piano on each floor, and singsongs and booze-ups every night – and they'd rounded them all up and put them in some stables down the road. And that was my first taste of what the Cold War was all about. They were fraternizing; they were having too good a time.

Paul Graven, prison guard officer
I was studying architecture at the University of Illinois, and was in the ROTC there, the Horse Cavalry, which was a requirement at the university. When the war started, of course we knew we were going to be called up. I was called up in my junior year, and went through basic training in Kansas; then I went to officers' training school at Fort Knox,

Kentucky and was commissioned in the armoured force, in tanks. Then we had three months' training as infantry officers at Fort Benning infantry school, in Georgia, because they weren't living too long overseas. From there I joined the 64th Infantry Division in 265th Battalion, trained for a while in Mississippi, and then we left from Boston and landed in Le Havre in December of 1944. We were attached to General Patton's Third Army, and fought our way east; when the war ended we were in Linz, in Austria. I was Marshal of Linz for a while, then we were sent to Czechoslovakia. During our military operations we visited Buchenwald; the colonel said, 'I want you all to go there and see what these people have done.' And of course it really got us mad, because we hadn't known about these things. It was a big shock. The bodies and the bones were still piled high, and the stench was terrible. There were some people walking around, who were so thin that I didn't see how they could stand up. It was the worst thing I ever saw in my life, I believe. It was quite a sight, and I don't care to see another one. I don't see how anybody civilized could have run a camp like that – could have seen what was going on, and yet worked there. Then we were sent to Dachau concentration camp for about two months; it had been fairly well cleaned up, so we didn't really do much except train and try to keep busy and to keep peace in the area.

Then the order came down to our regiment that they wanted an officer of the calibre of West Point or better, to go to Nuremberg, and I was chosen, along with one other person. I was always proud of that. When we got there we were introduced to Colonel Andrus, who was head of the Internal Security Detachment. All he had was a staff of officers, approximately twelve at that time. He had a house, with a dining-room where we all ate together, and it was real interesting to get his viewpoints. He was quite a man. He knew everybody – all the generals, all the way up. He was quite a taskmaster, too: when he said, 'Well, let's go swimming this afternoon,' we all went swimming with him. I thought he did an excellent job.

Joseph Stone, lawyer, Subsequent Proceedings

I did not have a war career. When the war started I was in the War Department in Washington; it ultimately became the Department of Defense. I left at the end of December 1942, and joined the Department of Labor in January 1943. This is of significance in terms of how I got to Nuremberg, because at the Labor Department I ultimately, somewhere in 1944 or 1945, began working for a Miss Bessie Margolin, who was the chief of the Appellate Division in the Office of the Solicitor of the Department of Labor. We wrote briefs for the Circuit Courts of Appeals and the Supreme Court. Marvellous lawyer, that woman. She argued twenty-nine cases before the Supreme Court, and won twenty-seven of them. She was very well known in Washington. In early 1946, Bessie went to Nuremberg, apparently to set up some kind of procedures between the main trial and the subsequent trials. Somewhere in the summer of 1946 I guess I wrote Bessie, and said I would appreciate her checking into some legal prosecution openings, I think in Wiesbaden. She wrote back and said, 'Well, if you have to come to Europe, you might as well come to Nuremberg.' And I wrote back and said that would be great. Around that time I got a telephone call from the War Department, saying they had a telegram signed by Justice Jackson asking me whether or not I was interested in coming to Nuremberg. Apparently Bessie had said something; it was obvious she had. I said yes, but I couldn't come at the moment, because I was in the middle of a love affair! They agreed to let me put it off for a month or two, and I left for Nuremberg at the end of September 1946.

I landed in Bremerhaven early in October; it was about a ten-day trip. The irony was that I, a Jew – not a terribly religious Jew, but nevertheless a Jew – was landing in Germany on Yom Kippur. It struck me as ironical, and most appropriate. I was there and Hitler was not. When I got off the boat, I remember they handed me a large army blanket, and I thought, 'Gee, what's this?' But after we got on the train for Nuremberg ... the train wasn't in the best of conditions and it was freezing. That blanket came in handy, and I must say that now, forty years later, by God I still have that blanket!

As early as 1941 the Allies declared their intention of bringing the Nazi leaders to account for their actions, and not long after this they began to discuss among themselves the question of how this should be done, even though they were not to be presented with their opportunity for several more years. The international route to Nuremberg was a long one, and made complicated by many things. The idea of putting Nazis on trial at all had to overcome opposition in some quarters, stemming from a belief that they should be summarily executed; after this point had been gained, it was necessary to settle the questions of where to hold the trial, which law or laws to draw on, whom to prosecute, and so on. And while these deliberations were going on it was also necessary to win the war, to make it all possible.

These military and bureaucratic strands can be traced in the personal routes to Nuremberg of the participants in this book. Some of them had been through a lot of fighting, while others had been behind a desk. Several had lived under the Nazis in occupied Europe. One or two were visiting Nuremberg from military zones elsewhere in Germany. Several, including the newspaper men, had seen some horrific sights. The experiences that they took with them to Germany in some measure helped to shape their reactions to the trial; another important factor, as we shall see in the following chapter, was the work that they did while they were there.

2. Work

Anna Cameron, secretary

I worked for a Lieutenant-Colonel Thomas Hinkle, who was interested in the economic 'phase' – what the Germans had done to the economy of the conquered countries, how they had dismantled whole factories and taken them back to Germany to foster their own war effort.

My working day started at 8.30 a.m., and it could go on till midnight if there was a case to be prepared. At one time we were told we'd get overtime, and none of us expected it, but we *were* paid overtime, and then we had to pay it back, because it was never authorized by Congress, and I suppose that after the war the Treasuries of all countries were pretty short of funds. I didn't mind working, because you were part of a great big thing, part of ... just, finally, bringing these cruel people to justice.

The Frank case was the one that Lieutenant-Colonel Hinkle worked on for four or five months. When his part of the trial was finished he went back to the United States for his discharge from the army, and I then went to work at the cable desk. This was where all the cables came in, from all over the world, and they were recorded and delivered to the various headquarters. Nobody thought much about it, except the Russians – they were very suspicious. I was supposed to call Justice Jackson's secretary if anything came in in the middle of the night; it was daytime in the United States. And it could happen with other countries too – everybody gave me the name and number where I could reach a responsible official or a responsible official's assistant at night. And when I went to the Russians, they said, 'What do you want to know *that* for?' So I explained; they spoke English very well. They consulted among themselves, and looked at me suspiciously, and then they said, 'Oh, that's all right. If any of our people wants to get in touch with us, they know where to go. They will call us. You don't need our night number.' Now isn't that typical?

Mary Burns, secretary

It was pretty routine. Mrs Elsie Douglas, Jackson's secretary, came from the Supreme Court and had all the right credentials for this work, so she did all of his dictation and personal negotiations, as did his son, who was a lawyer. So I kind of picked up the paper on the floor! But I did do a lot of document arranging and rewrites of papers that he was issuing and working on, and assisted Elsie when she was very busy and overloaded. It was kind of a piecemeal thing, but it was very pleasant. The hours were routine, as I recall, except when we got into a real bind, like when the Justice was preparing his final remarks, ending the prosecution. This was a big, big thing, and I think we worked half the night on that one, because in those days we had a big old-fashioned mimeograph machine to run off the copies. And the corrections, and the changes – as they advertise computers today, you don't have to throw away the copies; you can put new stuff in. But generally I think we were on a very even keel as far as hours were concerned. Mrs Douglas lived in the same house as the Justice and his son, and they could work at home; and the Justice frequently did this, which meant that Bill and I would hold down the office in the court-house itself.

Paul Graven, prison guard officer

When I got there, around August, there were twenty to thirty prisoners in the cells – we were just getting started and getting organized. They were working very hard at remodelling the building and getting the court-room set up. My assignment was as a prison guard officer. Every day the number of prisoners would increase. As far as I can remember, I was on for eight hours and off for twenty-four. It was considered very stressful, which was why we weren't put on for long. In the beginning we had men walking up and down outside the prison cells, looking in each window for a period of time and then going on to the next one. I was in charge of all the men that were doing that. All that changed after Dr Ley hung himself. He was sitting in his cell in a position in which the guard couldn't see him too well and couldn't tell what he was doing, and after about five or ten minutes the guard felt something was drastically wrong, and he called me out of the office. I happened to be the guard officer on duty at the time. We went in together and I cut him down. He had put a towel round his neck and over the back pipe on the toilet, and sat there. We called the prison doctor, and he came and pronounced him dead. Then I had to write a report on it. I was about twenty-one. It was quite stressful. And then, of course, I didn't know whether they'd blame me for not seeing that he didn't commit suicide, but it turned out to be all right. There really was no *fault* involved. After that, Colonel Andrus changed the procedure and put a guard on every single door.

One day, the guard on the door of Kaltenbrunner's cell was looking through the door. Kaltenbrunner had a plaid coat on, and on the door there were bars about an inch apart, going in each direction, and the guard kept passing out. So they came and got me again, and I stood and looked through these squares in the door at the checked jacket, and *I* became dizzy too! So we covered Kaltenbrunner up with a sheet after that.

We weren't supposed to talk to the prisoners, but I did talk to some of them. I was interested in Speer, being an architect, and I talked to him a little. I asked him about his architecture, and he talked a little about

American architecture. He could speak English very well; almost all of the prisoners *did* speak English. I asked Goering what he thought of the American Air Corps, and he said it was great. Goering was a very interesting fellow. He had beautiful clothes: gaberdine coats and uniforms.

There were various people going in to visit the prisoners. The prison psychiatrist, Dr Gilbert, was on Colonel Andrus's staff and I knew him well; there were also an American doctor and a German doctor. They all had passes, so they could go in and out without having to check with us. The psychiatrist would take the prisoner into a different room and test him, and he would tell us a few things about that at dinner. He wouldn't tell us a lot, because he was going to write a book, which he did! When the lawyers arrived, we would have a guard take Goering, for example, to a room in a different building, and then stand behind him all the time he was talking to his lawyer. I did that a couple of times, before I was given a different assignment. It was similar to any prison: he sat on one side of a desk, and there was a wall with a screen, and his lawyer sat on the other side.

Annabel Stover, secretary
We worked hard for a short period of time, and then there were great gaps of time when we had nothing to do, when the French presented their part of the case, then the English, then the Russians, then the German defence. So we had a lot of time to ourselves to go round and see the rest of Germany, as far as we could go; and some of us went to Switzerland, while others went to Paris. We were young girls, secretaries, and really had a good time. I don't know that I knew how important the trial was at that period of time. I knew that it *was* important, but I didn't realize that it would go down in history as such. I was just a small cog in the wheel.

Jean Tull, secretary
The working conditions were perfectly adequate. The American delegation was on the second floor, occupying the front and one side of the building, and the British had identical offices on the floor below. Those on the front were the grandest; I moved from a side office to one of the British prosecution staff's front offices at the beginning of the Subsequent Proceedings. We worked hard, especially when our case was about to start or an important piece of cross-examination was expected. When that happened, free evenings and weekends were non-existent. No overtime was paid; one just accepted it as an exigency of the situation. Some of the evidence and the exhibits with which I had to deal were pretty horrific. I remember particularly some of the evidence about experiments on the poor concentration camp victims, who were already half starved, to see how long people could exist in cold water, horrible things like that. And I can recall an instance where a witness got upset, retelling some of the evidence in the trial. But generally, I wasn't nearly as much affected by it as I would be now – youth makes one more resilient.

Seaghan Maynes, journalist

The press headquarters were in Schloss Stein, the great big grey stone castle just outside Nuremberg. It was built and owned by Baron Faber of the Faber family, the people who made pencils. We lived there. We were fed, it didn't cost us anything; there was a bar there, and we paid for that. It was all American supplies. There were about 200 correspondents in Schloss Stein, and the Reuter team consisted of about four people; it fluctuated, depending on the interesting developments in the trial itself. We'd take off in the morning and go down in the jeeps to the court. Inside the court-room, we would be on the right-hand side of the dock, not too far away – maybe eight yards – from the defendants. One of the oddities of the situation was that, while all these solemn events were taking place, we'd hear snatches of jazz coming in. The American guards in the building had radios, and they would play jazz or pop, and you could hear these strains every time a door into the court-room opened.

Whenever any statements were made, or there were any developments, we would write them down in shorthand; it was before the days of tape-recorders. This would go on for maybe a couple of hours. Then we would go back to our Reuter press room elsewhere in the building, and another Reuter man would go into the court-room. We did it in relays. Then we would transcribe our notes on the typewriter, belting out the story. We had our own copy-editor, a Reuter man, who would be getting all the copy together. Then we filed it out of the building to London. All the other correspondents were doing more or less the same thing, but we had to operate in relays because of the pressure of time. There was the Associated Press, Agence France Presse, the United Press, as it was known in those days, and all the other international news agencies, and it was imperative that you got your story out first. There was tremendous competition between the agencies, because a few seconds meant all the difference as to whether a subeditor on a newspaper got a Reuter story first. Even if it was half a minute, at least he'd got it, and then if AP came in, or Agence France Presse, the subeditor was already, in effect, mentally committed to the Reuter story. If you got the thing in first, it usually meant you were into the paper. If you *weren't* in first, the other side were in, so it was tremendously competitive.

The first few months were relatively boring, because it was the prosecution, and they were simply bringing up masses of documents and reading out this, that and the other. We would also be handed great sheaves of documents on the build-up of Germany's war crimes. The defendants were all just sitting there, not paying too much attention. We were always hoping that something would develop which would make the story a little bit more interesting. We were doing hard, factual news. You could put your own interpretation on it, such as 'Goering startled the court today with an outburst alleging that' something or other, and then give his quotes. Whereas the sketch-writer would say, 'Goering was giving the impression of a man who was so and so, and he was sitting as though nothing was happening', and so on. The sketch-writers' job was entirely different – there was no pressure on them. We had to be fast and accurate.

Dorothy Reilly, secretary

The day-to-day routine was to be driven from Hebelstrasse to the Grand Hotel for breakfast, and from there one could either ride or walk to the Palace of Justice. Either method involved passing the old city of Nuremberg, which was completely bombed out. Then we would begin the day's work, always showing the badge on entry. We would do what there was to do, and if you were free you could go into the court-room, on a pass.

Then lunch, which was ordinarily in the court-house cafeteria, the army mess. In the afternoon, if there was nothing to do, one went home and read. There was a great exchange of books. I shall never forget – Evelyn Waugh's *Brideshead Revisited* came out at about that time, and two people had copies, which were passed around. In the evening you would go out, if you were dating someone, or if someone was having a party, either in their own private villa or at the Marble Room.

Joseph Stone, lawyer, Subsequent Proceedings

You were given an office, and non-German-speaking personnel like me were given assistants – research analysts was technically the name they had – who were German-speaking. I was assigned a very young woman – she couldn't have been more than twenty-two years old. Her name was Ellen Levy. She was German, Jewish, and she had managed to get out of Germany before the war started. Her father had been a successful businessman near Frankfurt. Ellen was a very bright young lady. She spoke English, and she was back because she spoke German. We were sent down to the office of the Friedrich Flick Corporation; I was assigned to the Flick case. We were in this tremendous room, maybe fifteen feet wide and twenty feet long, and the walls were lined with bookcases and boxes of documentation. She and I worked there. It was easy enough to tell a dry-cleaning or grocery slip from something that might be of some value. Flick just saved everything in his life, apparently. Anything that looked unimportant I'd get rid of, and anything that looked important I'd hand to her, and she'd see what was in it. It was slow going; we were there for about five days.

Flick must have been in his late sixties at that point. There were about six or seven defendants: Flick and his top henchmen. One of these was called Weiss, and he was a very pleasant man, a financial genius of sorts. Part of our case involved breaking down the whole Flick organization: who was doing what, and who had responsibility for what. We were utilizing Mr Weiss in the office: he was helping us out because he knew the structure of that organization backwards. And you know what happens when you get personalized with somebody – you get very friendly. Well, the time came for the complaint, the document that we were going to file against these people charging them with all their various crimes, and Telford Taylor called us in. He was going over the whole thing, and we'd get to where each of the defendants was located, and he asked, where was Weiss? We said that Weiss was on the outside somewhere. 'You mean he's not in prison along with the others?' 'No, Weiss is floating around. We can get in touch with him any time we want.' 'Is he going to be a defendant in this case?' enquired Telford Taylor, and we said yes. He said, 'Well, he ought to be in prison.' Well, we tried to explain to him about the relationship, and why we didn't have him in prison, but he said, 'Put him in prison. If he's a defendant, he's got to come out of the prison.' So we had to do that with Mr Weiss, who I think probably was surprised. He must have gotten the idea that he was home free with us after all this activity.

Flick was a very, very interesting man. He had this tremendous empire of coal, steel and all kinds of manufacturing plants. But he himself was not a production man. His forte was financial figures, German mark figures. He knew how to acquire companies and merge them into his outfit. He was a brilliant man when it came to the financial aspects of business, and he had built this empire. As a matter of fact we convicted him of Aryanization of some coal-mines in Czechoslovakia, which were owned by the Petchek family. They had fled to New York with a few millions, so they weren't exactly poor. Flick took the coal-mines over, and he got convicted on that score.

Flick was a rather stern, dour individual – you didn't see smiles or any levity from *him*. But sitting in a court-room day in, day out for months with people sort of personalized the whole thing for you, so that when Flick had to go to the dentist, and was out of the trial for a day or two, upon his return your instinct was to ask him how he was. This was a man you were trying to convict; nevertheless, while you were there you were acting like human beings. Flick was defended by a Dr Dix, who was one of the leaders of the German Bar, a white-haired gentleman. He was an outstanding lawyer. However, in my book he was a little too old to learn new tricks, and I don't know that he really ever mastered the American technique of prosecution, and particularly of cross-examination. They don't have that in the European system: most of the questioning comes from the judges, and the lawyers do the expounding of the position but they don't do the examination, as I understand it. The trials followed the American procedure, and this threw some of the German lawyers, though it did *not* throw Dr Kranzbuehler, who had been General Counsel, I believe, to the German navy. Dix had to be in his late sixties or early seventies; Kranzbuehler, on the other hand, looked like he was in his mid-forties. A sharp cookie. I think he was the best lawyer in the defence team. He learned cross-examination very fast. I do not think that he ever became un-Nazified – I don't think his viewpoint changed one damn bit. There were several other lawyers who were somewhere between Dix and Kranzbuehler. They were certainly highly competent. There was no question that the Germans got as good a legal defence as was possible. Someone in one of the other cases hired some well-known American lawyers to defend him, and that was perfectly acceptable.

We got a great deal of assistance from a Dr Ungar, who was Czech. Apparently he had some kind of Jewish blood somewhere in his ancestry, because he went into a concentration camp. He was our expert on DPs [displaced persons]. He was a tremendously energetic man, and an expert in getting us contacts. Ungar would say to me, 'Joe, simply because someone was in a concentration camp it doesn't necessarily make him a nice person. I had to do things to survive that I'm not proud of. When they throw pieces of food at you, and all the animals go screaming for it, the stronger ones win and the weaker ones don't. So don't make the mistake of thinking every survivor from a concentration camp is a good person – not necessarily.'

Not everything was in documents that you found in an office. For example, before the Flick trial started I was given a translator, an army driver and an army vehicle, and off I went into Belgium, the Netherlands and France, looking for witnesses – all to do with Flick. We were on the road for several weeks. It was not a terribly successful trip: we may have gotten a couple of witnesses, not many. My translator was an American of Rumanian background, who spoke German, French, English, and his version of British! The reason I say that is that at some point we had to contact a British headquarters, in Belgium or Holland or somewhere, and I suddenly realized that he was speaking with a British accent. Pretty good, too, actually, to my untutored ear. I asked him about it later, and he said, 'Well, I thought it would help us along, you know. Doesn't hurt!' When we left Nuremberg, his wife suddenly appeared in the automobile with us, and he said he was going to drop her off in Paris. I said, 'Do you have travel documents for her?', and he said, 'No, no, no. Don't worry about it.' I said, 'What do you mean, don't worry about it? We've got to go through barriers.' I was a goody-goody American type. 'Don't worry, Joe, I'll take care of it.' Well, I was worried all the way up there. And sure enough we got to the border, and got asked for our credentials, all of which we had, other than hers, and then suddenly the auto takes off and we're in France. I said, 'How did you get her through?' 'Oh,' he said, 'I asked him the whereabouts of something, and when he began pointing we took off.' I said, 'He could have started shooting,' and he said, 'Oh, he wouldn't do that.' So I said, 'You get your wife back however you can, but I'm not going to go back with you!' And I did leave him, after we'd circled around looking for witnesses. I left him with the driver in Nancy, and took the train back to Nuremberg. The driver by this time had met somebody whom he was having a love affair with; he was very good at meeting girls. We left him in the auto one day to go into a hotel and talk to someone about billets, and when we came out he had an American girl sitting with him!

Ron Chapman, clerk

I was in the general administration office at that time. The British
delegation had one complete floor of the court-house. Our floor
consisted of a document room, a photostat room, various offices and
typists, the prosecuting counsel had their room, there were administration rooms, the pay office had a room. The Americans had their own PX,
then there was another PX which was the duty-free ration PX, as we
called it, for the other three nations. The American one was slightly
better, naturally, than what we had. We got 240 cigarettes a week, which
was a carton and two packs, for three and sixpence. That was the
cigarettes that we got from the Americans – you couldn't go out and buy
extra if you ran out. You got that ration and you could have a choice of
brand. But on top of that we got 200 free issue on the British side. It was
normally fifty a week, but being so far from the British zone we only got it
once a month. They had to send a truck up once a month, about 350
miles, with the duty-free cigarettes for the officers, plus all the wine and
spirit ration issued to the officers. They had a whisky, gin and wine ration
every month.

One of our jobs was finding witnesses. We might get Goering standing
up in court, giving a list of witnesses he wanted for the defence. The four
countries conducting the trial had to approve these witnesses. Say it was
Doenitz wanting a U-boat captain as a witness for the defence, it was then
the job of the various officers to find out where that U-boat captain was.
He might be in a prisoner-of-war camp up in the British zone of
Germany. If so, we then had to signal the Commandant of that camp and
say, 'Captain So and So is required by the International Military Tribunal
at Nuremberg as a witness for the defence on such and such a date.' Then
it was up to the Commandant of that camp to send him to Nuremberg
under armed escort. He was then lodged in the court-house gaol until
such time as he was to give evidence, after which he was escorted back.
Of course, if he was in the French zone, then it was up to France to signal
and get him there.

There were women – you know, those women concentration camp
people. Some of them were being held in the court-house gaol. Some of
them were actually being tried for war crimes themselves, up in the
British zone in Bad Oeynhausen, but they were also wanted as witnesses
at this main trial. So we often had them coming in under escort, and we
had to provide accommodation for the night for the escort that had
brought them down – they were usually military police. And women
military police brought the women down. A concentration camp
wardress was brought down by two British female military police, one
officer and a sergeant. The colonel was told that two military police
required accommodation, and he sent them up to the men's barracks,
thinking that they were male. Of course, when these two poor girls got
there, there were about a hundred men there, stripped to the waist,
washing and everything else. There was quite a hullabaloo, and when
they got back to the British zone they must have complained to their

officer. I remember the colonel reading out to us the letter he received
from their commanding officer, a woman, and she tore him off a strip –
'When our girls were sent down, they were expecting to be treated as girls,
and not put into this position,' and all this, then she really went to town,
and he was reading the letter out and saying, 'Look what she's calling
me!', and this was our colonel!

Priscilla Belcher, visitor

They brought the defendants into the hospital where I was working as a
nurse, and took them into the psychiatric ward, which was blocked off.
When Goering was brought in there was a tank sitting outside. I had that
ward, because I had worked with mental patients, and I'd go in with my
basket of goodies and check out who needed things like cigarettes, cards,
candy, handkerchiefs, books, pencils and paper. Somebody would say to
me, 'Try room 302!', so I'd knock on the door and open it, and there
would be a gun facing me, and I'd say, 'Can I do anything for you?', taking
a good look at the bed to see who it was! I saw Hess and von Papen;
nobody could get near Goering – they were so scared of plots to release
him.

In addition to working with patients we also did some work for the
UNRRA [United Nations Relief and Rehabilitation Association] camps.
The one we went to was for women and children only. They had been
rescued from concentration camps, and the children had probably never
known a home. We were helped by some Polish soldiers, who had been
released from concentration camps but didn't want to go back to Poland.
There were also a number of agencies that were working with them: the
Unitarian Church, Catholic charities, and so on. We gave parties for the
children and entertained them, while they were waiting to be collected by
relatives, if they had any left, or to have plans made for them. They were
pathetic when I first saw them: they were so small that it was difficult to
tell how old they were. By the time I left, nine months later, they had
fattened up a bit. We would turn over uniforms when the officers left, and
the uniforms would be made into clothes for the children, all dyed navy
blue. The poor little things looked so drab, we used to try and get white
ric-rac braid for them. They didn't know how to play. One little boy had a
beret which came down over his ears, and he just hung around all the
time; we were told he had been severely ill with typhus and lost all his
hair. The last time I saw him there, at Christmas time, he had little bits of
hair growing and he actually smiled. We tried to teach them things. They
didn't know about candy. The GIs made them a doll's house, because
they thought, 'Now some day they'll be going where there are real
houses.' And they furnished it so cleverly: they made ice-boxes with little
ice-cubes and cakes out of plastic. The children could hardly comprehend these things. And they couldn't comprehend some of the games,
either, the competitive games – they didn't want fighting games. They
were awfully sweet youngsters, but you had to be careful, too. You didn't
leave your jeep unlocked, or you'd find yourself losing all the parts. And

you hung on to your pocket-book when you went to certain places. This was what it was like – and then you'd go into the opulence that some of the lawyers were enjoying, in the Grand Hotel. It was a strange contrast.

Many of the GIs who were there had not fought in the war – they'd been drafted at the end – and so they were somewhat confused, and out for a good time. Some German nuns asked to bring in some children from their orphanage, to put on an entertainment programme for our patients, and when they came they were pink-cheeked, blue-eyed, blonde-haired, and the little girls had rabbit-fur coats, and they were the result of Hitler's programme to develop the super-race with his SS men and picked women. They looked so healthy, they were cute, they were adorable, and one can't fault them, but it made us furious when the GIs said, 'We'd rather have them than those other kids.'

Alfred Steer, administrative head, language division

I was the administrative head of the language division – I ran the thing. I acted as an interpreter on a few occasions, but I wasn't very good at it. You need a certain amount of absolutely iron nervous control, so that you can absolutely rely on the fact that you're never going to stutter or stop, ever. And I couldn't attain that sort of assurance. So I was fielding the teams, so to speak. We found that the job of interpreting was so nerve-racking that the individual could not do this day after day. The court was only in session from ten in the morning till four in the afternoon, but even so an individual interpreter would only be used for a portion of that time. If he interpreted from German into English, he did *not* do English into German, so he was spared from going back and forth in two languages, but even so we found that he could not do it day after day. So we had three different teams, which we used in succession.

We had repeated instances when an interpreter would simply fail, break down, be unable to continue, and we would have to put in a substitute at as short notice as possible, so that the court wouldn't be delayed any more than need be. Originally I put the stand-by people in a room nearby, and they complained bitterly that they didn't know what was going on when they were brought into the court-room situation cold like this, so then we arranged to have separate sound lines run from the court-room into this neighbouring room. The back-up interpreters were supposed to be sitting there with the headphones on, listening to what was going on in court. Frequently they could tell: before the interpreter in there actually failed they could hear him getting worse, and slowing down, and so forth, and knew that they were going to be called on any minute. I had to make the exchange. We had a system of two lights: a yellow one meaning 'Please slow down,' and a red one meaning 'Please stop the proceedings momentarily.' I'd press the red one, which was in front of Lord Justice Lawrence, he would stop everything and I'd make the shift. So one team would be in court, the second team would be in the room next-door, and then the third team would be completely off, studying the transcripts or doing whatever they wanted to do, because resting their nerves was the most important thing.

I tested something like 400 interpreters during the year I was there, travelling all over Europe. I found a large number of them in small countries like Belgium and Holland, and in the telephone services too. The Paris international telephone exchange was a superb place to pick people up, because they had to deal with conversations in all languages. But I found that only about five per cent of experienced interpreters could do this Nuremberg job, because of the nervous control that was needed, and because it was simultaneous. Actually, the interpretation was not exactly simultaneous, of course. There should be a lag of about eight to ten seconds between hearing a word in the original language and the appearance of its proper translation in the language interpreted into. If the lag got longer, the interpreter would soon get into trouble, because you can only hold a limited number of words in your memory under those conditions. My Russian was never very good, but I would take a split set of headphones, listening to the Russian in one ear and the original in the other ear, and I would listen for the cognates. For instance, their word for 'tribunal' is 'tribunaliye'. So if I didn't get it within about eight seconds, that interpreter had to be replaced. I was running the thing behind the scenes, most of the time.

We were turning out vast amounts of mimeographed materials in English, French, German and Russian, which was the daily transcript from the court reporters, and the justices asked us to look into the possibility of having this stuff printed. So we set up an international committee, and I worked with Barton, the chairman, who was a very able man. We decided that we would print the transcript, but we would need to clean it up a bit. For instance, people would get up in court, and instead of saying 422 they would say 244, things like that. Constant little errors were being made, and everything needed to be checked. So we set up a special section of reviewers, who would take the transcript as it came out of the court reporters' hands, and check back if necessary with the speaker of that day. Then we would send it off to be printed. Actually it fell far behind, and wasn't completed until after the trial was over. Nevertheless it was a final summation in print, and is a valuable historical record, of course. The woman in charge of the whole reviewing effort, about sixty people, Marguerite Wolf, was a native of Berlin, Jewish, whose family had moved to Britain some time long before Hitler. She was an absolutely charming person, very upper-class-sounding, and she had one of those idiotic little pairs of gold tweezers to hold a cigarette. I'd never seen one before, and I would just stare in fascination and watch her get the last eighth of an inch off that cigarette. We originally had her in as an interpreter, but she, like some others, did not have that iron nervous control that you have to have for simultaneous work under pressure.

We also compiled a glossary of legal terms in each language for the use of interpreters. This was done by Major Egbert. We had been trying to find a job for him, as he didn't test out as an interpreter, and at his rank he was useless as a group administrator. One day Sigmund Roth, then head of the interpreters, came into my office saying, 'Al, I've solved it. I've told Egbert that we need a glossary of legal terms. I've got him a room up in the attic, and by golly, he's at work!' I forgot the man for three months, completely, and all of a sudden here comes this apparition out of the past; I vaguely remembered the face, you know? He said, 'Well, it's finished.' I said, 'What's finished?' He turned out later to be quite good as an editor, and he helped to edit the record.

The judges called me in one day, and notified me that it was quite tiring for them to listen to heavily-accented English for six hours a day, and was there anything I could do to take some of these interpreters, who were obviously skilled people, and help them to reduce their accents? I said I'd see what I could do. I chose about six whose accents were particularly bad, and who were interpreting a good deal, and took them down to the sound lab organization, and set up a place where each of them could record himself and then hear himself. I said, 'I want you to hear what you sound like, and then you're going to work with people here, who are going to point out to you certain things that you do which make understanding difficult and which I think can be improved.' One of the Russian–English interpreters was a former Czarist officer, Colonel Schilovsky; he was about six feet seven, enormous. As we were walking away down the hall after the session, Schilovsky said to me, 'You know, Commanderr, that iss the first time I ever hearr I speak with haccent.' I loved it, I just loved it!

Virginia Grey was a German-American from Milwaukee; her parents were German. She adopted the attitude that many second-generation German-Americans do: German is what they speak at home, and when they go to school everyone speaks English. Therefore German is something that they're a little ashamed of – they don't quite admit it. They get into the habit of speaking no German whatever: their parents speak German to them, and they understand every syllable, but they always answer in English. I had a number of friends like that in college, and I'd noticed this. Virginia Grey was a very smart girl, a very nice girl. We got one of those concentration camp guards on the stand, who was an animal. He used the most incredibly filthy, derogatory language you could imagine. I'll use some bad language here – let's say he said, 'You just had to piss on the Jews.' 'Auf die Juden pissen.' *She* would say, 'You just had to ignore the Jews.' I heard that, and during a few moments of recess I grabbed her and pulled her aside, and said, 'Look, young lady, you can't *do* this!' She replied, 'I'm not going to use those words!' She taught Sunday school back home in Milwaukee, and she wasn't going to say those things. 'Look,' I said, 'you are a servant of the court, and the judges are relying on your interpretation to get their opinion of what that man is saying. It's *your* responsibility to give an accurate, complete translation, even if it *isn't* in harmony with your ideas.' I could see she was going to give me an argument; she wasn't about to say 'Yes, sir' at all. So to cut it off I just walked away – the coward's response! When the court reconvened, I had to do something else, and I didn't get back into the court-room till it had been going for about ten minutes. I slid into a seat, and all of a sudden I heard a gust of laughter sweep the court-room. But this was no laughing matter – it was just impossible. Virginia Grey was sitting in the interpreter's box, beside a British Captain Mackintosh, who was supposed to do French into English. He knew German just as well as he knew French. She would say into her microphone, 'You just had to ...' and then there would be a clipped Scottish accent saying 'Piss', and she would continue, 'on the Jews.' Well the contrast of these two voices, you see, midwestern American female and clipped Scottish male ... so then I took her out and made somebody else do it.

I remember one interpreter I brought to Nuremberg – she was in her thirties, with a Jewish background. I worked with her on our training programme; before we put them in court we'd give them several days of mock court work. After a while I considered that she was ready to go into the court, and I made a point of being there to see how she was doing. And she just froze. She couldn't say a word. It became obvious, and I looked over at her, and she was getting red in the face, and then the tears started. So I punched the red light and told Lord Lawrence that I had to make a substitution, and by the time I got somebody else in she was out in the hallway, and she was crying. I said, 'What happened? I thought you were well prepared to do this job.' 'Well,' she said, 'I looked right over there and I saw those men, and I thought to myself, "Because of those men, twelve of the fourteen men in my family are dead."'

At the end of the trial, the question came up of how the translation of the verdict was to be taken care of. The judges asked me to translate the verdict in advance. I pointed out that this brought up a security question, and they said 'Well, what we can do is give you the verdict and simply leave out the sentence.' So we appropriated a German barracks in Furth, outside Nuremberg – it was easy to seal off – and I took about twenty-five people with various languages and put them there for two weeks to translate the verdicts. They had to be absolutely isolated: there was no telephone; we took food out to them. As part of their payment they wanted to be in the court-room to hear the verdicts, so we reserved seats for them.

After the verdicts were given out, one of the press boys came running into my office, saying, 'Have you heard the latest? Schacht is going to hold a press conference!' Hjalmar Horace Greeley Schacht, by his full name, was one of the three who were acquitted. So we went downstairs to see it. Finally the guards brought him out, and took off his handcuffs – from now on, you know, he's a free man. There was a big table there, with four or five microphones. He sat down and they started throwing questions at him. Then he said, 'Wait a minute!' Of course he spoke perfect English, having been brought up in Brooklyn. He wouldn't speak a word of anything but German in the court. He said, 'You want me to co-operate with you reporters, and I'll be happy to, but I'd like to ask you first if you'll co-operate with me. When I walk out of here today I have nothing but the clothes on my back. I own nothing. It has all been confiscated. I don't have a penny, or a mark, or a house. What I am going to be forced to do is go to my daughter's home in Heidelberg, and I think she'll take me in. But she has children, and I've never been to her house and visited my grandchildren without taking them a gift of some sort. So if you gentlemen could spare a candy bar or a packet of cigarettes, I would be very glad to co-operate with you.' The next thing you know there's a heap of stuff on this table, and I thought to myself, 'That old son of a bitch! He isn't out of prison and he's in business!' The last time I heard of him, he was called in by King Farouk to reform the Egyptian economy, which he probably did at a fantastic fee.

Peter Uiberall, interpreter
I got to Nuremberg before my boss did, and I was immediately put to work on translation, as most of us were. My first job was to translate the interrogation of the former Austrian Chancellor, Kurt Schuschnigg, who had been in confinement under Hitler – 'honourable confinement', they called it, but it was still confinement – and who was freed with many others when the Allied armies came into northern Italy. He had been brought to Nuremberg and was being interrogated, and in the interrogation he described what went on at the Anschluss, and the scenes in Berchtesgaden, including the very famous one where Hitler opened the door and showed him the generals all lined up and ready to march. So it was very interesting working with some 140 pages of interrogation and translating them from German into English. The interrogation had been done with an interpreter. And I did the best job I knew how to do. I knew the circumstances; I was quite familiar with them. I certainly didn't miss any names or places or anything like that. Eventually I turned it in, and my boss, a woman army officer, said, 'You know, I'm terribly embarrassed, because that so-and-so denied the whole thing and said his interrogation was mistranslated.' In my experience it was fully in character for Schuschnigg. He refused to testify, and nobody wanted to force him. He went to the United States and became a college professor. But I was hurt. This was my first job in Nuremberg, and I was told by no less a person than the former Chancellor of Austria that I'd mistranslated his interrogation. A few days later, thank goodness, my colonel arrived, and we started work on the preparation for the trial.

The court-room was being worked on busily and there was no chance to do any practice trials in it. They had to fly in a rug from Belgium, the nearest place where such a big rug could be found. Germany was desolate – there were no rugs left that could fill a court-room in Nuremberg. The machinery wasn't there, the benches weren't there, there was nothing to sit on. We were given a space in the attic of the court-house, and in there we set up a mock court-room. There were hills of evacuated German law books standing everywhere. Colonel Dostert and Major Vincent worked out and tested the system, assisted by a whole group of officers, including myself. We played various roles, which we had to guess at because nobody had seen a war crimes trial before. Some of us played the prosecutors, defence counsel, witnesses, and so on, making up the text, while others among us were doing the interpreting into the microphones. And we discovered a number of things that we had not thought of before. In the first place, there is a certain speed beyond which you cannot possibly hear and talk, so there had to be a system to keep people from getting too fast. Then someone came up with the idea of light signals: a yellow light coming on for 'slow down', and a red one for 'stop'. The latter was for situations where the interpreter could not carry on because he had a coughing spell or something – it happened once or twice – and then you pushed the red button, and everything stopped until you were ready to go on. You had to have somebody who observed this, and the need to stop, and that was the monitor. He had two channels on his earphones, one for each ear, and sometimes he held one earphone away from his ear and listened to the actual room sound. It wasn't so much a matter of having to understand whether the interpreter was doing a good job or not, as of listening to the way he was speaking. Was his breathing showing trouble? Sometimes you could see this. On a number of occasions I did that monitoring job, and sometimes it was possible to step in and help. The monitor sat very close to the German-English interpreter; on one or two occasions he had some problem, he handed me the microphone and I was able to help. That was the monitor's job, invented in these mock trials. Eventually, when we had some of these problems ironed out, we set up mock trials in the court-room once it was ready.

While this was going on in preparation for the interpreting, there were a lot of people doing translation of documents, and I did some of this too. The problem was that we had nothing to sit on. The court-house had been hit by one or two bombs; it was patched up, and there was no furniture. The army had brought in some field folding tables, and most of the translators, in the first week or so, were given these long court benches to sit on, old-fashioned German court benches with a high back. I remember many a night, when we were working through the night, by about five or six o'clock in the morning you would see one or two of the translators stretched out, taking a few winks on the court benches, because we had deadlines to meet, and it was extremely difficult to keep up with the mass of German documentary material that was coming in. It had to be translated into the other languages in order to make it available to the prosecution, so that they could use it to prepare their cases.

Before 1945, simultaneous interpretation had not existed in the form in which we used it at Nuremberg. At the League of Nations there was a form of simultaneous translation, however, that was pre-translated speeches that were read simultaneously in the different languages; there was a selector switch and you could choose the language in which you wished to listen to them. That was called the Filene-Findlay system: Gordon Findlay was the man who devised the system of different channels, and Filene was the Boston businessman and philanthropist who financed the thing. Our work in Nuremberg was based essentially on the Filene-Findlay system, but something entirely new had come up: we had to do *spontaneous* interpretation, *immediate* interpretation. I don't personally like the word simultaneous, because it *isn't* really simultaneous – first you have to hear, then you can speak. And nothing that I have heard at the United Nations is as difficult as any of the things we had to do with our witnesses, because we had no way of anticipating what they were going to say. To make a comparison, the speeches at the United Nations very often start with, 'It gives me great pleasure to add to the words of my distinguished colleague,' etc. etc. Much of this is code, and all you have to do is know these things by heart. And you can wait as long as you want – you don't lose anything – and you can rattle it in any time you want, and some do. We had incredible problems in the court, because nobody had thought of them before. For instance, in German, where the verb comes at the end of the sentence, you do not know at the beginning of the sentence what he's going to say. A classic example that actually happened in the Nuremberg Trial: a former Nazi official on the witness-stand is asked, 'Did you know Mr Schmidt?' (I'm making up the name.) And let us say Mr Schmidt was a concentration camp Commandant, and having known him would be incriminating. The witness starts, 'Ja, den Schmidt, den habe ich im Jahre Fünfunddreissig oder nein im Jahre Sechsunddreissig, da habe ich den Schmidt ...' You still don't know. Has he seen him, has he known him, has he spoken to him, has he heard of him? All this can follow in the verb at the end. So the poor interpreter cannot start, unless he does what they used to call in German 'eine Eselsbrücke bauen', which is a German term, very difficult to translate, meaning something like 'building a donkey's bridge'. It doesn't exist in English. That is to say, 'Yes, er, no, er, Schmidt, well, with regard to Schmidt, was it in thirty-five or thirty-six, was it in Leipzig or was it in Dresden, I'm not quite sure, it was then that ...' You have to turn the sentence around completely, in order to be free to speak when he speaks, or else you lose him and you cannot catch up. That is one of the very characteristic problems of simultaneous interpretation.

Another one, the worst, is when you don't understand the word that you hear – when you have never heard it before. The United Nations has a principle, which I dispute – I'm nobody, so I can dispute it! – that they employ people to translate *from* the foreign language *into* the native tongue. The fact is that our experience in Nuremberg showed that the people who are best at simultaneous interpreting are the ones who understand every word that comes over the phones, and then are somehow capable of putting that into the other language. If you don't understand it in the first place, namely, native tongue understanding, then you can't do anything with it. There's a very important difference here. We preferred people like Wolfe Frank, who had native tongue German but who had lived long enough in an English-speaking country and had enough experience with the English language, in different fields of professions and endeavours. It helped me a lot at Nuremberg that I had worked in agriculture; I had worked in all kinds of fields. The interpreters need to have the vocabulary of the language they translate *into*, but they must have the full *understanding* of the original. I was once in the court-room when a very, very good interpreter was sitting at the German–English microphone, and a witness on the stand was talking about somebody who had been an alcoholic, and who had been sent to an institution to dry out. This is the way it came out in German: 'Und da wurde er in ein Sanatorium gebracht, wo er sich einer Entwöhnungskur unterziehen musste.' This simply means that he was brought to a medical institution, where he had to subject himself to a withdrawal treatment. The poor interpreter had never heard the word 'Entwöhnungskur', for which I don't blame him – many native tongue German people hadn't, and he wasn't native tongue German. I was sitting in the visitors' gallery, which we often did in order to find out how our friends were doing, and I heard the German, and I said to myself, 'Oh my God, he can't handle that! What's he going to do?' I saw an expression of utter consternation on his face, and he said, 'And he was – he was – taken to a hospital, where – where something terrible happened to him!' He had no idea what it was, but he knew enough to know that it was something very unpleasant!

Upstairs in the court-house we had a section which was called the reviewing section, where the transcript of the preceding day was gone over by interpreters of the third team. It was absolutely necessary to have three teams of interpreters: two teams alternated in the court-room, with one team on stand-by in the radio room behind, with phone connection, and the third team was up in the reviewing section, going over the previous day's transcript word for word: hearing the original, seeing the text of the translation and correcting it. We had to fight for the third team: the personnel people could not understand why the interpreters needed three teams.

Sometimes one of the interpreters would say, 'Do you mind letting me go on the mike for the next one?' For instance, Wolfe Frank did all the final statements of the defendants; we had an agreement on that. Early in the trial he had said, 'Please, whatever we do, let me do the final statements!' And he did a beautiful job. There would be long periods in court when your language was not spoken and you sat there doing nothing, but then you might suddenly have to go into action if your language came in. German–English, which was my spot, was pretty busy, because most of the language spoken in the court was German. The prosecutor might speak English, French or Russian, but there was almost always a German answer, so the interpreters interpreting out of German were almost always busy. Sometimes we had to have a special interpreter because of a particular witness. I remember there was the case of the university library in some great Belgian university town, that the Germans were accused of having stolen, lock, stock and barrel, and somebody on the witness-stand testified in Flemish; we had a Flemish–English or Flemish–German interpreter standing next to the witness, and the interpreters picked up from there.

One of our first stars in interpreting came from the States, and was a student of German. He had lived in Germany, and had probably studied at Heidelberg or Göttingen or somewhere, and he was a graduate of Pennsylvania State College. He did very well at the beginning of the trial. Then, one day, we had a witness on the witness-stand who was a witness for the defence, and he wanted to show that not all people in concentration camps were mistreated – some had a wonderful, clean and healthy life in agriculture, working on the fields. There are a lot of fields around Dachau, and he was talking about that concentration camp, describing in detail how you go about cutting up seed potatoes and planting them, and then 'hilling' them, 'häufeln' in German, where you make these hills around them. I was monitor on that day. The monitor sat close to the interpreter, and if he had problems the monitor could sometimes help. I heard him slowing down, and I realized that he could have handled Nietzsche and Schopenhauer very well, but that he had absolutely no idea of agriculture. He couldn't figure out for the life of him what 'eyes' had to do on potatoes! So in such cases, of course, the reviewing section had a lot of work to do. Sometimes the German defence counsel, who listened in both German and English, jumped up and said, 'This is not what the witness has said!', and so on, but they didn't protest this time; it wasn't really very important.

That interpreter sooner or later went back to the States. He was very highly specialized in sophisticated vocabulary, and that is not what you need in simultaneous interpreting – you must be very broadly informed about vocabulary. Otherwise you can't handle it, because you don't know what people are going to say next. Sometimes things were sprung on us. Baldur von Schirach, the Reich youth leader, was also Gauleiter of Vienna, and that was his greatest undoing, because he was responsible for the deportation and death of many, many Jewish families. He was one of the few defendants who made what you might call a confession of wrongdoing on the witness-stand. I happened to be on duty on the morning when he came on to the witness-stand in his own defence. I was on the German–English mike. I came in, got into my seat in the interpreter's box, the defendant was brought in by the guards and led to the witness-stand, and he stuck his hand into his tunic and brought out a prepared statement. To the interpreters, that is very bad, because it means the man is going to speak fast, faster than he would if he were speaking freely; it means he doesn't have to wait and think; and the interpreter has an awful time keeping up. Normally, if it was at all possible, the defence counsel would see to it that the interpreters got a copy, which helped. You had the text in front of you: if you missed something in the hearing, you could look it up. But on this day, I think Baldur von Schirach wanted nobody to know what he was going to say. He started out, 'It was my guilt, that I loyally served a man who committed murder a millionfold.' The original German text read, 'Es war meine Schuld, dass ich getreu einem Mann diente, der millionenfach Mord begangen hat.' I translated that immediately, as well as I could, and I thought I was right. When the thing was printed, the editor changed it to 'a million murders', and I've been furious ever since! There *were* such disappointments, and of course we made mistakes too. Simultaneous interpreting is not very high in quality, especially when it has to be done in a court-room in a hurry, and a professional linguist can quibble with it very easily, because you can sometimes see that what the interpreter says, although the meaning is exact, is not *literally* the translation of what he hears – very often it cannot be.

Colonel Dostert was chief interpreter first, then Wolfe Frank was, then I was. When I became chief interpreter I instructed all the interpreters that when they had a witness on the stand and he started with the German word 'Ja', they were never to translate that as 'Yes' until they were absolutely sure that that was what he meant. Because 'Ja' in German is 'Well', among other things, the typical 'Well' that President Reagan, for instance, started with in his press conferences when he got a question that he had to think about. This is what a German does when he says 'Ja'. Very often a witness was asked about something, the answer to which could be incriminating to him and others if it wasn't very carefully thought out. And he might answer, 'Ja, das war nämlich so', of which the only correct translation is, 'Well, let me show you, this is the way it happened.' It's completely different in word material in English from the German, and yet in a court of law this is the correct way to translate it, or else you're hanging a man, wrongly. Because once that 'Yes' is on the transcript, the man is stuck. Interpreting in these cases had a lot of pitfalls, and very often at the end of the day we were not exactly overjoyed at the way it came through. We would run upstairs to the reviewing people and say, 'Hey, that wasn't exactly the best way to do it. Have you checked that?' You had a lot of safeguards against mistranslations – I don't think any that occurred remained in the transcript.

The defence had their own English experts in the court-room. And there was a very good German lawyer who also knew English, Professor Hermann Jahrreiss, who acted as adviser to the court, and in the publication of the trial record. So there were many, many ways in which everything was checked and double-checked before it was actually printed or used by the judges as material for their considerations.

Maxwell-Fyfe was fabulous, he was magnificent. And Goering was very good, very quick. Our chief prosecutor, Justice Jackson, was a very erudite gentleman, a fine lawyer and a wonderful legal writer – his indictment was marvellous – but with less trial experience, I think, than Sir David Maxwell-Fyfe. He once put a question to Goering that was strictly a question of law, and Goering said, '*I* can't answer that question, since *I* was not the leading jurist in my country, thank God!' It was intended as a direct slap at Justice Jackson, who had been Attorney-General in the United States and was a justice on the Supreme Court. But Sir David was fabulous. We all admired him. He was very fast, so he was a problem to us interpreters. But then, of course, the presiding judge, Lord Justice Lawrence, watched for that, and many a time he would take his pencil – he didn't use a gavel – and tap it, which made a terrific noise because the microphone was standing right next to it, and he would say, 'You're going too fast! Slow down!' That was when the yellow light button had been pushed by the monitor. Of course, if the *monitor* wasn't on the ball there were problems. We very rarely used the red light. Even if the interpreter had a coughing spell and was physically unable to go on, we would much rather have a stand-by slip in and take over the microphone. Once, early on, we had a Russian witness on the stand, and the Russian–English interpreter was one of our senior interpreters, who had a long experience of conference interpreting and wasn't really fast enough for simultaneous. He jumped up in the court-room, pulled off his earphones, and shouted, 'Get me out of here, I can't stand it!'

The turnover was considerable, but this was mostly because people did not come with the expectation of staying that long. They were borrowed from various agencies, or they left their professions on leave of absence, and they simply couldn't stay. We had some *very* good people, who were by no means over-strained, but they had to go home when their time was up. The man who had trouble with potatoes, for instance, came back later for a second tour, in which he was more fortunate and did quite well.

There is a certain age beyond which you are not fast enough. *I* couldn't do simultaneous interpreting now. You pick up the telephone and dial the weather service, and while you are hearing the forecast you tell someone else in the room the same information in French. That's the way it is. Then again, the weather forecast is code – it is something that is anticipated, you know the terms. It is much easier to do that than translate a witness on the witness-stand. And the older people very often had trouble. We had a marvellous British linguist, probably the best German–English linguist we had, who was in her late fifties, and she started off as a court interpreter. It didn't work; it was much too fast for her. Another thing: the trained linguist, who has gone through a good school and done, say, book translation, cannot stand what he or she has to do in simultaneous interpretation, because you cannot verify, you cannot check by going back to a dictionary. There is no such thing as an exact translation of any word – only non-linguists think that. So that is why a very precise and well-trained linguist doesn't by any means make a good simultaneous interpreter. They can't reconcile all that they know and have learned about language work with the business of giving an instant solution, as you have to.

You didn't have time to think about the content of what you were saying, but it came back to you in your sleep, in nightmares. You couldn't possibly handle the information about concentration camps all day long without being affected by it. Nobody could. We had among our interpreters some who had been in concentration camps, and they were the best, of course, for that kind of material. But it was probably very hard for them at times, to be brought back to it again. *I* didn't particularly have nightmares; some interpreters did, and told me about it. But you couldn't distance yourself from it.

John Pine, visitor

I was working as a British prosecutor in various military government courts. Many of the cases were concerned with the illegal possession of firearms, and whatever sort of 'arm' you had, if it could fire anything at all, that was a capital offence and you were liable to have your head chopped off. I was attached to a judge, Colonel Fenton-Atkinson, and I remember him saying to me, 'You know, when one gets back, one will have to be extremely careful if one ever sits on the bench again, because you'll only have to hear about a pea-shooter and you'll say "Off with his head!"' One got into this very regular habit: one was attached to a judge, and one used to do a circuit, and what it amounted to was that one used to go round beforehand to the various military headquarters and Kreis headquarters, and they would give you their papers. They had little idea, of course, how to formulate any charges, or anything like that, so you had to formulate the charges, and, so to speak, arrange the calendar, and go back to your headquarters – my headquarters then was Hanover – and get your judge organized, get your transport organized, and then get on tour, round the circuit for a week or so.

A terrific lot of the cases arose from the displaced persons' camps. They were, of course, very full indeed, full of every known nationality, virtually speaking. All people who had been slave labour to the Germans – in the main, possibly farmers – on the land, and there they were, incarcerated in these camps with nothing to do, little provided for them, and minimum rations, and so forth, and not unnaturally they didn't take all that kindly to it, particularly bearing in mind the type of life they'd been subjected to for years past, under the heel of the Germans. They felt that, having won the war, they were deserving of something better, and one thing they had very much in mind was to sort out the Germans for whom they'd been working and slaving for so many years. The tendency was for six or eight of them to band themselves together in the camp. And come nightfall, out they would go and commit the most heinous crimes, with the possession of firearms, mainly sawn-off shotguns. They would go – where better? – to the farmer's house where they'd been incarcerated, or the outbuildings, and beat him and his wife up, plunder the whole place, fill themselves with loot, threaten him with their guns and so forth, rape his daughters, generally misbehave themselves, packing up all the farmer's stuff that they wanted, stuff that would be useful in the camp to make themselves more comfortable. And come four o'clock in the morning, coming towards light, when they'd gorged themselves well on the farmer's provisions and had a jolly good meal, which the farmer's wife had probably been made to cook for them, they would then leave, and as an encore would probably shoot the farmer and his wife dead. Then they would go back to the camp. It was a thing that, not unnaturally, the civilian police and courts couldn't deal with at all; we had our own police, but *they* couldn't effectively deal with it; and neither could the German courts deal with it. And to re-establish law and order the military government courts had to take over and deal with all those things, particularly the possession of firearms.

Looking back on it, one sometimes wondered if there ever was a Nazi in Germany at all; there certainly never was an SS person! Everybody, as soon as they were picked up by the military government authorities, had to fill in what was known as a 'Fragebogen' – a general questionnaire – as to their background, and so on. And it was always a case of, 'I was never a Nazi, I was never in the SS, or anything like that.' I have seen somebody in court, whom I was cross-examining myself, literally vomit over the side of the witness-box when I said to him, 'Now you were in the SS, weren't you?' It was quite pathetic to see the fear on his face when I said this. I remember cross-examining the Duke of Oldenburg in relation to the possession of firearms, and it came out that his possession was – being who he was – quite innocent, but the fact remains that it *was* a capital offence. I knew the Director of the Military Government's Court Branch, Sir Charles Gerahty, very well: it was his job to review all capital sentences and advise the Commander-in-Chief as to whether or not they should be carried out. He used to have a terrible time, in his own mind, as to what he should advise. They had a very neat little machine thing that worked electrically, with a knife that came down and chopped your head off before you knew what had happened to you, and it went into a basket in front. It certainly left me with very strong doubts about capital punishment, particularly when one realized, when once the head's off, you can't put it back again if you made a mistake.

Roger Barrett, officer in charge of documents

My first assignment was to go to a rather secret British intelligence organization which had reports from inside Berlin during the war, and I gathered evidence of atrocities while the big shots were agreeing on the structure of the court. My one aim in life was to get inside the court-room if the trial ever started, and I realized that, being then a lieutenant – the highest I ever got was a captain – I would not be very likely to get into the court unless I had some special function. Rank was very important at the trial: we would go to a meeting where the highest-ranking American was a general and the highest-ranking Russian was a colonel, and the next time we met that same Russian would come back as a general, having been promoted! And neither my rank nor my stature warranted any great recognition at the trial. So I started to husband all the documents, and every time I found captured German documents or witness transcripts I piled them up. When we moved to Paris on the way to Nuremberg, I was made head of the American document section of the trial, and as the trial became more formally organized I was also put in charge of the relations between the counsel for the defendants and the court. In connection with the actual presentation of the case, I documented, from one document room which served all the countries, the presentations that were made in court.

My principal activity was in connection with the documents. The problem was to assemble all the documents that might be used at the trial, to get them translated into four languages, to get them sufficiently analysed so that their significance would be readily apparent and you could decide how they would fit into the case, and to reproduce them. Not the least of the problems was the reproduction of documents. We had our own reproduction machines, but we had to have generators for electricity, and we had to use German prisoners of war to sit on planks to make the documents flat so that they wouldn't roll up when you read them. Living conditions were rather difficult, and our equipment was somewhat primitive, and to process millions of documents and cull from them those that were significant, and then get them introduced into evidence in a very short time, was quite a logistical problem.

I had a young corporal working for me named Cardozo, known as Ben, and one day I gave him a paper bag to be delivered to another officer, and told him to be sure and not look inside it. I was sure that he *would* look at it and tell everybody about it as soon as he left, and a moment after he went outside there was a big scream and he came running back in. He had in his hand the head of a Polish prisoner of war; he had been hung, because the rope mark was around his neck, and then the head had been shrunk to about six and a half inches in height. It was one of the pieces of evidence that we thought we might use at the trial, and it was quite a shocking thing even if you knew what was in the bag, but it was doubly shocking for him! We also had a collection of tattoos which were cut from the chests of prisoners at concentration camps and made into lampshades, slippers, etc. The Germans seemed to be fascinated by the tattoos. When we started gathering evidence, I looked for things like witnesses who'd witnessed particular mass killings, and things like shrunken heads, and I was disgusted, revolted, by the evidence I was dealing with. Incidents which involved only twenty or thirty people were not significant enough for the trial, and individual atrocities weren't either. I became hardened to the experiences that I heard or read about and the exhibits that I saw, and I really didn't react in the way that a normal human being would, because I was so immersed in it. After the trial, and after I went back into civilian life, I used to lecture on the trial, with particular emphasis on what bigotry and prejudice can do to the human outlook, to a country, and so on. I was trying to impress the people who'd led a rather sheltered life in the area that I come from, with what really happened and how horrible it was. And I remember describing one incident, which I had gathered for use at the trial but which was never used, and the host's daughter in the front row passed out. I really lost sight of how horrible these things were, until I came back and tried them out on other people. I felt that people in my part of the middle west ought to to know something about these things; I was surprised at how little people knew even after the war, even after newspaper publicity.

Because of my work with the documents, I worked quite closely with people like Justice Jackson – indeed, my relationship to the top-level people was closer than either my importance or my rank signified. I had access to them. One of the principal motivations which Justice Jackson had in proceeding with the trial was to create a record, by documentary evidence that couldn't be challenged, of what actually took place. First World War atrocities were not believed, the few Germans who were convicted were released within a year or two, and we were afraid that unless a record was made which was tested by American-style and British-style cross-examination, future generations would not believe how horrible the truth really was. And of all the documents that were introduced at Nuremberg, hundreds of thousands, I don't remember one that was challenged for authenticity.

Occasionally I would meet with the Russian staff to deliver documents, and I had a document problem to take up with them on Christmas Eve. I went to their offices, and the secretary said that the whole staff was in conference. She was very unco-operative, and I was very pushy. Finally I said, 'I know they want to see me,' and I pushed my way in, and they were all on the floor on their hands and knees playing with wind-up toys which they'd gotten from the PX!

I think that, professionally speaking, one of my most colourful experiences was when I was assisting Sam Harris, a former officer of the Securities Exchange Commission and a very brilliant lawyer. He later became a senior partner in one of the most important law firms in the United States. Sam was, like me, a nervous young lawyer, and he stood up to address the court on a presentation that he'd worked on for several months, and I sat in front of him to hand him appropriate documentary material. As he stood up to talk, in front of the four judges and their assistants, in a court-room with John Dos Passos and Rebecca West, and world press, his first words were: 'The sound you hear is my knees knocking, and I haven't been this nervous since the day I proposed to my wife!' Then he went on with a first-rate presentation. But it was frightfully embarrassing, and Gordon Dean, the head of our press relations, immediately gathered together the press people, saying it would ruin this poor young man's career and make a joke of the trial, and they were to keep it out of the press, which they did. Sam said to me afterwards, 'How did it go? I had a vague feeling that I said something before I started.' I said, 'Nothing of any consequence,' and no one else said anything to him. At four in the afternoon, Sir Norman Birkett called and said he would like to see Captain Harris, and I thought, 'My goodness! He's going to be sent home, he's going to be cashiered!' We respected Sir Norman more than any of the other judges on the bench, as a judge and as a person – at least I did. Sam came out after spending half an hour with him, and I said, 'What happened?' And he said, 'It was just delightful. We had tea, and Sir Norman told me about his early days at the Bar, and some of the things he did were sort of embarrassing, and he made some mistakes and so forth, and isn't he a wonderful person?' And Sam was a hero among all of us, because he'd had tea with Sir Norman. The next day, when Sam found out from others what he'd done, the curse had already been taken off by Sir Norman's kindness.

At first it amazed me that the Germans hadn't tried to destroy any of the documents, but – although I hate to ascribe characteristics to a race – it *is* a German characteristic to have that methodical record. The best example was the Mauthausen concentration camp book, which was one of the documents that I had: in it was listed every person who came into the concentration camp, and every detail about them, including how and why they 'left'. They had to account for everyone who came in and went out, because of their tendency to be so methodical, so these people died in alphabetical order, at intervals of a minute. For the first hour everybody would die of heart failure, and for the second hour everybody would die of a stroke – you know. The cause of death and the time of death were ridiculous, on the face of it, but they accounted for every single human being. One investigation brought to us the total archives of the German navy, which were found intact underground – I think the OSS people found them by accident. There were trucks and trucks of key archives. I collect literary and historical manuscripts as a hobby, and my father did, so I looked at these things as though they were great historical treasures, many of them, and even though many people pinched souvenirs, I didn't. But one of the ones which I would have treasured was a letter from Goering – I've forgotten its subject-matter and addressee – which said, 'When you have finished reading this, be sure and destroy it, because some Jew like Roosevelt will use it to try us as war criminals!' There was document after document which said 'Destroy immediately after reading', which turned up at the trial.

Andy Wheeler, lawyer

My assistant Frank Wallis and I spent a lot of time on Jackson's speech, when he took on Goering. There were a lot of errors in it, and Wallis and I worked late into the night correcting them.

My major contribution, I guess, was to get things started: to get the different systems going, move people from London to join the group in Nuremberg. My function during the trial was to work under Justice Jackson to co-ordinate the collection, classification and translation of the various materials that were to be made available to the court, and to assist him in making decisions.

One thing disturbed us and slowed us down: the judges decided to allow these defendants, instead of just answering the question, to make a speech in reply. And that went on for ever. The defence counsel didn't know the first thing about our system of cross-examination and confrontation, so they would listen to some defendant, and when he mentioned *another* defendant, the first thing a lawyer over here would do would be to say, 'Stop that! You have no business to talk about my client,' but they just allowed him to do so. So I'm sure that the defendants didn't get as good a representation as the defendants in the Japanese trials did.

They had English and American lawyers, who incidentally came through Nuremberg on their way to Japan, and consulted us on how we were doing and what they should do. I think we told them quite a bit that helped them.

The only time I actually addressed the court myself was after Christmas, when I held forth on the suppression of the Christian churches in the eastern territories. By that time it was just a question of reading a prepared memorandum, but it was an honour and I was glad to do it. Otherwise my efforts were directed towards sifting out what we had to present, in such a form that it could be used. There was an enormous number of documents, and Roger Barrett, who was only a lieutenant at the time, had immense responsibilities, and carried them out wonderfully, for making documents available, getting translations, and so on. He had a lot to do with things going as well as they did. Justice Jackson was not a very good administrator, and he hated to rule on who should do this and who should do that, so he welcomed concrete suggestions that we were able to make to decide those questions. He was magnificent at putting words together, but when he came up against Goering he wasn't well-prepared.

Daniel Margolies, lawyer

I started out in the documentary section, and then I was transferred to the interrogation section. Tom Dodd, who wasn't a senator then, had been on the Labor Committee briefly with me, so we knew each other, and he quickly attached me to his group. He didn't know any German, so I was rather useful to him. We went around interrogating the prisoners, many of whom had by this time arrived and were locked up in the cells of the court-house. They were bored stiff because they were all in solitary confinement, and they were delighted when anyone called them out to be interrogated. All those interrogations, I believe, are now published.

A furious debate broke out as to whether the trial would be based on documents that we would introduce, which we had accumulated and which were quite incriminating, or whether we would have witnesses on the stand based upon the interrogations that we had held. One theory was that all you had to do was put the documents in, and that showed what happened and who did it, and you didn't have to bother with the case of people getting up and either telling the truth or not, as the case might be. But others said that you would put everybody to sleep if you just had people standing around reading documents to the court – that if you were going to have a trial, and all the press of the world was there, and it was the first trial of this sort in history, you'd got to have a certain amount of action, suspense, and the way to do that was to have witnesses. And then, of course, it did dawn on them that you could have both – I mean, you could have documents, and confront the witnesses with them. I don't know why ... whenever you get two lawyers together you get competition. I think we really ended up with a documentary trial, based on the documents, but we produced witnesses who would identify the documents.

It was only later, in what we called the Subsequent Proceedings, that the German defendants woke up to a rather ingenious defence, which was: 'Yes, this document has my signature, but there's not a word of truth in it.' That didn't occur to them at Nuremberg – they were still somewhat dazed, perhaps, by the defeat, or something. None of them came up with this ingenious notion that the documents were all fanciful affairs that they wrote up for some reason that I never quite understood.

We had a bunch of rooms where we interrogated people. We had the interpreter, and one of the defendants, and Tom Dodd, and me handing him notes; and he wouldn't have an attorney, but he would have a soldier or two behind him to see that they didn't escape or anything. Dodd would say something in English and the interpreter would say something in German which approximated to what Dodd had said, and the prisoner would respond, and it all got written down. And then we would say, 'Well, here's a document that you issued, saying that all the inhabitants of such and such a town should be shot – is this your signature?', and 'Why did you do this?' And he would say, 'Well, somebody or other had destroyed a truck,' or something, 'and we had to maintain a certain amount of respect ...' At any rate, we went through weeks of interrogation. And then they plotted out the trial, and divided up the defendants among the Russians, the French, the British and the Americans. Meantime, we also had Benelux observers on hand, who were there to make suggestions.

The Germans never did understand the concept of the trial, which was based on the American notion of 'conspiracy', which is a favourite American legal device for dealing with organized crime. I don't know if the British use it much or not, but it's very common in the United States. The point is that if you have a group of people with a common objective, they are in a conspiracy, and any act done by any member of the conspiracy is attributable to the conspirators as a whole. Any statement made by any member of the conspiracy is binding on the conspirators as a group. It's a very convenient way of convicting a large group of people, like what we in America call organized crime, if you get these people together. Now, I don't believe that under the Napoleonic code this rather convenient method of prosecuting large groups of people had been developed – they may have had other techniques for that. The result was that you could well be indicted along with someone you had never met, as happened in this case. One of the defendants was that horrible man from Nuremberg who wrote that anti-Semitic newspaper, Streicher, who was not a particularly prominent member of the Nazi Party, although he was prominent in other respects – at any rate, socially he wasn't all that high. We had the Foreign Minister, and Mr Schacht, and other people, and they found themselves sitting alphabetically, Schacht and Streicher, and Mr Schacht found Mr Streicher a very distasteful person to sit near, and he kept pointing out that he'd never met Mr Streicher, and he rather resented being on an indictment that had him and Streicher as co-conspirators, of all things. And they never did quite understand how that worked.

Actually, Streicher was convicted and Schacht was acquitted. Schacht had been in charge of the financial aspects of Hitler's regime, which were very ingeniously and, I must say, very dishonestly managed, with great success. And without his efforts the Nazis never would have gotten anywhere. On the other hand, there's nothing in international law that says running the affairs of a country with great ingenuity, even without honesty, is a war crime, or a crime against humanity. So he was acquitted on the grounds that he was not a very nice man, and he managed to finance a movement that was quite distressing, but it wasn't exactly clear why that was a war crime. Von Papen was acquitted. Now, von Papen had played a prominent undercover role in charge of spies in the United States during World War One, and was prominent in connection with blowing up a munitions factory and killing a number of people – the Black Tom massacre in New Jersey. Mr von Papen pointed out rather plaintively that this was, after all, World War Two, and that being tried for crimes that he'd committed during World War One didn't fit within the framework of the indictment. He actually had been Prime Minister and had arranged for Hitler to take over power: I don't think Hitler would have gotten in quite as easily as he did without the connivance of von Papen. It's not clear exactly why *that* was a war crime: I mean, it's not clear which Convention – the Geneva Convention, or some other – says that you can't assist somebody to take over power.

Tom Dodd was a leading Catholic, who played an important role in politics in the United States, and we also had in our group Father Walsh, who was a geopolitician of some eminence, a professor at Georgetown University in Washington, which is a Jesuit school. He was brought along by Mr Jackson because of the fact that the Catholic Church had been one of the targets of the Nazis, and we had hoped that the Vatican would lend its influence, and give us supporting documents to the extent that they had any. Father Walsh was brought along to negotiate with the Vatican on these matters, which he did with great success. The Pope in fact submitted an affidavit with a lot of documents, which led to one of the more extraordinary scenes of the trial. The Attorney-General of the Nazis, Mr Frank, who had a somewhat sinister record as Governor-General of Poland, suffered a change of conscience and felt that his life had not been perhaps as exemplary as it might have been, and he turned to the Catholic Church for solace. He became a Catholic, and he sought forgiveness for his sins. His confessions must have gone on for a long time, but at any rate he did become a Catholic. He was sitting there, and to his dismay the Americans submitted an affidavit from His Holiness the Pope, along with a whole series of shocking documents as to what had happened to the clergy in Germany – the priests at Dachau, the medical experiments that had been worked on the nuns, and so on. All that was spelled out – Father Walsh had done an outstanding job in getting this together. And Hans Frank rose up among the defendants, and protested that the trial was illegal, the proceedings were a farce and a mockery of justice, and that for His Holiness to participate in them was an offence against the Church, and that unless the Pope saw fit to withdraw his affidavit within twenty-four hours, Mr Frank would withdraw from the Church. He withdrew from the Church. People were not impressed.

Whitney Harris, lawyer

Since I was more or less an expert on German intelligence, I was given the primary responsibility for the prosecution of Ernst Kaltenbrunner, the Gestapo and the SD [Sicherheitsdienst, or Security Service]. These two repressive agencies were under the umbrella of German intelligence, and my major task at the beginning was to prepare the case against them.

The United States' case was what we call the 'common plan', and that embraced the entire history, the conspiracy, of the Hitler regime. As part of that, we had to present the evidence against the individuals who had been indicted, and also against the organizations. This was quite unusual in a trial, to have organizations named as accused. The British assignment was primarily with respect to crimes against peace, violations of specific treaties. The Russians had the responsibility of handling war crimes and crimes against humanity in the East, and the French had the same responsibility in the West.

At the outset we had some problems between the lawyers who came from the civil law countries, France and Russia, and the lawyers who came from the common law countries, Britain and the United States. They had some differences in concepts. Under the civil law an accused person is not permitted to testify under oath in his own behalf, but he *is* accorded that right under the common law. But under the civil law the accused person is permitted to make an unsworn statement at the end of the proceedings: he can say what he wants. That is not allowed under the common law. To accommodate these differences we allowed the accused both privileges: that is, they were permitted to testify under oath and also to make an unsworn statement at the end of the case. Similarly, in the civil law the method of procedure is usually the preparation of a dossier on the accused person, containing all the evidence the prosecution has, which is presented to the judge, and then the judge decides which witnesses will be called. The trial is more or less controlled by the judge. Under the common law we don't proceed that way: the evidence is introduced as it comes along, by the prosecution, and the trial is primarily controlled by the prosecution. Again we combined, to some extent, these two procedures. What we did was prepare dossiers, which were summaries of all the evidence including documents supporting the charges, extracts from publications and so forth. These documents were then read into evidence – so, in the case of Kaltenbrunner, I prepared an extensive summary of the case against him, supported by documents, and I then read that into the record. That was the initial presentation. This was the capacity in which I served, but other lawyers were in charge of interrogation, for example. They took care of the witnesses: they would decide if each one was suitable, and if so, what witness would be called to give evidence and be cross-examined. Those lawyers spent more time in the court-room than the lawyers in my capacity did, although as time went on I was permitted to cross-examine defence witnesses and to take a more active role in the trial.

I think that the staffs were extremely competent. This was an international trial, a trial of the vanquished by the victors, and the integrity of the trial depended completely upon the reliability, the honesty and the fairness of the lawyers – and I include the judges, because they're lawyers too – who conducted it. At the outset, Justice Jackson made the point in his opening statement that history would judge *us* according to the manner in which we conducted *ourselves* in handling this trial. The trial throughout was very quiet – there were no histrionics, there was no abuse of any witness by anybody at any time. Lord Lawrence was just an unbelievably marvellous presiding officer: calm, cool, deliberate, very fair, and extremely strict on the prosecution. We had problems over the translation of documents, and of course we had to make documents available to the defence, and we had to make our witnesses available to the defence, too. When there was a mix-up in translations he was very severe on the prosecution staff. So the trial was certainly conducted in a marvellous manner; there couldn't have been a more dignified proceedings.

The accused were permitted to have a lawyer of their choice, and these were all German lawyers, whereas in the Tokyo trial, which followed our trial, United States officers acted as defence counsel. So these defendants at Nuremberg selected their own lawyers, and they could be members of the Nazi Party – there was no prohibition against that. But as far as I know they all conducted themselves very well, as lawyers should. Some of them were a little bit wordy, but for the most part I think they did an excellent job.

After we had rested our case, then of course we were not permitted to introduce new evidence, and the defence went ahead with *their* case. I received word that Rudolf Hoess, the commandant of Auschwitz concentration camp, had been captured by the British, so I immediately asked if he could be brought down to Nuremberg so that we might interrogate him. I spent three days with Rudolf Hoess, the greatest killer in history, and during this time he told me that they'd killed two and a half million people at Auschwitz while he was the commandant there, and I took this sworn affidavit. This was without a doubt the most significant document in this area of the case that we had come upon, because here was a man who was actually the commandant of Auschwitz, who had testified that two and a half million people had been murdered there, with all the details supporting it. The problem was how to get this evidence into the record, since we had rested our case. Of course, when I had finished interrogating Hoess he had to be turned over to Kauffmann, Kaltenbrunner's defence lawyer, and he got the same story. In the end,

Kauffmann called Rudolf Hoess to the stand as a witness for the defence. Why did he do this? Because here was the worst concentration camp in the whole regime, here was the worst person in the whole regime, and Hoess testified that Kaltenbrunner had never visited Auschwitz, which was Kaltenbrunner's defence throughout – that he had nothing to do with the concentration camps, that it was all handled by Himmler. And Kauffman felt that if he presented the very worst case, then Kaltenbrunner might be acquitted. So the evidence went into the record after all.

As far as trial lawyers like myself were concerned, it was no different from any other trial. I was out to convict Ernst Kaltenbrunner, and I got all the evidence I could find to use against him. That didn't mean I was going to fabricate evidence against him or anything like that, of course, but this was a lawsuit and we were out to win it if we could. There was never any suggestion from the top that we had to convict these people – if there had been, the lawyers would have walked out. There was no thought of that. We just put the evidence together, presented it and let the court decide. And we didn't completely succeed, either – three of the defendants were acquitted.

Bernard Meltzer, lawyer

I co-ordinated a group that worked on the economic case, which consisted of the charges involving slave labour, the pillaging and plunder of property in the occupied territories, and related matters. That was my primary job. It happened that while we were working on that job, problems surfaced in connection with the presentation that was being prepared on concentration camps, and I was asked if I would take over that preparation. I think that request came about ten days before the presentation to the Tribunal was scheduled. I didn't read German so I got the help of a couple of lawyers who did, and we worked as hard as we could and finished a statement on concentration camps that became the basis for the presentation to the Tribunal.

Those were my basic responsibilities. In carrying them out, I interrogated various people, including Schacht, Goering, Funk and various minor figures. I remember that during the interrogation of Funk, he wept. He was the head of economics and also president of the Reichsbank, succeeding Schacht in both of those posts. In the bank were found gold teeth and all sorts of jewellery that had been extracted from concentration camp victims. When he was confronted with that evidence during his pre-trial interrogation he burst into tears. Goering I remember even more vividly. He never lost his arrogance and his willingness to defend the Nazi regime. He was very skilful with words: he was a natural-born lawyer. He understood English, I think, although we worked through interpreters. I think I interrogated him about the struggle for power involving Schacht and Goering among others. One of the questions that troubled various members of the staff at the beginning was whether we had a case against Schacht. I myself was dubious. I was to present the case against Funk; I was also asked to present the case against Schacht, and I said I was perfectly willing to do it, but the American press, particularly on the Left, was indicating that Schacht would be acquitted because of his linkages with American bankers, and I pointed out to my superiors that if they sent somebody who was as young as I then was to take on Schacht, and Schacht was acquitted, as I expected that he would be, they might be criticized for sending a boy to do a man's job. So somebody else, not very much older than I, incidentally, did that job. Schacht, of course, was acquitted. The press, however, didn't give as much attention as I had feared to the relative youth of Schacht's prosecutor.

The preparation of the written materials for the overall case was broken down first into subject areas and then into areas of the personal responsibility of each of the defendants. So, for instance, the concentration camp case would be concerned with the responsibility of the whole regime for what had been going on in concentration camps, and particularly those outside Germany, set up after the outbreak of war in 1939, because a technical problem arose in the Tribunal's dealing with essentially domestic problems within Germany. Then the case against Schacht or Goering or any other individual defendant would pinpoint his responsibility for the offences that had been established generally during the subject-matter presentations. In presenting the case against Funk, my job was to show his responsibility for the offences with which he had been charged.

The concentration camp case had been handled, for a long time, by a Judge Advocate General's unit. That unit had an enormous room, crammed full of documents, and I think one of the problems was that they had not digested the mass of pertinent documents – I'm not sure what the problem was. In any event, the powers that be, about ten days before the presentation, recognized that the material that had been prepared needed further work and asked me to take it on. For me the problem was not so much evidence-gathering as organizing and writing up the mass of evidence available. Dan Margolies, a lawyer on the staff, read German, and there was another lawyer on the staff, Sidney Jacoby, who had gone to an American law school but had been educated in Germany, and was quite fluent in German. And they ran through these files in the time that we had, and fired up the stuff to me. I did the drafting; they made the suggestions. You must remember that three of these ten days had to be reserved for translation and the making of copies and so on, so we just worked as hard as we could during that seven-day period.

As for the economic crimes, our group prepared briefs on all aspects of the case, presenting and analysing all the evidence we had. When the entire case was divided among the staffs of the four countries the Russians got the economic crimes in the East, and we took all of our briefs, with all the supporting documents, and handed them to the Russians, saying, 'Here you are – this is part of your case.' Throughout, to the best of my recollection, everybody was trying to be as helpful as possible to the Russians, but it was a one-way street. The American case, of course, involved the possibility, and indeed the actuality, of poaching on all other cases. We had the conspiracy count, for example, and showing acts in the furtherance of the conspiracy involved some overlap with areas that had been assigned to other countries. None the less, our group, and I think other groups, made everything that was pertinent to the Russian case available to them. But they did nothing for us.

Before I got involved in the trial and the concentration camp case in particular, I had a general sense of the uniquely monstrous barbarities perpetrated in those camps. None the less, there were a couple of items that were especially appalling when we came across them, and that had an enormous impact when they were presented to the Tribunal. These were the so-called concentration camp 'Todesbücher', 'death books', and either Margolies or Jacoby discovered them. They were just lying around loosely, not having been previously integrated into the case. They contained lists of people who had died in a particular concentration camp, and they had died in alphabetical order, at fixed intervals of time, and the cause of death in each case had been heart disease. There was something about the German mentality that required record-keeping, even though those records, obviously, were quite incriminating. It was strange throughout to see how slavish the Germans were in making a record of so many things that would be damning later on. This evidence was presented without a single word of editorializing, and you could hear the hush in the court-room.

Brady Bryson, lawyer
I began my work as a liaison officer with the Russian staff in about September of 1945. The trial was to open in November. And it was total confusion. People had been working on it since early in the year, and literally hundreds of thousands of documents had been captured – the Germans were known for their meticulous records of everything. I think at times they found complete files of German cabinet members, and other things of that character. All these documents had to be translated, and there was a big translation operation going on. Of course we didn't have Xerox machines as we have now. And then determinations had to be made of how relevant given documents really were as material for these trials which were being organized. So in retrospect it wasn't too surprising that there was all this confusion. Meanwhile, the legal work had to be advanced, because the opening of the trial was approaching. It was a huge undertaking.

I didn't have ready access to Colonel Storey, but finally I did get to him. He gave me the name of the chief counsel for Soviet Russia at the trials, and suggested that I go to their offices and introduce myself, and indicate my availability to be of service, to suggest that if at any time they were having any difficulty which they attributed to language problems, I had a legal background and some knowledge of Russian and would certainly try to do what I could. So I did that. They were polite and friendly, and I told them how to reach me. I had gotten from Colonel Storey an assignment to a desk someplace in the Palace of Justice. I didn't have an office, but I had a desk there, and the receptionist knew my name and how to locate me. I began reporting in every morning at a reasonable hour, staying a reasonable period of time, and going back to the hotel at will. In the course of the day I would talk with anyone around who was free to talk, picking up information about the staff people, what was going on, what people were trying to do, and so on. But after a period of several weeks nobody had asked me to do anything, so I began to get restless. However it was interesting, amusing, and I was entertaining myself in my free time, of which I had quite a little bit.

One day, a middle-aged Russian woman came in. She wore a very dark dress, really rather reminiscent of the old-fashioned feminine clothing you see in Sicily today, and she had asked for and been sent to see me. She came in, and in understandable but broken English indicated that she needed something in the way of a document that she thought was in the possession of the American staff, and would I be good enough to try and find it for her? She gave me instructions how to get it to her; she wrote down her name and how to direct it. Then I spoke to her in Russian. Well, she was totally astonished. I don't think it had ever occurred to her that any American could say one Russian word. And that probably had been the experience of most of the Russians at Nuremberg, and elsewhere in the world, no doubt. Until I went to the Russian language school, I didn't know any American who could speak any Russian in my civilian life in this country. So she was first astonished, then on second thoughts she didn't know what to make of this, and became suspicious. She wore a smock, something like an apron, and she threw it over her head – she was so taken aback. She let it down again, and looked at me *very* suspiciously, a very hard look. Then she said goodbye, turned on her heel, and walked out. This conveyed to me a message, namely that the Russians really weren't prepared for much contact with Americans. So I began to enquire about this, and I found there was a general understanding in the American group that the Russians had no interest in working with the Americans on this undertaking, except at arm's length and in a very formal way. I think that was my first realization that while the American military forces and the Russian military forces had worked towards a common goal, that is, the defeat of the Axis forces – I understood that the Americans had supplied immense amounts of equipment to the Russians, and I'd always thought of them as allies – their alliance was at best pragmatic, and the truth of the matter might well be that the Americans and the Russians weren't cut out to collaborate. Now I don't say I arrived at a conviction on this subject at that moment, but looking back, I was aware of it.

In any event, after more delay I went to see Colonel Storey, and said that I didn't feel I was rendering any worthwhile service, and further, that I had serious doubt that the Russian staff felt any need for such service, and I didn't think it likely that I would find, if I stayed there, any real opportunity to contribute anything that was needed. Of course I was still in military service, and I indicated that if he agreed with me, and thought it appropriate, he might as well send me back to the States. We chatted a while, and he discovered I had a legal background of some consequence. I'm sure I seemed very young to him; actually I had a very rapid early start in the practice of law. I'd done extremely well at Columbia University, and by the time I entered the service at twenty-nine or so I was already a partner in a major law firm. Colonel Storey was from Texas, I think, but knew my firm by reputation, and he indicated that he would speak to Robert Jackson about the fact that I was there. It turned out that Robert Jackson was a lifelong friend of one of the older partners in my law firm; I believe he got in touch with this partner and apparently received some favourable response. Storey got back to me and asked whether I wanted to stay on and accept an assignment on the trial staff, which I agreed to do. So I sort of backed in.

I rather think I was the youngest member of the trial staff. There was, however, a slot that needed to be filled. One of the members of the staff, Murray Gurfein, was a very experienced trial lawyer in New York city, and later became a federal judge. He had come early to Nuremberg and was, I believe, one of the leaders in the recruitment of staff. For some reason he had left. I heard indirectly – and I'm not sure of the validity of this – that after studying the materials that were collected and making an effort to develop the case, he didn't feel that a case had been collected, at least as far as the American evidence was concerned. There was disagreement about this, I believe, and it was a question of policy within the trial staff. I don't know, but I assume Jackson himself decided the question, and it was concluded that the American case should go forward. In any case, a slot had become vacant on the trial staff, so I was fitted in. They put me in charge of a small team, to work on the assembly and organization of American documentary material and the preparation of what was known as a 'trial brief', on the subject of the persecution of the Jews. There were one or two other more senior officers – although the trial wasn't really organized on the basis of military rank – who had been assigned this subject and had been there for some months. But they needed somebody really to take charge and organize the collection of so-called evidence and the preparation of a memorandum which could be used by the trial counsel presenting the evidence in the tribunal and could also be filed with the court for the use of the judges and their staffs.

I had about five or six people altogether, and we worked very hard there. We organized all the materials in a systematic way, assigning different concentration camps to different people. The documents were drawn from the archives unit in a controlled way that brought us the right material to put together the requested memorandum. It was my function to know what they were doing, to supervise their efforts, to collaborate with them in the formulation of our techniques of working, and so on. And then I had the responsibility of actually preparing the document, the trial memorandum, which was well within my capability, because that was the sort of thing that I'd had lots of experience in over a relatively short period: three years in law school, where I was a *Law Review* editor, and then five years in practice. The assignment was given to an army major, who was a couple of notches above me in this hierarchy, by the name of Walsh, to present the evidence in court, and to take the court through the memorandum. He did it quite satisfactorily. I think he knew it was a good document for the purpose, and he followed it very closely. He had no difficulty with it, as far as the court was concerned, and while the defence counsel occasionally objected to this and that, on the whole we survived very well in getting the evidence that we wanted introduced into the record. There were corresponding legal staffs for the other participating countries – England, France, Russia – and each did its own thing on any given subject. So there were other sources of materials of this kind which were presented by other people.

After that job, they turned over to me another file that had been in the possession of Murray Gurfein, as I remember it, on which no one had done any further work since Gurfein had left. It related to the prosecution of one of the individual defendants in the major war crimes trial, Dr Hjalmar Schacht. It had been expected that Gurfein would present the American case against Dr Schacht, but as I say, he had departed the scene, and somebody was needed to take it over. I was asked whether I thought I could do that, and I undertook it. I remember that there was little to be done in terms of the collection and classification of available materials, because, of course, that kind of work had all been going on for many months. What we had on Dr Schacht, which wasn't all that extensive, was pretty well collected. As a matter of fact Murray Gurfein had prepared a sort of preliminary summary of his material, and the beginnings of a rough outline of how the case might be organized for presentation in the court. I found this in the file; I never had any conversation with Gurfein himself. I was provided with whatever I needed in the way of access to translators, and staff lawyers who might do some kind of research for me if I wanted it, but fundamentally I was given the dossier, and there were papers up to the point where work on it had ended.

I put together a lengthy statement on the subject, a so-called trial memorandum, which I'd started off from scratch. The time came for me to do my bit, and I remember that Telford Taylor was at the counsel table because he was to follow me and present his case on another defendant. I think *his* defendant was not an individual, as mine was, but rather one of the organizations. I recall that it started first thing in the morning, when the court opened, and I think it continued through the entire morning, and the afternoon after the recess. I think there were a few questions from time to time from members of the court. There were several American trial lawyers sitting at the counsel table, one of whom was in charge of the trial team for the day. He didn't really function except to be present and ready to take over in an emergency if any lawyer didn't seem to be able to handle it. At one point, counsel for Dr Schacht rose, asked permission to address the court, and made a series of objections to the information and

evidence that we were presenting, objections of a legal nature. Of course
he was doing this in German. I had one of those sets of headphones
equipped with a switch, and I tuned in to the American interpretation
and made notes in the event of being expected to respond. Finally he
finished, after perhaps ten minutes, and sat down, but he didn't appear to
make any kind of a procedural motion – he didn't appear to be asking the
court to do anything except, when it considered the case, to disregard
everything that I had been putting in as evidence. So I looked at the
lawyer who was in charge of the trial table, and just by a signal we both
understood that there was no need to respond to that, and I should just go
right on. So I got up, and said nothing about it, and went on with my
presentation. He made no further objection; no judge made any
comment on that way of handling it. That's the way the procedure
seemed to go a lot of times there, I think, partly because there was no
single system of jurisprudence in operation, no detailed rules that would
control what, procedurally, was happening at that moment and what
obligations they might put on either side.

So I finished my presentation, and offered to keep myself available if
there was any question. The judges conferred back and forth with each
other and finally said, 'Thank you very much, lieutenant,' and I was
dismissed. I spent some time sort of tidying up the files and making
memoranda of the materials that I'd studied that I thought might be
useful at some time, so as to leave the thing in good shape. For the
moment, I was free again, and I began to think that I might now consider
going back home. But I realized that at some point other lawyers from
other countries would presumably be putting on similar evidence in the
case of Dr Schacht – I believe we had gone first – and that I, who knew
these materials, might have an obligation to stay around and hear what
they had to say. And then, of course, there would presumably come a
period when there would be some defence, and there would be some
possibility that Dr Schacht, who wasn't obliged to, would take the stand,
at which time there might be an opportunity to examine him. The idea of
it rather appealed to me at that time, as a young lawyer – to have the
opportunity to do that in a trial of this kind.

Well, it turned out that they had organized the thing in a peculiar way.
Maybe it was necessary; I shouldn't call it peculiar. But they didn't take a
defendant and complete the case with respect to that defendant in one
continuous operation. They sort of took it piecemeal: there would be a
time when America would present its evidence about Dr Schacht; at
some uncertain time in the future France would present *its* evidence;
then at some time Russia and England would do the same; then at some
point the defence would be reached. Here were a couple of dozen
defendants. Who knew just when each would be reached? Who knew
how long each would take? So there was no way that Colonel Storey
could give me any particular assurance about how long I would be
detained there if I decided I would like to see it all the way through. He
did indicate that it was open to me to do that if I wished. He also indicated

that he didn't feel that I should have any sense of obligation or compulsion simply because I had done the initial work, and if it were necessary, some other lawyer in due course could pick up the file and study my materials as I had studied Gurfein's, study the record that I had presented, and go forward.

I decided that I would try to go home. I had in the meantime discovered a general in charge of the military organization at Nuremberg, which had responsibility for the safety of the area. I guess technically he was in command of all the military personnel who were assigned to Nuremberg, including me. I said that I needed to leave officially, and didn't want to turn up AWOL someplace, and I just hoped that he would understand the mechanics of that, and put me straight on how to go about it. He said it was very simple. He said, 'I have some very important documents here that have to be carried by hand to Washington, and I need a young officer like you to take them back. If you'll undertake to do that you'll travel as my courier. When you get to Washington, go to the Pentagon and deliver these papers.' And then he said, 'I would just recommend to you, lieutenant, that you stop at the office of the Bureau of Personnel of the United States navy, and ask to have your file brought up, and discuss with the person there your stance in the military and what the possibilities are of your being released. I wish you luck!'

So I made my way back, going to London first. Our small military plane landed at Heathrow, and I had all my possessions in one of those universal Val-Pack travelling-bags that everybody used in those days. It was heavy, and I was immediately offered a ride into town by a strange Englishman and his wife, in a very small car – I was wondering how three of us could get in it and where in the world would they put my Val-Pack? But they sort of roped it on the top, and the wife got on what was more or less a ledge in the back, but could be used as a back seat. They took me right to the office of the United States navy in London! The people there found me a billet in a very comfortable hotel. I had read the military papers I was carrying, and I didn't think there was any great urgency about delivering them. I took my chance on that, because I didn't know when I'd get another chance to be in London. You weren't as accustomed to those things as you are today. But the time came when I headed out for Washington. I handed in the papers at the Pentagon and went to see the Bureau of Personnel. As predicted, they summoned up my file and went through it with me. They had a system of calculating points for different kinds of service, and you got extra points if you were overseas. They added it all up, and said I was two points short out of forty-odd that were required for me to be released. And I said, 'Well, really, do you think I should go back to Nuremberg, for two points?' There was a little huddled conference in another office, and they came back and said, 'Your release has been approved.' So I got out, and very quickly went back to my legal career.

With four different Allied delegations at work in the court-house, there were opportunities to study the people with whom one's fortunes had been linked for the past several years. How well did the victorious powers manage to work together?

Mary Burns, secretary

My impressions of the other Allies were very good. I thought all of us got along fine. I was a very young girl at that time, and probably there was some friction – it wouldn't be normal if there *wasn't* friction, at the higher levels. In any law case in the world, there would be a difference of opinion. But I wasn't in on any of that kind of thing at all. Just seeing it offhand, I think it was a wonderful performance of unanimity and fairness, and a good example of getting along. It really was almost a predecessor of the United Nations: there's friction, but it's lasted. People have serious criticism of the Nuremberg Trial, but I wouldn't be able to take a stand on it except that they're all wrong! That's a biased opinion; I'm not a legal scholar!

Anna Cameron, secretary

At first we got along very well with the Russians. At all the parties which the officials attended, they always asked us young girls, Czech, British and American, because there was a shortage of women around. Colonel Volchkov was a very fascinating man; he'd been in the movie business before he got into the army. He always used to dance with me, and the American men joked that I'd penetrated the Iron Curtain! I used to love talking to him; he would talk about how you'd put a movie production together, how you would assemble characters for a picture. I could sit and listen to him all night. But one time he was walking in the hall with General Rudenko, and I saw him and said 'Good morning'. He looked straight ahead and didn't reply. Apparently he wasn't supposed to be so sociable.

Annabel Stover, secretary

The Russians, the lower echelons, I think would have liked to be more friendly, but they really kept to themselves almost entirely. They didn't eat at the Grand Hotel with us – it was just an American mess – but they were allowed to come in and have cocktails at the bar. For the most part, the Russians stayed by themselves, and when we went to Berlin to hand down the indictment it seemed that we were there unnecessarily long, because whatever decision was made, the Russians seemed to have to get back to Moscow to get directions as to what to do next. They couldn't make any decisions themselves; it would take two or three days each time they had to make a decision of any kind.

I don't recall having much association with the French. Some of the English girls we were friendly with, and I think they were billeted along with us at the place we called Girls Town. But as a rule the various countries had their own little enclave of groups of people living in various German houses that were close to one another.

Dorothy Reilly, secretary

I found the British staff really superb. They chose their best people. I didn't know the French very well; those whom I met, I liked. The French invited only Resistance workers to come to Nuremberg. Of course they had a very bad time; they got very little of Germany. Judge Biddle got along fine with them – of course, he was born in Paris. The Russian staff we never saw at all, except occasionally. I remember one time – we must have been at the villa in Duisberg – we were invited to a luncheon which the Russians were giving. The food was great, and the flowers were in bloom, and I recall doing a German waltz, or something that resembled it, with General Nikitchenko. I know he spoke English, but ordinarily he was never allowed to be near an American without an interpreter present. However, I got two or three words in English out of him while we were dancing, but shortly after the music stopped, every Russian in sight was gone. That was in the days when they thought their thinking might be turned by too much contact with free Americans and British.

Andy Wheeler, lawyer

The Russians were difficult to work with – they were only concerned about what had happened to Russians, in Russia, at the hands of the Germans. Similarly, the main effort of the French was to portray what nasty people the Germans had been in France. The British were the most co-operative, and they shared a lot of their information with us, but they didn't have a very big staff so they relied a good deal on the Americans to put in most of the stuff.

Hume Boggis-Rolfe, visitor

We always seemed to be getting ready for a meeting between the four powers, or else winding up after one. We were aware of the Nuremberg Trial in so far as papers crossed our desks from time to time – we used to receive reports. I got to know my American opposite number well, and still keep in touch with him, and I also got to know some people in the French section. But the Russians one knew less well, because they weren't allowed to circulate. When we travelled around Berlin we could cross over into the French and American sectors, but we weren't allowed to enter the Russian sector without an invitation. And in the business of running the quadripartite government – meetings, decisions, and so on – the Russians were, in a good many things, out on a limb, while the British, the French and the Americans would be more likely to be in agreement.

Alfred Steer, administrative head, language division

The Russians were extremely difficult to work with. We found very quickly that we intensely disliked the men, but we were extremely attracted to the women, and we couldn't figure this out. Everybody had the same reaction. We finally put our heads together and decided that the men whom we saw there at Nuremberg were people who had worked their way up through the communist hierarchy, and had gotten where they wanted through soft soap, flattery, subservience, this sort of thing, and we reacted very negatively to that sort of person. We figured that the girls didn't have that necessity pushing them down, and they could be natural. They weren't particularly pretty, but they could be just charming. They would get together, and when we had a wait they would start a folk song – they were bubbling over with good humour. We just loved them to pieces. We quickly found out that if we wanted something done, it was better to get the girls. 'See if you can talk your boss into this,' you know? Even then it sometimes didn't work. When the lawyers made their speeches they referred to a lot of documents, and we quickly found out that it made things a lot easier if we could have the documents in advance and translate them. But I always had difficulty getting anything in advance out of the Russians. I went to see Pokrovsky, the Russian prosecutor, and said, 'Please will you let me have your speech and your documents in advance, so that we can translate them? My interpreters can listen and translate as they hear it, but they frequently make little slips, so your presentation would be much more effective if we could have a chance to put this into good English, good French and good German.' 'Of course,' he said. 'As a matter of fact the papers are now ready, and I'm just waiting for the OK from Moscow.' This was three weeks before he was due to give it. Do you know when he got the OK from Moscow? The night before! The incredibly clumsy Soviet centralization made efficient work with them almost impossible.

Most of the French were very poor, very close with money. They were quite good, what there were of them, but there were very few of them. And there were several notorious black market types, that got me in all kinds of trouble. One of them, whom we disliked intensely, we nicknamed 'Le Jerque'.

We liked the British, and got along very well with them. Again, we thought they were poor – in other words they didn't have anywhere near the number of people that we did. But the people they did have were of top-notch quality. So if you took a group of translators into English, let's say, sixty per cent of them would be US and forty per cent of them would be from Britain. Mr William Mercer, he tickled the heck out of me. He was a little bit straight-sided. He was something in British intelligence; I used to tease him about it but of course he would never admit it. He was in charge of all the British civilian personnel, including a lot of girls and typists and so on. Apparently one of these, who came over from Britain, decided that sex was a wonderful thing and she was going to try out all the men in Nuremberg. Well, you can guess what happened: she got 'tooken pregnant', as the saying goes, without too much delay. And of course Mercer was right in the middle of this. They instructed him from London to find out who was responsible. So he called this girl in, and asked, 'Who is the father?' 'Oh, I've no idea – how can I tell?' Well, of course, she got shipped home to Britain. Mercer was a little upset – he was a very proper sort.

Lord Justice Lawrence, I thought, was the outstanding personality of the trial, by all laws. I thought Justice Jackson, on the American side, simply wasn't in his class. For example, I had people working for me on the US army payroll, the navy payroll, the civil service payroll, the army of occupation payroll, and so on and so forth. I had all these payrolls, and no opportunity of paying them overtime. For instance, when that Russian came in the night before and gave us all that stuff, we couldn't possibly do a proper job, but we did as much as we could and our people worked overtime. I could only offer them compensatory time off, not the usual extra overtime pay. I mentioned to Lord Lawrence that this had happened several times, and that I was having difficulty in getting these people, who were living in difficult circumstances, to work overtime because I couldn't pay them overtime. About four or five days later, someone came down and asked, would it be convenient for Lord Lawrence to visit some of the translation sections that day? I said yes, and I took him around. He came down the hall with his wife, and she was the perfect British lady – the parasol ... I think she would fit right into a garden-party, you know, or a tea. I couldn't believe it. He walked into the first room that I took him to, and made a little speech. He said, 'Commander Steer tells me that you people have been working overtime, and I want to assure you that we appreciate this, that the job of this tribunal is important, and even though you may not be working in the court-room you are an essential group of people and we are much in your debt.' Then he went round and shook hands with everybody. And from then on all I had to say was, 'Lord Lawrence has requested that you do a little overtime if you can.' They admired and respected him, you see. That's the kind of guy he was.

Peter Uiberall, interpreter

We had pooled our interpreters, pretty well – I mean the Western nations had – so that at the German–English desk there could be American or British interpreters. But the interpreters into Russian were all Soviets. They were all excellent. There were quite a number of ladies, whose names were usually Vera or Nadia, and they were usually in Russian army uniform, although they were just administrative uniforms, issued, as one of the girls told me, for the occasion of coming to Nuremberg. Once I asked one of them, ' How long have you lived in America?', because her pronunciation was excellent. I was trying to trap her, I have to admit. She said, 'Not at all. I was never in the States.' And a long time later I found out that some of the Russian training camps were complete with a model American small town – with a drugstore and various other things – so that the trainees could live there, *in* the language. I understand the RAF had a similar language camp for Russian at one time. The Russian interpreters were excellent – I never saw them flounder. And it is very difficult to translate into Russian, for the simple reason that Russian is so much longer: there are more words, so you have to speak faster and get more in during the same period of time.

I had a little difficulty with them when I was monitor, because my job was to go out during recess to the open area where the interpreters were, behind the court-room, and to ask them to take their seats, and the Russians never paid any attention. I would say, 'Nehmen-Sie Platz, bitte, asseyez-vous, s'il vous plaît,' and so on, and I went to one of the Russian interpreters and asked him to teach me the Russian for 'Take your seats.' So next time I went out there, and the interpreters were milling around, I started off, 'Nehmen-Sie Platz, bitte, asseyez-vous, s'il vous plaît, take your seats, please', and everybody moved except the Russians, who did of course understand these languages – that's what they were here for. So I shouted at the top of my voice, 'Sodyeetis pozholouste!' And they swung round and came at once. One of the girls said, 'I didn't know you spoke Russian,' and I said, 'I don't – I just learned it to get you people into your seats!' It worked for a while – they were amused and they thought it was OK – but after a while the same thing happened again. It didn't matter if I said it in English, German, French and Russian – they were still out there, and we had to wait till they took their seats. I had found out that one of their group, a very intense, serious-looking young man, was their KGB man, because they were always very deferential to him, took instructions from him – you could see that. So I called him aside one day, and I said, 'I have to talk to you about your interpreters.' He said, 'Yes? Please?' He was very polite. 'I have this problem of getting them back into their seats after the recess. One of these days, when they stand outside, I will not do anything further, and the session will start. The presiding judge will say, as he always does, "Is the prosecution ready?" The senior prosecution counsel will say, "Yes, your honour, the prosecution is ready." He will say, "Is the defence ready?" And the German defence counsel will say, "Yes, the defence is ready." Then he will say, "Are the interpreters ready?" And being the monitor, I will say, "No, your honour, the interpreters are not ready." He will ask, "Why aren't the interpreters ready?" And I will say, "Because the interpreters of the Soviet Union are not in their places." And then he will ask for the bench interpreter, and say, "Will you please enquire of the judge of the Soviet Union why his interpreters are not ready?" Would you like to have that happen?' It never happened again. That was all that was needed. But I thought I had to be very descriptive about the situation that might occur. They were very, very nice when you used the right method of explaining everything carefully.

Whitney Harris, lawyer

The people who would have lined the defendants up against a wall and shot them were the British, Churchill in particular, and it took a great deal of persuasion on the part of Justice Jackson to bring them around to the idea of conducting a trial. There was a great deal of controversy about it in the United States as well. The Russians were in favour of the trial from the beginning, but the problem was that they took the view that the guilt had already been determined by the heads of state at the Yalta and

Crimea conferences, and that therefore this trial was primarily to determine punishment. This produced perhaps the most severe crisis in the negotiations before the trial; Justice Jackson immediately dissociated himself from this position, and said that if there was going to be a trial it had to be a real trial, with the Tribunal deciding the question of guilt, and of course the British went along with this completely. But the Russians did dissent from the three acquittals. So that was perhaps the greatest problem that we had with them.

The concept of conspiracy was completely unknown in French law, and they didn't care for the idea at all. And we lost on that issue: we didn't get the general conspiracy charge that we were seeking to get. The reason that Justice Jackson wanted the conspiracy charge was that he wanted to be able to get into the record the entire history of the Nazi regime, and it was very, very important to him that this be accomplished. But the French, who don't think in these kinds of terms, simply couldn't understand it at all. That's why the general conspiracy charge was dropped, but it came in in the definition of aggressive war, and so we were able to get all the evidence into the record.

Roger Barrett, officer in charge of documents

There were a great many very talented and dedicated people, at very low levels, who hadn't yet made their mark in their own country. I think perhaps the British lawyer at my level by whom I was most impressed was Peter Calvocoressi. The American higher-level people were sometimes people who wanted to become senators, and did, or wanted to become head of the Atomic Energy Commission, and did, and wanted Nuremberg as a star to put on their career. The younger ones were just hard-working lawyers, and didn't seek glory, and didn't get much glory, but most of them were equally talented, if not more so. Many of the most important presentations were prepared by the younger lawyers, and merely presented by the senior ones. In the British staff there was a very high level of competence all the way through, I thought. I don't have that many recollections of the French staff, and I only knew one of the Russian lawyers well. He was from Georgia, and had gotten to Nuremberg through his friendship with Stalin.

As for the defendants' lawyers, I remember that at the time of the selection of lawyers, Krupp's son, Alfried, appeared in my office. As distinguished from most of the Germans and most of the defendants, this was one of the most sophisticated, intellectual, well-bred and obviously wealthy people I've ever met in my life. All the defendants, with maybe a few exceptions, got the lawyers of their choice, and we went to great extremes to find the individual that the defendant requested. The Krupps had first-class lawyers, and most of the defendants' lawyers were very competent, and had substantial reputations in pre-war Germany.

Bernard Meltzer, lawyer

Our working relations with the British were excellent. I mean, they were open and helpful colleagues, and if I had a problem, whether of analysis,

Above: Outside the Palace of Justice, Nuremberg, 1946.

Below: View of the court-room. The four judges and their alternatives are on the left of the picture.

Right: 'The Nuremberg Trial, 1946' by Dame Laura Knight.

Left: Members of the Press Corps wait to go into the court-room on the opening day of the trial. Eddie Worth (profile, standing) is in the lower right-hand corner of the picture.
Right: Report, submitted by Paul Graven, on the suicide of Robert Ley.

PRISON OFFICE

SUBJECT: Statement concerning Suicide of Dr. Ley.

TO   : Major Teich

        At 2010 25 October 1945 the Corporal of the Guard,
Cpl Glaskell, came into the prison office and asked me to
come to cell# 9, Dr. Ley's cell immediately. I rushed to
cell #9/in the latrine recess with a rag stuffed into his
mouth and an improvised noose around his neck fastened to
the latrine flushpipe. I tried to lift him in order release
the noose from the flushpipe but he was to heavy. The
corporal of the guard cut the material and Dr. Ley fell
forward. I caught him and we laid him on the floor.
I told the corporal of the guard to get our German interned
doctor, Dr. Pfluecker, and tell him the situation AND TO COME IMMEDIATELY

        The Sergeant of the Guard, S/Sgt John J. Daley, was
told to remain in the cell. I returned to the prison office
and called Dr. Juchli, informing him of the situation.
I told Dr. Juchli to inform the colonel. He said he would
and he was coming right down.

        I returned to cell # 9 and found Dr. Pfluegker and
our German interned dentist, Dr. Hoch, giving Ley one cc
of cardiazol and one cc of lobulin. The German doctor
then ordered Ley to be placed on the bed, which the sgt and
corporal did. I told the Sgt of the Guard to go out and
check the posts on the first floor. The German doctor
began artificial respiration at approximately 2020.
I told the corporal of the guard to assist Dr Pfluecker.

        I checked the guard on post # 8. Questions asked at
this time were later covered in detail by Major Teich in
his talk with the guard. I then checked the remainder of
the guard on the first floor and returned to cell # 9.
Dr. Pfluecker then told me that Ley was dead and to the
best of his knowledge had been dead about fifteen minutes.
He continued artificial respiration. Col Juchli, Maj Teich
and Lt Durkee arrived at 2028. Col Juchli examined the
body and pronounced him dead at approximately 2032.

        The door to Dr Ley's cell was kept closed. There was
little confusion or noise. I returned to my normal duties.

                              PAUL H. GRAVEN
                              2nd Lt Infantry
                              Ass't prison Officer on Duty

Left: Keitel comes out of the lift into the dock.
Below: Goering (left) and Hess (right) in the dock. Doenitz, wearing dark glasses, is behind them.
Right: Goering on the witness-stand. Peter Uiberall, with his face turned towards Goering, interprets.
Below right: Ribbentrop confers with his counsel.

Top left: Listening in the court-room. Joseph Stone (chin on hand, no earphones) is one of the lawyers sitting at the tables.

Left: Paul Graven (black helmet, flanked by two 'snowdrops') visits the court-room to check on the guards. To his right are Colonel Andrus (back to camera) and Dr Gilbert, the prison psychologist. The letters on the armbands stand for Internal Security Detachment.

Above: Alfred Steer in front of a photo mural of the court-room, explaining the simultaneous multi-lingual interpreting system.

Right: Hess reading Grimms' *Fairy Tales* in the dock.

Above: Goering on the witness-stand. In the corner of the court-room Eddie Worth operates his still camera.
Left: Hess suffering from stomach pains.

Above: Alfred Steer with the group of translators who, at the end of the trial, agreed to be locked up (for security reasons) to translate the verdicts.
Right: Fritzsche and Schacht sign autographs at a press conference after their acquittal.

Opposite page, top: The Flick Trial, Subsequent Proceedings. Joseph Stone is sitting at the table, beside the window.
Opposite page, bottom: Nuremberg: the ruins.

Above: Nuremberg: women selling and buying bread.
Below: The Grand Hotel before the war.

Opposite page,
top: The Grand
Hotel, 1946.
Left: The Faber
Castle at Stein,
outside Nurem-
berg, where the
Press Corps was
billeted.
Above: Signposts
in the Hindenburg
Platz, Nuremberg,
1946.
Right: Annabel
Stover (centre)
with two coll-
eagues entering the
Palace of Justice.
Russian guards are
on duty.

Left: Eddie Worth surveys the site of the Nuremberg rallies.
Right: Leonard ('Andy') Wheeler, 1945.

Left: Priscilla Belcher and two convalescent GIs entertain concentration camp children at a Christmas party at the American Red Cross hospital, Nuremberg, 1945. The children were survivors of concentration camps.
Right: Jean Tull in the garden at 75 Parkstrasse, 1946.

Above: Annabel Stover in Nuremberg. Photograph taken by Paul Graven. **Left:** Ron Chapman, 1946.

evidence or anything else, there was absolutely no difference in my reaction to the British and my reaction to my American colleagues. We also had good relations with the French, but not so close as with the British. Perhaps that difference resulted from our not having a common language and a common legal culture with the French. We never could reach the Russians; we never could get a scrap of paper from the Russians, no matter how many demands we made. I don't believe *anybody* got a scrap of paper from the Russians. When we socialized with the Russians, the Russians were always in groups of at least three. So far as the Russians were concerned, I never had a sense of developing any sort of personal relationship. I believe everyone on our side had a similar reaction. One was dealing not with individuals but with the Kremlin. I remember a party at which a very attractive, very well-gowned young Russian woman, who spoke very good English, had quite a few dances with a British officer, and two days later she was gone. Her English was awfully good for her staff position, and whether she had any extra-curricular activities, such as intelligence, I don't know. But relationships with the Russians were very disappointing, because one of the justifications – not the major one, but a secondary one – for the trial was that it would be an opportunity for international collaboration, particularly with the Russians. And there was really no positive co-operation that I remember. An anecdote about Jackson and a watch makes that point nicely. During World War Two, a lot of GIs had watches with Mickey Mouse on their faces, and the Russians were ecstatic when they got a Mickey Mouse watch. Against that background, Justice Jackson had a birthday at Nuremberg. We had a little PX there, so somebody picked up a very modest Swiss watch, and it was presented to the Justice at his birthday party. He said, 'It's a very nice watch, and thank you very much. Where did you get it?' And somebody cracked, 'Well, we got it from the Russians.' And Jackson, quick as a flash, said, 'That's fine. That's really fine. Up to now, I haven't been able to get even the time of day from them!'

Daniel Margolies, lawyer

Birkett was the one who wrote the 'Opinions'. He was the deputy to Lord Justice Lawrence. He was a great lawyer. The four judges and the four deputies got together, and they all agreed that Birkett's 'Opinions' were perfect. And then the French judge looked at the translation that had been prepared by the staff, and said the French was execrable and he would put it into proper French, which he did. It took him a week, and I'm told, though I haven't bothered to compare them, that the French 'Opinion' and the English 'Opinion' bear very little resemblance to each other. At any rate, during that week the Russian judge got word from Moscow – evidently, though I don't know – but within that week he came back and said he had reconsidered, and he no longer could vote for the acquittal of Schacht, and von Papen, and I don't even remember the name of the third man, who was so insignificant; he was a minor official in the Goebbels organization [Fritzsche]. The only reason he was indicted was that the Russians had very few people. All the prisoners had managed to escape to the West, except for a few that the Russians got their hands on – one admiral, Raeder I think, and then this rather insignificant member of the Goebbels organization. They arrived in Nuremberg with their confessions completely filled out, saying they were guilty of Article 1 and they were guilty of Article 2, and so on. We explained to the Russians that under our form of law you can't plead guilty to Articles of the indictment in that form – you have to say what you did, and not merely that you are guilty of such and such a crime. And they hadn't said they'd *done* anything – they'd merely said they were guilty of all this. The Russians thought it was a great waste of time.

The Russian judge was really quite a nice man. His deputy, I believe, was KGB, because he kept giving orders to the judge all the time on how to behave: the judge used to come to our parties and dance with the girls, and the deputy judge would glower at him from time to time, and rebuke him rather openly. They wore their military uniforms. At any rate, the Russian judge said that he had thought it over and that he could no longer concur in the acquittal – he had to dissent. It would be a three to one vote. And Lord Justice Lawrence said it was too late – he had already voted for the acquittal. And the French judge said that you had to look at it from the point of view of history, and this was the first trial of its kind in history, and if you started writing dissents and things this would weaken it. The American judge, Mr Biddle, said he saw absolutely nothing wrong with dissenting. He in fact had just written a book on Oliver Wendell Holmes, the 'great dissenter', and he had a copy of the book which he was happy to offer to his colleagues, and if the Russian judge wished to dissent he thought that would only be appropriate, and the sort of thing that an eminent judge might well do, which left the British and the French judges rather hanging in the air. So the Russian judge was allowed to dissent. And later that evening, as Mr Biddle was sitting in his office, the Russian judge called upon him, and said he had had very little experience writing dissents in Russia, and any assistance that Mr Biddle could give him in drafting a dissent would be much appreciated. I thought that was rather nice. I'm sure that there were very few occasions for dissenting in Russia.

We were supposed to have subsequent proceedings, and General Telford Taylor was brought along by Justice Jackson to negotiate with the French and the British and the Russians on which group of defendants would be selected for the next international trial. And they reached an agreement. Now Colonel Gill was our chief administrative officer, and the arrangement at Nuremberg was that this was an enclave of an international sort, that didn't fall under General Clay's responsibility although he was Commander-in-Chief of the zone. Nuremberg had a special status, and the Russians could come and go as they saw fit, and so could the British and the French, without General Clay's control. So the Russian administrative officer came to see Colonel Gill and said they had a body they wanted to send back to Moscow. And Colonel Gill said,

'What body?' And the Russian administrative officer said, 'Well, you know, the understanding we had was that we wouldn't go into all these administrative details.' And Gill said that he did want to know what body it was, and it turned out that it was the general who was negotiating with Telford Taylor on these subsequent proceedings. And Gill said, 'Well, that's dreadful! What happened?' 'He was shot,' said the Russian. 'Shot? Who shot him? What happened?' 'Details, details!' said the Russian. 'Well,' he said, 'he was cleaning his gun.' Anyway, that was the end of the Russian general who negotiated the agreement. That's one way in which they brought an end to negotiations for subsequent proceedings. The Russians were not pleased with that trial. It went on for a long time – it was around February, I think, that the prosecution finally closed its case, and the Russians then pressed for an immediate verdict. The British and the Americans and the French pointed out that the defence had not been heard from, and the Russians said that, considering the nature of the evidence, there wasn't really any point in wasting people's time with the defence. But they did, and the trial dragged on for five more months or so. And the Russians thought it was all a great waste of time.

The participants in this book did such different kinds of work in Nuremberg that there are few common denominators in their experience. Many of them, however, do seem to have shared the feeling that they were being given an opportunity to do work which was necessary and important, and to do it well. They also speak of the feeling of being part of a great endeavour, however unsung they may have been on an individual level. At the same time, work had for many of them painful and sometimes shocking aspects: Priscilla Belcher was working with concentration camp victims; lawyers such as Roger Barrett, Bernard Meltzer and Whitney Harris were investigating – and Peter Uiberall was translating – evidence of terrible atrocities; Paul Graven, as a young prison officer, had to cut down Robert Ley after he hanged himself in his cell. Not everyone became inured to the things that they were dealing with, as Al Steer discovered on several occasions when he had to withdraw interpreters from their duties.

The basic reason for everyone's presence in Nuremberg, whether they worked at the centre of the trial or on its periphery, could be found in the court-room. In the following chapter the participants, both workers and spectators, recall the time that they spent face to face with the men on trial.

3. The court-room and the defendants

Andy Wheeler, lawyer

Goering had been on drugs, but by the time the trial started he was off them and alert again, and had lost a lot of weight. He stood up one day, at the beginning of the trial, and wanted to make a speech. Judge Lawrence said, 'The defendant Goering will please be seated,' but Goering remained standing, so Lawrence said, 'Did you hear me, Goering? Will you please be seated?' But Goering still wouldn't sit down, so Lawrence ordered, 'Put him down!', and a GI standing behind him grabbed him by the shoulders and made him sit down. And that was the end of his efforts to conduct the trial for all the defendants. All he wanted was to tell everything that he knew in return for being shot instead of hanged, because it was a great disgrace to be hanged.

Brady Bryson, lawyer

As far as the defendants were concerned, they were impassive. They sat there in the dock, and some listened more than others. Occasionally there would be a little flutter, but on the whole they weren't demonstrating anything, or protesting – they were just sitting there and sort of taking it.

Dorothy Reilly, secretary

I found it exciting in the court-room; it required some concentration. Some of the interpreters were exceptionally good. Then there was a kind of fascination in looking at these defendants. Goering first, who seemed to enjoy everything, Hess, von Papen and all of them. Goering liked to watch the ladies. There were a couple of attractive court reporters in whom he showed great interest.

No German was allowed in the court-house, except workers. I do recall being in court one day, sitting in the visitors' gallery. I saw a lady coming down the aisle, and I noticed her shoes. Nowadays one would think nothing of it, but her shoes were heavy, like ankle boots. I guess I was accustomed to everybody wearing ordinary shoes, in spite of the rubble. The only time you put on flats or tough shoes was when you were going on a walking tour. I said to myself, 'That's *got* to be a German.' I just took this in. There was an imperceptible meeting of the eyes with the defendant Frick. So that evening I was talking to one of the G2 officers, and I asked, 'What's going on?' There was a lot of fuss, and people running hither and yon. 'Was there by any chance a German in the court-room?' And he said, 'How did you know?' I was right. I was so pleased, secretly, that I had been that observant. No one seemed to know how she got the pass. It was rather sad, in a way.

I was in the court-room the day Hess refused to answer questions, and the tribunal decided that he wasn't competent to stand trial. And I was in and out of the court one of the days when Kaltenbrunner was questioned. That was four solid days of 'Nein'. No matter who said anything, it was 'Nein'.

I was present for the judgments. The court-room was so crowded, though, that you had to take your turn – fifteen minutes, or maybe twenty. Everyone was extremely anxious to be there.

Seaghan Maynes, journalist
The dominant character was Goering. He just dominated the whole trial. He was shrewd, very intelligent, extremely quick on the uptake. He also bullied, in a way, the other defendants. He was wearing a pearl-grey uniform, with no insignia, nothing. The only other people in uniform were the army people, Keitel and Jodl. The navy people, Doenitz and Raeder, were in civilian clothes. Hess was gaunt, and just not 'with it', as we'd say nowadays. He wasn't taking any part at all in the proceedings, just gazing vacantly around the court. I'm no psychiatrist or psycho-analyst, but he looked to me like a man who had completely withdrawn from life and the developments around him. There was a chap called Funk, who was president of the Reichsbank. I often wondered, 'What the devil is *he* doing in the dock?' It was like bringing in the governor of the Bank of England. It was said, of course, that he'd been involved in looting other countries, and so on. The other defendants didn't make much of an impact. The military men were very austere types, very dignified in fact, and like the admirals they didn't seem to be able to understand why they should be in the dock at all. Streicher the Jew-baiter – that was one of the terms that the press stuck on people, like the Beast of Belsen. We used to sit around Schloss Stein, with people thinking up their pieces and hoping to hit on some tag or name to stick on something which would carry the story. But he didn't create much of an impression in the dock. For the first five months or so they all just sat there and did nothing. The prosecution was making its case, and they weren't allowed to interject. Goering was the central figure, and there was the rather pathetic figure of Hess, but the rest of the defendants didn't make much of an impact. The strange irony in the case of Hess was that he was the only man in the whole Nazi hierarchy who had tried to get peace. He had flown in somewhat mysterious circumstances to Britain in 1941 – parachuting into Scotland – in a vain effort to get peace negotiations started with the Allies. His life sentence eventually became more than forty years' solitary confinement.

I don't know of any other human being who suffered that penalty in the interests of justice.

The boredom really ended when the time came for the defendants to put their cases. This was when the news stories really began to materialize. When Goering came to give evidence the whole court wondered what was going to happen. He went on the offensive immediately. There was none of this craven 'I didn't do it, I'm terribly sorry, it wasn't my fault.' His attitude was, 'What the hell do you expect? We were fighting a war for our survival.' When it came to his cross-examination, the prosecutor was Justice Jackson, who was one of those tough American lawyers, you know, third-degree type. He started to give Goering the third-degree treatment, but I imagine that Goering had third-degreed more men than Jackson had ever met, because Goering simply wiped the floor with him. He reduced Jackson to such a state of impotence and fury that Jackson actually had to appeal to the president of the court for protection against the witness he was supposed to be interrogating! He threw down his headphones and looked as if he was going to give up altogether. Of course Goering was enjoying all this tremendously – he was an actor on the stage, in all the limelight. But the thing that caught him was Sir David Maxwell-Fyfe, the British prosecutor. Whereas Jackson had said things like, 'I put it to you, Goering,' when Maxwell-Fyfe got up he was the soul of politeness and deference. He would start by saying, 'Herr Reichsmarschall, perhaps you would be good enough to study the document you have now been handed. Please don't hurry – take your time and consider it properly,' and he would get an answer out of Goering, who was flummoxed by this sort of approach.

One of the things which bothered a lot of us in the press corps was the hearsay evidence. I'm not promoting the defence of the German defendants, but the legality of a lot of the evidence brought against them just didn't exist. There were, I suppose, about 200 witnesses against the defendants, but a lot of documents were produced, sheaf after sheaf, consisting of 'Statement by Katusha Misleva from the village of X, who testifies that she heard from her cousin Maria Blobova of the village of Y, who had been told by somebody else that so many people had been executed by the Germans in such and such a place.' This was the sort of stuff that used to pile up, and it was completely unnecessary. There was enough concrete evidence without it. And as for the possibility of the German defendants getting witnesses to come forward – they would be as scarce as holy water in an Orange Lodge. What German was going to get up and give evidence for Goering, or Streicher, or Kaltenbrunner? They had to live in Germany under the Allied occupation. Some Germans, military men and officials, came and gave evidence for the prosecution, and the press people in my circle didn't have a great deal of sympathy for them, because they'd lived high on the hog while their bosses were in power. Here under the occupation, with the winners conducting a trial, a lot of these people were trying to get themselves a good deal.

Funk used to cry often, especially when they were showing those films of the atrocities and the camps – hour after hour of bodies piled up, skeletons, and that sort of thing. The bankers and industrialists and so on were the ones who showed more emotion. It appeared to me genuine that some of these people in the dock were completely unaware of the camps. That was the impression we had. Another thing some press people felt was that very little attention was paid to the Christians who died in the camps. There were millions. And Russians, Poles, gypsies, clergymen, social democrats, communists, the royal family of Italy, some of whose people died in the camps. One got the impression that only Jewish people were exterminated, because world attention was focused on the Jewish victims. But the whole thing was a terrible tragedy anyway. I mean, to kill one person is as big a crime as to kill a thousand.

Annabel Stover, secretary

I attended some of the proceedings, but a lot of it was very boring, because it would go on, and you would have to hear translations in whatever language you could understand. So whenever we knew that someone we knew was presenting the case – Justice Jackson, or Sidney Alderman, or someone like that – then we would make an effort to go, and get passes to go into the trial. I dated one of the boys who was a guard for the prisoners, and he was able to get me the autographs of the prisoners at one point.

Keitel and Jodl wore their uniforms to the trial and held themselves very erect. Some of the others – Frick and Frank – looked like very disgusting types: I had no love for them whatsoever. I thought they should get whatever the tribunal handed out; they were certainly guilty of those crimes.

Roger Barrett, officer in charge of documents

Goering was perhaps the most fascinating person at the trial. People ask what he was like, and I say that if you were going to have a cocktail party and wanted somebody to be the life of the party, that's the person you'd have. He was completely amoral. At the time of the Roehm putsch in 1934, he gave a party, and the people who were going to be executed were invited to the party so that they could be fingered more readily on the way out of the party. One day I took a document down to him, to talk to him about the document and the meaning of it. He always acted as if he didn't know English, always requested an interpreter. I knew German, but it was our policy always to have an interpreter. He thus had the benefit of thinking longer before answering the question. When I said something humorous he'd smile before it was translated, so I knew very well that he could understand me. He was sitting there in a powder-blue or very light grey uniform, very elegant except that the buttons were all removed, so that he couldn't injure himself, I guess. He was no longer on dope. As we talked I smoked a pipe, and I offered him cigarettes, and he said, 'Captain, you don't do this right. If we'd won, we wouldn't have done it this way – you'd be standing up, and you wouldn't have your uniform on, you'd have a black-and-white prisoner's suit, and there would be two SS men standing behind you, sticking you in the butt with bayonets. And when you answered questions you'd say, "Yes sir, Herr Goering, no sir, Herr Goering." That's the way you ought to treat us!' Even though it might be detrimental to our treatment of him, he was frank enough to say that.

During the trial we had in evidence a written transcription of conversations between Goering in Germany and Seyss-Inquart in Austria, listed as 'Luftwaffe Record'. The contents were very dramatic. Goering would say to Seyss-Inquart, 'I think that over this weekend there should be some destruction of synagogues. Burn down five,' or 'I think that there should be disturbances at certain intersections,' and then on the following Monday Seyss-Inquart would call back and Goering would say, 'How did it go?' 'Well, there was a fire at this synagogue, which was burned down, and we arranged this...' The various steps that were taken in the weeks immediately preceding the Anschluss had been scripted by Goering, then when the time came for the Anschluss he dictated to Seyss-Inquart a telegram which Schuschnigg was to send to Hitler. And when Hitler said he came in at the request of the Austrians, it was a telegram that Goering had dictated! When this session in the court-room ended, before he was led back to his cell, Goering called me over and said, 'Captain, you identified that document as the Luftwaffe record of conversations. That wasn't the Luftwaffe – that was Hermann Goering. The only reason the name of the Luftwaffe came in is because I used their transmission facilities.' In other words he wanted credit for this marvellous accomplishment, and he was very proud of it.

On another occasion, we put together a movie from captured German films showing the rise of the Nazis, with a second half showing the fall. While the first half was showing, with Hitler, obviously, featured in many of the tapes, I passed Goering, and he said to me, 'Couldn't you just feel the magnetism of that wonderful man?' He relived his early days and his admiration. At the end of the day, when we had shown the fall, including the concentration camps and so forth, most of the defendants had tears in their eyes, but I didn't notice any tears in Goering's eyes.

One of the things we had in the document room was a collection of transcripts from conversations called 'Ashcan and Dustbin'. One of the ways that I analysed the documents was to make a list of names and subjects, and when a document came in I would have people find out what people it involved and what subjects it involved. As a result of that, when the time came to select the defendants we used the documentary material we had. The people who weren't going to be selected as defendants, and the people who were, were kept in two camps, called by the Americans 'Ashcan and Dustbin'. They were interrogated regularly, and many of their American interrogators were like me, not international in knowledge or outlook or background – they didn't know a great deal about some of the subjects that were going to be covered in the interrogation. But we all learned quickly. One of the ways was to interrogate the people in Ashcan and Dustbin. These people were kept isolated from the time they were captured, but they were allowed to use the latrine cubby-holes next to each other, so they could talk through the partitions. The cubby-holes were bugged. They were very anxious to talk to each other, about their experiences since they last saw each other, when they were in power, sometimes about documents which had been stashed, and usually about the stupid questioning being done by the American interrogators, and what had been missed. As a result of these transcriptions, our interrogators were able to make up for their stupidity by what they learned from the latrine.

Mary Burns, secretary

I didn't get into the court-room very often, because with the Justice and Elsie Douglas working at the house a lot, and Bill doing so much liaison work with the people who were doing interrogation and preparing the presentations, I was in the position of holding down the office, if somebody dropped by. It wasn't a casual office by any means, in those days, and I didn't often get over to the court-room, for that reason. And the court-room didn't accommodate very many people. I had a pass, but if there's no place to sit, you don't get in.

I found it very exciting when I was there. Of course, the times I wanted to go there were when the Justice was interrogating, or delivering one of the briefs. It was when he was there that I really had the most interest. It was exciting for me to see him, because he had great presence, and he was so highly respected.

You'd see the defendants shifting around. Goering was a big man, you know; he shifted around and didn't really sit up straight. Hess sat there always in the same position, just like he was wound up to sit there and then he would go off. The Admirals sat there in fine military style. But Goering was dominant. Other than that I don't really recollect them, because I think I was more interested in the movement of the prosecution.

Anna Cameron, secretary

I didn't get down to the court-house as often as I would like to, but whenever I could I went down and listened. I remember going there one day and seeing them demonstrating the lampshades made of human skin. That made me feel the trials were worthwhile. They tattooed the skin. That I can understand – you've got to keep track of the enemy. But to read about putting children and women in ovens and burning them like so much charcoal – it's inhuman. I don't think even the worst savages would do what those so-called well-educated people would do. I never could understand – and I still can't now – what makes people want to do a thing like that. People sat stunned, I guess, because we were observers from another country. There were a lot of American Jews there, and I'm sure they cried in their hearts for their cousins and aunts and uncles who were there. The defendants looked like men who had once been important, and they hadn't forgotten that they'd once been important. But you sensed that they knew that this was defeat, the end of the line. Goering stood out in the dock. He would be the one who would shake his head angrily when he disagreed. He didn't say anything, but oh, he'd look fierce and shake his head. Hess just sat there as though he were in a dream world, but I think he may have been acting – I don't know. But the other men, they sat there like the important people they had been. They held themselves up.

Priscilla Belcher, visitor

I went in to several of the sessions in the court-room. The first time I went, there was a big tank outside, and everybody had to show their credentials, and so forth. I walked in and sat in the balcony and looked down at the court-room and all of these impressive people. The Russians always wore uniforms; the others were in civilian dress. We all stood up when the judges came in, and then in marched these men that we'd seen on newsreels, that we'd heard about, that we'd read about: Goering, Hess, von Ribbentrop, von Papen, Streicher, all of these men who had done these awful things. To be there, looking at them, was a *very* strange feeling. I was interested in the byplay amongst them, sometimes more than in what was being said. I went to von Papen's cross-examination, and he was trying to proclaim that he came from an old family and he was all for Germany, that he was not a politician, and this, that and the other. I noticed that Goering turned to Hess, and a guard told me afterwards that he had used one of his favourite expressions, the German version of 'Crap!' In the afternoon session Sir David Maxwell-Fyfe confronted him with some letters and things, and he couldn't explain how he could have saved 10,000 refugees from a concentration camp, when before he'd said he didn't know anything about the concentration camps. This was the thing that got me in Germany – nobody knew anything about them. But if you took the train from Frankfurt to Munich, you could *see* Dachau, and you could *smell* Dachau. We visited Dachau, and it was ... very difficult. I don't know how people faced it; well, I knew some of the doctors who went in at the beginning, and it was just horrifying. And to hear some of these men say, '*I* didn't know anything about it!', scapegoating each other ...

I also saw Doenitz and Speer being cross-examined. Speer admitted that he was using labour from the camps, but not very much, and he said that in 1943 he knew the war was over, and he thought about killing Hitler but he never did it. According to one of the guards, Goering said, 'Well, why didn't he do it, then?' The old guard, officers such as Raeder and Jodl, always sat very stiffly and didn't horse around at all. It was a *strange* feeling, looking at these men. I can't describe it. And then to go outside and see the results, and work with the results of what they had done. And to hear somebody like Jodl declaring that all the deaths at Rotterdam – he had called for Rotterdam to be wiped out – was not as bad as the Allies' bombing of Leipzig when the war was practically over ... The psychology of their thinking was, well, I don't know. You wonder sometimes, when you're in a situation like that, seeing the people there scrounging around and black marketing, what would *you* do if you were in their situation, conquered?

Peter Uiberall, interpreter

Everybody was very interested in Goering, who was undoubtedly the most intelligent of the bunch, in a rather bad way – a *Condottiere* type, a Renaissance type, who apparently had no ability to distinguish between good and bad. He was one of the biggest robbers in world history; he stole, or ordered to be stolen, some of the greatest art collections of European countries. He was an early Nazi; he was with Hitler in the Munich putsch, and when he was injured he was smuggled into Austria and taken to the castle of an acquaintance of his, where he was nursed. When he came to power one of his first acts was to put that man in a concentration camp and take his castle. Cesare Borgia couldn't have done a better job. So from that point of view, in a sort of negative sense, Goering was always very interesting.

Hess was also very interesting to me. I did not have the impression at any time that Hess was crazy. The entire episode of Hess's flight to Scotland will sooner or later be cleared up to a point where it will be understood that Hitler *must* have known about it: Hitler wanted his trusted and – he thought – accepted deputy to go to Britain and persuade the British to join forces against the Soviet Union. Had that succeeded, it would of course have been a great coup; since it did not succeed, Hitler had to denounce Hess, as he did, and disavow him and replace him. I think Hess was sane. It is interesting to read the various evaluations of the psychologists. He had times of mental disturbance, according to some of them. I remember the scene in the court when he got up and said something like, 'I want to announce that from now on my memory is fully at the disposal of the court.' That doesn't sound like an insane person. He *could* have had fits of amnesia, without being insane. He was a well-educated man, who had lived in foreign countries. He was probably responsible for more of *Mein Kampf* than Hitler himself. So he is also interesting, in a bad sense, because though he could not actually be charged for what happened in Germany while he wasn't there, he was to a high degree responsible because he laid the groundwork for much of it.

We became sort of acquainted with them from daily observation – hearing their lawyers, and hearing themselves if they went on the witness-stand. You did have a wonderful opportunity to observe them if you were an interpreter, especially since you were not always busy. Of course we didn't know what they talked about among themselves, since they didn't do very much of that in the court-room. I would say – speaking also for some of my colleagues – that our favourites were probably Speer and Schacht, for very selfish reasons: they were both very good in English! Schacht was perfect in English, fluent. His name was Hjalmar Horace

Greeley Schacht – I think his mother was American. And whenever an interpreter got stuck on some technical term that a German witness used, you would see either Speer or Schacht or both quickly whip out a piece of paper, write the English term on it, and send it along the line to the defendant who was sitting closest to the interpreter, who slipped it under the glass partition. So we were grateful to them. They were interested in good translation, as we were, and were helping where they could. In the case of Schacht it was a very 'innocent' friendship, because he was acquitted; in the case of Speer it was less so, because he was undoubtedly heavily incriminated and served twenty years.

Streicher was a despicable individual. I can only compare him to the head man in a lynch mob, and that's not strong enough. There was nothing particularly significant about him, other than his inexorable hatred of the Jews, whom he held responsible for everything evil in the world. He was certainly not an intellectual. He was the type of person who most clearly represented everything that was rotten and bad – the mob side – about the National Socialist movement. He was pretty much shunned by the others. But that was very often quite hypocritical, because the others had sometimes committed much more heinous crimes, while he was fighting mostly with words. He was small fry compared with some others.

Funk was also a small individual. So many of them were little people who had been propelled into high positions in the Nazi hierarchy by their talent for being followers of Hitler. Funk was the president of the Reichsbank, the national bank, and he had said in his defence that he didn't know about the concentration camps or any of these things that were going on. And then came the day when the film was shown in court, and it showed among other things the gold teeth and fillings and the hair of concentration camp victims, and the dolls of the children who were taken to the camps. All this material had been collected and shipped to Berlin, and had been found after the war in the vaults of the Reichsbank building, the bank of which Funk was president. And that was when he broke down, because he could no longer deny that he knew about the concentration camps.

One time Goering lashed out at a witness who testified rather damagingly against him and other Nazi leaders. His name was von dem Bach-Zelewski, and he was a high-ranking official in the SS. He had been on the witness-stand for quite some time and had been interrogated by prosecutors of the participating nations. As he walked away from the witness-stand and out of the court-room he had to pass by the corner of the defendants' dock, where Goering sat. Goering jumped up and lunged at the witness, trying to slap him, shouting, 'Verfluchter Schweinhund!', which means 'Damned pig!' He was restrained by the guards, of course, and the witness was safely conducted out of the court-room, and at the end of that session, while people were leaving the court-room, Lord Justice Lawrence announced that he wanted the defendant Goering, his defence counsel and a guard to remain in the court-room, and also a

German–English interpreter. Since I was on duty I was the one to stay behind, and when the court-room had emptied the presiding judge gave Goering a lecture about behaviour. He told him that if this happened once again, he would be put on rations of bread and water, deprived of his exercise rights, etc. etc. And I found myself, a former refugee, in the enviable position of being able to deliver that lecture, in German, to Hermann Goering. It was a strange impression, the man in this much-too-large uniform – he didn't look like anything, let alone like the feared Goering who was responsible for so many terrible crimes. He didn't seem real. There was no feeling of triumph in my mind. It was just an unusual situation, and the sort of thing you don't forget.

If my colleagues and I were not on duty in the court-room, and we knew that Sir David Maxwell-Fyfe was going to be 'on', as we called it, we made sure that we were present to listen. And everybody respected the presiding judge, Lord Justice Lawrence. It was fabulous how he control-led the proceedings. The young lawyers had a hard time sometimes, because he would cut them back if he thought they were too long. So many times I heard the phrase, 'Is all this detail really necessary?' One day, I remember, he seemed to doze off. I've never forgotten that. There was German being spoken on the stand at the time, and the German–English interpreter lowered his voice and then SUDDENLY SPOKE LOUD. We could see Lawrence's head bob up, and we smiled at each other – we had done it without disturbing anybody! We liked him very much, especially since he was the saviour of the interpreters when some speaker was too fast, or wasn't close enough to the microphone, which also happened sometimes. The speaker would turn his head to the right or the left, and we wouldn't get it, you see. And he was absolutely impartial. There was never any doubt about that. The fairness of the Nuremberg Trial is something that impressed me at all times. There were many war crimes trials after World War Two, none like Nuremberg. The standards of fairness that were applied in Nuremberg were unique – they were unfortunately not copied everywhere else – and we were very proud of that. The court-room procedure was based on the procedural law of all the participating nations, and especially in the sense that any feature which favoured the defendant was to be included.

Alfred Steer, administrative head, language division
The defendants behaved on the whole very well. You see, this was the first time that this interpreting system had been used, and the general judgement was that it wouldn't work. And when the defendants first came into the court-room you could see that they, too, were sneering at this dumb idea that the Americans were putting on. However, it tickled me no end that Speer was the first one to grasp that this idea was workable and was saving an enormous amount of time. He became very much interested, and we called him our assistant. I would put in a new interpreter, for instance, as I was constantly having to do because of the turnover, and he would spot the new interpreter immediately. Of course

he spoke French and English quite well. You could see him tuning in to the new interpreter, and he would listen for a little while and then look over at me and make some appropriate sign, either a thumbs up or a sign meaning 'He'll never make it!' And he was right every time!

Some of the defendants pretended to pay no attention. This was particularly true of Streicher. I don't think he was normal – he was subhuman. The others, I think, accepted it. Goering was an extraordinary individual. He had this characteristic we now call charisma to an extraordinary degree. I never saw it fail. I think anyone who went into the court-room and watched him for any period of time felt this, and I would have people, American officers from outlying places, saying to me over and over again, 'Gosh, I'd like to get that man out of that gaol cell and have him over to the house and fill him full of a couple of beers, and it would be a lot of fun to hear what he has to say!' Over and over again we got this reaction. We could also see very clearly how he leered at every nubile female in sight. There were two French court reporters particularly, one of whom had a very decided bustal development, and he would just – the German word is 'glotzen', meaning 'to devour with the eyes' – as she came and went. The court reporters took down everything verbatim, and they could not stand to stay there a whole session; they would take only half an hour. So they would be constantly coming and going. That Goering. What a scoundrel! But, charisma or not, he was a proven criminal.

Hess was a very strange case. As you know, he was examined by a number of different psychiatrists and specialists of various sorts. I talked to one of them, who sat in the court-room for days and days and did nothing but simply observe Hess. He came to the conclusion that Hess was suffering from a kind of intermittent insanity: his mind came and went more or less at will. There were times when he could behave almost like a normal individual, and there were times when he was simply completely off. This psychiatrist did something which I thought was very interesting: he placed a number of small lights along the railing of the dock, which would throw a light on the faces of the defendants when they showed movies of the terrible situation in the concentration camps, these things that used to make me wake up screaming in the middle of the night for weeks thereafter. He would watch their faces, and he said that when these things came on the screen there was a triumphant leer on Hess's face. Nuts, completely nuts.

Jodl was a little, short, sawn-off fellow. He was a very smart man, and he had heard us preparing document books in advance, and observed that the presentation of the case concerned was made more effective when the interpreter had a written version rather than simply interpreting it as he heard it. The defendants were told that they were going to have an opportunity to make a final statement to the court in their own defence, and he passed me a note in the court-room, asking, if he wrote out his defence statement in advance would I translate it for him in advance? I said of course I would. So he sent me over a single half-sheet, very neatly written, saying this: that when he had entered the military service and then entered the war, he had done so under the impression that loyalty to one's nation was the highest loyalty that could be demanded of one – there was no obligation to a higher entity or set of values at all – and that this trial had seemed to indicate that that conviction was in error, that there *was* a higher morality to which he and all other military men should owe allegiance, although of course the nation was important. And he said that if this trial established that precedent, he was willing to accept whatever punishment this court meted out and he would be satisfied. Well, I mean, there's a man. I admired that man, I certainly did. He was the only one who had anything positive to say: all the others were complaining, or making wild accusations, and so on. This was a man who looked straight at the facts and made a logical conclusion, in spite of the fact that it involved his own execution.

The judges had a special room in the court-house where they could meet to consider requests by the prosecution and defence, and talk these things over in private. So we set up a special miniature simultaneous system in a small room, and I put in four interpreters whom I considered particularly gifted and particularly discreet. They were used a good deal.

Justice Jackson – I didn't much like that gentleman. His cross-examination of Goering was a flat failure. I thought Goering was far superior to him. He was way ahead of him: he could foresee what Jackson was going to say next and take a position, and make Jackson's question when it came sound kind of ridiculous. There was no mystery why he was the second man in the Third Reich. He was not only a charismatic ladies' man; he also had a superb mind. Maxwell-Fyfe was far superior to Jackson in cross-examination. He would just bore in and bore in. At one point Goering was waiting for the interpretation, and he said, 'Well, witness, you understand English quite well, don't you? Suppose you answer right away?' He was pushing him, pushing him. This is what you need in a cross-examination, and what you expect an able attorney to be able to do. And Jackson didn't do it.

Bernard Meltzer, lawyer
One couldn't spend all one's time in the court-room and get on with one's work, so I was in and out. I was there, for example, when Jackson made his splendid opening statement, and when Goering was cross-examined, but it would be very hard for me to say how much time I spent in there. In fact, the longer you were in Nuremberg, the more tedious the court-room became.

I was disappointed by Jackson's cross-examination of Goering. I was disappointed in his having to appeal to the court for help in controlling him. I was also disappointed for another and perhaps less well-known reason: there was a lot of stuff kicking around that would have been helpful to Jackson, and the junior staff didn't know whether that material was being processed by his immediate staff, and whether it would be intrusive to volunteer, and, rightly or wrongly, they were waiting to be asked. So as the cross-examination evolved, some of the staff had more or less clear recollections of material that, if only it had been presented to Jackson, might have been helpful. Beyond that, I think Jackson was victimized by a mistaken translation. Anyhow, overall the cross-examination was, to put it mildly, a disappointment. My recollection is a bit fuzzy, but my impression is that it did get better when Maxwell-Fyfe came in, although it might have gotten better because the subject-matter had changed. I remember one aspect of the cross-examination which involved some German documents that were marked 'Top Secret', and Jackson made quite a point of that, and Goering said that *he* was not accustomed to reading about the plans of the American military in the *New York Times*. Here was Jackson, who had all the chips, on the surface, losing his cool, while Goering maintained this cool, arrogant defiance throughout. Goering was a clever man, and he had decided to play a role that showed no penitence, no guilt – the uncompromising defender of the Reich.

I remember that Raeder maintained his dignity, and I remember Rosenberg saying, 'A thousand years will not erase the guilt of Germany.' Funk was kind of insignificant. I remember Keitel bristling under some of the charges, when his military honour was impugned. When their uniforms and medals were removed, it made a great difference to the way they looked. They were in the dock, you know; and some of them were quite big and dominating physically, but the aura of power was gone if you looked at them as a group. Part of the power, of course, had been the context, and that was all changed. It was hard to believe that that group had almost conquered all of Europe.

Daniel Margolies, lawyer
Mr Jackson came very seldom to the trial. I don't know what he did – stayed at home, or stayed wherever he was – but he asked Mr Dodd to attend the trial on a daily basis as the main US prosecutor. Many of the American lawyers on the staff had had very little trial experience. In many instances leading American lawyers have never set foot in a trial court. Distinguished British barristers are in trial courts very often. Our better-known lawyers are frequently in the higher courts discussing legal subjects and writing briefs, but they are seldom in trial courts interrogating witnesses, in the trenches, as you might say.

I thought Jackson's cross-examination of Goering was a disaster. Everybody did. Among other things, he got caught up on words when his German translation led him astray. The 'Freimachung' of the Rhine was one of them: he thought that was the movement of the German troops into the Rhineland, but it turned out that he was discussing the time that the Rhine had frozen over and they managed to get the ice broken up, which was scarcely a war crime. He had the two confused, and Goering, gloating over that, was really quite upsetting – I think it threw Mr Jackson off his stride. That's one of the things that I recall. Anyway, Jackson had a great command of language – he wrote beautifully and he made excellent speeches – but he wasn't a first-class trial lawyer.

Speer is an interesting case. There's no reason for sending a man to gaol as a war criminal because he mobilized the resources of his country to defend itself, or to carry on a war. That's like Schacht's activities, in which he managed to default on all the German bonds, and barter deals with countries in which he lied, and one thing and another. Speer was extremely able and intelligent – his personality was outstanding. And he managed to run the war economy with great skill. That's not really a war crime. A main reason he got sent to gaol was because of part of a brief that my wife wrote on him. He had the misfortune to have his picture taken with Himmler, walking through a concentration camp discussing, as it turned out, how they could use this body of labour for war production purposes. They did, in fact, take the concentration camp people who were simply being starved to death, and put them to work – they didn't feed them, but they figured they might at least get such energy as they had out of them before they died. And he worked out a technique for this. I think Himmler probably thought it up, but Speer was looking for a labour supply and he used it. He may not have liked the arrangement – I don't know. But he did it. If you read his autobiography, he doesn't mention this. If you read the trial records, you'll find the part of the brief that my wife prepared around this picture of the concentration camp. There was some interrogation and he admitted it. That is why he was convicted – if he hadn't arranged for the use of concentration camp labour he might have been acquitted. They had some problems with Streicher, by the way. I mean, he did write terrible stuff, but you normally don't hang people for writing terrible stuff. As I recall they scrounged around and found he'd killed somebody. Somehow, nobody wanted to acquit *him*. He was a very unsatisfactory human being.

Whitney Harris, lawyer

Hess paid very little attention to the proceedings, and sat there most of the time reading a book or with his head bowed. When he was brought from England to Nuremberg, he was of course interrogated, and he maintained as his defence that he was suffering from progressive amnesia and could not remember anything beyond two weeks in the past. He was confronted with Goering, and showed no signs of recognizing him at all, and Goering left the room shaking his head. One remark that Hess made made the lawyers a little suspicious: he made reference to the fact that Belgium was in the war. So the lawyers thought, well, now we have him. 'How did you know that Belgium was in the war, Mr Hess, if you can't remember anything beyond two weeks?' And he replied, 'When we flew over from England, I saw these bomb craters and asked where we were. We were over Belgium, so naturally I concluded that Belgium was in the war.' I must say that the lawyers were rather sceptical of his plea, however it was necessary for the Tribunal to appoint a medical commission to enquire into Hess's condition. And I was in the court-room when the commission's report, having been received by the Tribunal, was presented, in effect, to Hess. The commission concluded that Hess was suffering from a loss of memory, but they felt that he probably could defend himself. It was not really proper for them to do that: that was a legal conclusion. Anyway, it looked to me and others that very likely Hess would have to be excused, because if he couldn't defend himself, how could he be brought to trial? Lord Lawrence turned to Hess and asked him if *he* had anything that he wanted to say in his own behalf, and Hess stood up and said he wanted to explain to the Tribunal that he had been feigning this loss of memory ever since he was in England, because he didn't want to be interrogated any more, that his lawyer was completely innocent and knew nothing about it, and that he remembered everything and was perfectly able to defend himself. So that statement kept him in the lawsuit, and convinced us lawyers that he really was not very sound of mind, because he was out of the case and he'd talked himself back into it. But he didn't participate very much, in the event. He made a final statement, not under oath, which was wild and rambling. He was just getting to a point where it sounded like he was going to refer to mistreatment in England – these men had, I think, fifteen minutes to make their final unsworn statement – and everybody was quite tense at that moment, wondering what Hess was going to say now, when Lord Lawrence quietly intervened: 'Mr Hess, your time is up.' And that concluded Hess's final statement – we never knew what he was going to say. But he was so rambling, and I remember him saying that there were always these eyes upon him. He was obviously not very sound of mind, at *that* point.

My defendant, Ernst Kaltenbrunner, had suffered a stroke, and at the beginning it looked like maybe all my work was going to be in vain. But he finally came back. He was a very tall, grey-haired man, with fencing scars, which gave him a rather fierce appearance. His position throughout the trial was that his function was only to take care of intelligence, and that he had nothing to do with the concentration camps, the killing of people, and so forth. His position was one of aloofness. Goering was always very self-assured: he felt that he was, and acted as, the leader of the group, and he made an effort throughout to defend the regime in every way that he could. He tried to get the others to stand fast, and that is one reason that he was disgusted with Hess, because Hess was really not with it at all. Schirach, I think, always felt that he really didn't belong in this group. Streicher was much as he'd always been – blustering. For the most part the defendants didn't have much to do except sit there in the courtroom, until their moment came when they took the stand.

I was Justice Jackson's assistant during his cross-examination of Goering. He conceived the idea that he would try to prove, through his cross-examination of Goering, the entire Nazi conspiracy. This was an extremely daring thing to do, and particularly with someone like Hermann Goering, who was very alert and knowledgeable – more knowledgeable than any of us. Jackson proceeded with the cross-examination extremely well, going into the idea of how the Nazis took over, eliminated opposition, set up the concentration camps, and so on. So everything was going pretty well, but then Goering began to expand on his answers, and use any opportunity that he had to go into a long explanation of irrelevancies. And unfortunately, we felt, Lord Lawrence was much too easy on him. Eventually Jackson had some words over this, and complained to the Tribunal that the Tribunal was letting Goering go too far. I might say that, during the negotiations in London, this was one of the main concerns, and this was one of the reasons, I'm sure, why the British, early on, felt that executive action was the right procedure. I'm sure some of them felt, 'What are we doing allowing these people a forum, from which they're going to propagandize? We've killed I don't know how many million soldiers to get rid of these people, and now we're going to turn around and let them make speeches! Is that the way to go about this?' And there's a lot to be said for this. Executive action is not all wrong. I'm very grateful that we had the judicial proceedings – I think it was the right choice – but they disposed of Napoleon by executive action, at least they put him away, so there's nothing too wrong with it in international law. But there had been great concern about this in the negotiations, and this was the first witness, the strongest witness and the most dangerous witness, and he began doing that very thing.

Jackson thought that the best thing would be for Goering to be instructed to save his comments for re-examination – that is, he would have to answer categorically yes or no at first, and he could make his speeches when being examined by his own counsel. But Lord Lawrence seemed not to understand this at all. He did not rule in favour of Jackson, and he pretty much let Goering do what he wanted. That was the problem, if there was a problem. But as we went on, Goering himself recognized that he was going a little bit too far and more or less quietened down, and then when we got into areas where he was completely vulnerable, he just faded away. So I thought that ultimately the cross-examination came off extremely well. It was a very difficult case, extremely hard to do. And there was another thing that was hard. My function in assisting Justice Jackson was primarily to sit there and hand him documents. We had translations of documents. Justice Jackson would be reading the document in English, and Goering would have his own copy in German. He would look at it and say, 'Well, I don't think that's right,' or 'No, it doesn't mean so and so', and then we'd get into a big argument over what the document said. That happened throughout the proceedings, of course, inevitably. But in the ultimate, there is no question that the cross-examination of Goering by Justice Jackson demolished Goering. The facts were indisputable, and there wasn't really any way that Goering could get out of it.

John Pine, visitor

I went to Nuremberg in the spring of 1946, with Colonel Bown, a judge of the military government courts before whom I was then prosecuting, and we spent a few days there. When we first went into the court it was in session. One's attention seemed automatically directed towards Goering, who was sitting comparatively near one in what had been one of his uniforms, stripped of all his medals and decorations and with a few of the buttons of his tunic undone. He seemed to dominate the scene, judges and all, and to me he was a most powerful personality, with an obvious sense of humour. Next to him was Hess, who automatically seemed to draw one's attention with his brightly shining, withdrawn eyes. To me he looked the perfect illustration of 'as mad as a hatter'. His movements of his hands rather substantiated this, and his whole behaviour seemed to be rather what one would have expected having regard to his background. He had been incarcerated in some mental hospital in Abergavenny whilst in the UK, and rather an amusing cartoon appeared around that time. In the early stages of the trial, they had shown a number of films of grandiose parades, each bigger and better than the last, all designed to show the grandeur of the Nazi Party and those who had organized it. Goering took obvious and great pride in these films, and the cartoon showed him watching one even grander parade than the others, and digging Hess in the ribs, saying to Hess, 'There now! Where were you when that was taking place? Nutting around in Abergavenny.'

Next to Hess was Ribbentrop, who seemed the perfect illustration of someone who had had the wind knocked out of him: very deflated, and the complete negation of his former arrogance. Nothing really to attract one's attention as with the former two, Goering and Hess. And then I recall well Keitel, Jodl, Raeder and Doenitz, all of them stripped of their medals and decorations, and I think their metal buttons too. All four of them seemed very deflated and lacking in any dynamism – certainly not a C-in-C among them. What a difference a fully-dressed uniform makes. But even so, I don't think that any of them had much to draw one's attention to them. And then there was Speer, and von Papen, and von Neurath, but I remember nothing special, really, about *them*. I don't think that I ever took in much about all the others – I only seemed to have eyes for Goering and Hess, with Ribbentrop a poor third. But Goering dominated the court.

The interpreting machinery was remarkably good, and you could tune into four languages by putting your earphones on. I believe it was the first time this was ever done, and it was noticeably good, particularly when one had been toiling for so long in the ordinary military government courts. There so often one had four or five languages going, but just in terms of interpreters – no earphones. Sometimes you could tell that the interpreter wasn't translating exactly what you had said – he was translating what he thought you *ought* to have said; in other words he was filling in slightly. The judge got very cross about this on one occasion, and gave the interpreter a going-over in front of everybody, saying, 'Now look here, I want you to translate *everything* I say, *exactly*. Do you understand?' The interpreter nodded, and the judge signalled to me to proceed, saying, 'Yes, Mr Pine?', whereupon the interpreter said, 'Ja, Herr Tannenbaum?'

Ron Chapman, clerk

Occasionally we would get into the actual court-room where the trial was taking place – not often. Occasionally we would take messages through to the prosecutors from their secretaries. We would leave a slip of paper on their desk; naturally we never spoke. I remember walking in one day with Anadins for Mr G.D.[Khaki] Roberts. He had a headache and he phoned through for some. I do always remember that particular time, because as I walked in Goering was right on the end of the front bench. He was leaning on the end, and he turned round and looked up as I walked over to Mr Roberts. I tried to walk out without looking at him. It was like a magnet – you wanted to look, and yet you felt embarrassed.

The most amazing thing in the court-room, I think, was the translation, the interpreting side of it. Four languages had got to be spoken and heard, simultaneously. The British Signal Corps did all the wiring, and laid many miles of wire in there. It was a very sophisticated network. The interpreters couldn't wait until the whole question had finished, and then translate it, because it would take so long, and it would lose its continuation. I know for a fact that it was such a stressful thing for these translators that two or three of them had nervous breakdowns during the trial. It was really terrible, because they could not afford to get a word wrong or it could give a different meaning to the question. Mind you, when documents were being read out it was easy, because the documents had all been prepared in four languages, and all the interpreters had to do was sit there and read from a document.

You went and sat in the visitors' gallery, which held about 150 people and was up at one end of the court-room, looking down on the dock. You had a little dial on the arm of your chair, with S, 1, 2, 3, 4. That was Speaker, English, German, French and Russian – I can't remember the order exactly. So if a British prosecutor was speaking you could get him on either S or 1. If a French prosecutor was speaking, you still turned to 1 and you got it in English. You got different translators' voices coming over the earphones. If Goering was talking and you wanted to hear him in German, you turned to Speaker and you got Goering's voice coming over the earphones. The eight judges – two from each nation – had their own earphones, so that they could follow every word.

The British judges lived not far from us, and they went to the court-house every day in a bullet-proof car. They were also escorted by a jeep, and two motor-cycles with military police. Sir David Maxwell-Fyfe, who was known as the Tiger of Nuremberg, was the cleverest of all the prosecutors. And Goering was no fool, believe you me. He was the fat field marshal, he was baited and laughed at, but he was a very clever man, not the fool that a lot of people thought. They reckoned that when Maxwell-Fyfe cross-examined Goering it was the most exciting time of the trial. They were both clever, they were both fighting each other in their questions and answers. And the way Maxwell-Fyfe fired questions at Goering, the translators were getting absolutely hot under the collar, they were coming over so fast. Goering didn't have time to think: as soon as he'd given an answer there would be another question.

The prisoners themselves ... it was very strange to watch them. The majority of them spent the day sitting in their pews, in the dock, in dark glasses, with their heads on their chests. You couldn't really tell if they were listening or if they were asleep. Lots of films were shown in the court-room during the trial. They had a special screen. There was a lot shown there that I don't think the public were shown, but they still sat there with their heads on their chests and their dark glasses, as if they were in a hypnotic trance. Hess was a very strange character. He had a lot of stomach cramps, and he was often going out of the court, with an American guard. You would see him say something to his defence counsel, and they would have a word with the American officer in charge of the guards. Then you'd see him come back perhaps an hour later, depending on what the doctor had said. Kaltenbrunner was another one who spent a lot of time absent – they did say he had a brain haemorrhage, although he was hung all the same. Very few of them took any notice of the proceedings – just the odd one or two. Goering was usually listening, with his hand on his chin, taking it in. Hess ... well, you didn't know *where* Hess was. Streicher, the Jew-baiter, *he* paid quite a bit of attention. Doenitz was very sombre. They just had these fixed masks. I don't think they really worried if they were in or out, themselves. Most of them, I think, were very accepting of the fact that they'd just had it. They accepted the fact that they couldn't get away with it. Except Goering. He must have known that he was going to be found guilty, but he still fought in his cross-examination, and it was as if he was fighting to the end, you know. Perhaps inwardly he knew, but in his other mind he was hoping that he could get away with it.

The actual summing-up and sentencing took four sessions in the court-room, two a day, and for all NCOs, corporals upwards, they had a draw of tickets for the visitors' gallery, and I won a ticket for one session. At the time I was in Nuremberg Hospital: I had these terrible boils on my arm. The medical officer sent me up to the military hospital, because they'd got penicillin, which we hadn't heard of in those days. I was due to come out on the fourth day, and I'd got a ticket for the session, and I asked to see the American major who was in charge of the hospital. He was quite nasty to me. I said, 'I'm a British corporal working at the court-house and I've got a ticket for a session, and I'd very much like to be released so I can attend it.' My major had arranged for one of the chaps to pick me up and get me to the court-house. And he was nasty: 'How did *you* get a ticket? What are *you* doing with a ticket?' Thought I didn't deserve one, I suppose. But I managed to get there, and I did get into the first session, which didn't actually include the sentencing; it only included a lot of the summing-up.

Patrick Cooper, airman

I was never in the court-room. It *was* open to the public, in principle, but in practice nobody got in unless they had a good reason to get in, and a pass, and what not, and the likes of me weren't allowed. But I often passed by the Palace of Justice. One of the things that I remember from very early on is that there were knots of people hanging about outside, and one didn't quite know who they were; they were usually shooed away by the MPs [military policemen]. They weren't demonstrators or anything like that; they were just curious people wondering what was going on. Another thing I remember is once or twice, when I happened to be passing by the Palace of Justice, seeing the families of the various defendants going in, presumably to visit them, because they were kept in cells quite nearby and brought to the court-room every day. I saw these families being brought there and getting out of their cars, and going into the Palace of Justice. You remember the most curious things ... such odd things stick in your memory. I remember a lady – somebody said it was Frau Goering, but I'm not sure – a very distinguished-looking woman. This was still in cold weather, so it would be early 1946. She was wearing a fox thing, you know, and a marvellous wide-brimmed hat, of the sort that was much worn in the late thirties and early forties. I can see her now; if I met her I would recognize her. She was wearing those T-strapped shoes ... it's funny, the things that stick in your mind. They looked ... it was a curious combination of sullen and shamefaced, if you can imagine such a thing. And a sort of shock, too. I didn't have any personal contact with these people; I'm just talking about being there and seeing them from a distance. But I'm a painter, and accustomed to using my eyes, so I probably saw a lot of things that boys of my age and experience at that time wouldn't see.

Eddie Worth, photographer

At the opening session of the trial, we saw that in the corner there was a great big camera – I forget how many thousand feet its reel was. None of us had anything like that over there. And it was Leni Riefenstahl, the woman who had made the films for Hitler – her studio was going to record every minute and word of the opening session: all their pleas, and this, that and the other. We were allowed on the floor. There was a great big dock, and at the back of it was a little door which was actually a lift. The lift came up, and there were two guards and one defendant. They all came up in order of precedence: Goering came up first, went to his seat and sat down. I photographed him close up. Then Hess came – he still had his flying boots on, from the time he flew to England. And as they came in, one by one, they all bowed to Goering, the former Reichsmarschall.

When I went up to photograph old Schacht, the financial wizard, he turned to the others and said, 'This is my old friend from London,' which didn't please me very much! What had happened was that I had photographed him several times in London with old Montague Norman, the Governor of the Bank of England, who was as nutty as a fruitcake. Schacht used to come over from Germany and fiddle the currencies. He got away with it at the trial, and afterwards he went out to Brazil or somewhere and ended up sorting *their* finances out. He was a very clever bloke.

I photographed all these people, and then we had to get out. But I had said to the German crew, 'I'm not in on the opening session, but I'd like some pictures, so that we can have negatives of the opening session. Does anybody in your crew know how to use a still camera?' And the very fellow I was speaking to said, 'Well, I'm the studio still man!' So I gave him my camera, and a special lens which was a 15-inch Ross, absolutely perfect for the job. When the opening session was over, he came out and gave me the camera. All the pool material had to be handed into the American army film unit, who were going to develop it and wire it to London and everywhere else in the world. I didn't much fancy doing that, because I wasn't supposed to have this film, so I wrapped it up very neatly and took it out to Furth, just outside Nuremberg, where there was an Advance Delivery Letter Service: a Mosquito used to fly back to London every hour, with papers and stuff. I put it on one of those, and it whizzed back to London, where a motor cyclist took it up to the Associated Press and they developed and printed it. The next evening we were all in the mess, and the newspapers came. And every newspaper was flooded with these pictures; we were studying them, and thinking, 'This is a bit odd – they don't look like wire photos!' It turned out that the Americans had mucked it all up – the wires weren't working very well – and all the photos in the newspapers were my originals! So then there was a great enquiry as to how I'd got them, and one of the people in Keystone accused me of stealing their film. But unfortunately for them we still had the whole lot in London, numbered from one to twelve, so they were shot down in flames, and we scooped the world with it!

My daily routine was this: I would get up and have one of those sumptuous breakfasts, and then I would be carted off to the court-room. Most of the photographers lost interest in going there every day, but I had a little camera stand in the corner. You weren't allowed to use flashes, so the photographs had to be very slow exposure, so my still camera was on a stand. I used to listen to all the evidence about the terrible things the Germans had been getting up to: slave labour, experiments, all sorts of things. At one point, terrible as it was, the court-room burst out laughing. The Germans were finding that sailors and airmen who were dropped in northern waters were freezing to death, and they were trying to find out ways of reviving them. They would put slave labourers into a bath, and then slowly reduce the temperature of the water until they were nearly frozen to a block of ice, and when they were near death they would try and revive them, by injecting them and all sorts of things. And they came to the conclusion that taking them out of the bath and putting them in a bed with a couple of slave girls revived them much better than anything else. That made the court laugh.

I don't think people cried. It seemed so unreal, you know, you could hardly believe it was happening. The Germans were the most arrogant people on earth, before the war. There was an edict put out in triplicate to all the commanders, that any escapees were to be handed over to the SS for liquidation. They put it in print. They never *dreamed* that they would lose. And of course that was one of the indictments: that after the breakout from Stalag Luft III, the fifty airmen who'd tried to escape, and were caught, were all murdered. That was one of the things that nearly brought tears to my eyes when I heard it, because I'd been mixed up all the time with these young flyers. I used to go to the American bases, and all these young lads – they were boys to me, really ... To think that this was the flower of our youth, and fifty of them had been murdered by these beasts. So I felt no compunction – I'd have shot the blooming lot of them if I'd had my way.

I photographed Hess one day; he had a book in his hand and he took no notice whatsoever of the trial. He'd be either reading or dozing. His book intrigued me, because it looked like a very old book, and I asked one of the guards to find out what it was. The next day he said, 'You'll never believe what it is. It's Grimms' *Fairy Tales*!'

Goering was a wonderful character. He certainly kept the dignity of the court. He ruled it, really. We were all very pleased when he committed suicide, because the prison commander [Colonel Andrus], an American ... oh, he was an objectionable beast. He used to boast that they couldn't even breathe without his knowledge. He was a real horror. We all had a good laugh when it was announced that Goering had done himself in!

Streicher was an absolutely abominable creature. He *looked* the lowest of the low, almost subhuman. None of the other defendants could stand him; they ostracized him. The German generals were very correct: their uniforms were very smart, and they were always taking notes and things. Unless they were mixed up in the atrocities I don't know why they were convicted, because they were no different, really, from our generals. I suppose they had the stigma of only being where they were because of Hitler; all the old type had disappeared.

One day one of the guards said to me, 'If you come round the back of the court-house at lunchtime, you'll see an interesting sight.' So I went round, and lo and behold, there were nearly all the defendants' wives. Apparently they came in for a free meal: they used the tradesmen's entrance, and took a tray, and got a decent meal. That had been going on for ages, and nobody had picked the story up, that they were getting a handout. It was a very strange business, that court: all sorts of things were going on all the time.

Paul Graven, prison guard officer

Just before the trial started, I was promoted to the job of exterior guard officer. I would have a guard mount outside the building every morning, and then I would post the interior guards throughout the Palace of Justice. We'd have guards on every corner of the building, all the different quarters. It was my job to go round all day long and see that they were performing their duties, and find out whether there were any problems and that sort of thing. That enabled me to get into the court-room, which I did. That was very interesting. If you weren't there all the time it was pretty hard to follow – you'd come in on various subjects that they were talking about. But I enjoyed listening to some of the proceedings and seeing the prisoners. I thought they looked older than I remembered them from their pictures. I would say they had a tough life in prison, though we did give them exercise every day, for about an hour – they would walk around the courtyard. We'd send two or three at a time, and we wouldn't let them walk together, because they weren't supposed to talk to each other.

Justice Jackson was excellent. In the books I've read, it says that he made several mistakes, but I didn't realize that – I'm not enough of a lawyer. The audience, who all had their headphones on, were very attentive; we had no trouble that I recall, in the court-room, with disruptions and that sort of thing. But of course it was pretty well restricted: you had to have a pass to get into the Palace of Justice, and then there were guards at all the corners to check you again as you were walking around. I knew some of the guards who stood round the court-room. They said it was rather boring standing around all the time, not understanding much of what was said, because of course they didn't have the advantage of headphones with the translation.

Jean Tull, secretary

Although I was a 'back room' girl, I and the other secretaries could get tickets to the court-room whenever our own work permitted and particularly when any interesting cross-examination was expected. One of the American prosecutors, Justice Jackson, was having a difficult time cross-examining Goering, who was running rings round him, and they brought in Sir David Maxwell-Fyfe to save the situation. Well, everyone wanted to go in for fifteen minutes to listen to that.

The German lawyers looked rather formidable, in long black gowns. It was noticeable that there was a preponderance of Jewish lawyers among the American delegation; they felt it rather deeply.

I remember that Goering had a bit of a roving eye, particularly for one very attractive British officer who was there called Esmé Sherriff. She had come via the Bletchley Park group, working on the Enigma code. There was quite a little posse of them at the trial. I should imagine she was in charge of handing documents to the prosecutor. Goering was looking her up and down, and smiling, and nudging his companions. He had been a very large man, but had got very thin in prison: his clothes hung off him. He did rather dominate the court-room, especially when he was getting the better of Jackson. Hess looked a poor creature: he always seemed to be half asleep. Baldur von Schirach, the youth leader, was about the best-looking of the bunch. They were a grisly lot, on the whole. They all just sat there, but some paid more attention than others: Goering, Ribbentrop and Speer were probably the most alert.

Hume Boggis-Rolfe, visitor

I was at Nuremberg for only two or three days. With the exception of Hess, the defendants mostly had their headphones on and looked fairly attentive. Now and then one of them would react to something said by a witness, but in general none of them reacted much to the evidence – you wouldn't expect them to, would you? They didn't look particularly depraved, except perhaps for Sauckel, Seyss-Inquart and Streicher. The military figures looked as you would expect them to, like senior servicemen on the other side. And von Neurath just looked like a distinguished old diplomat. One of the things we used to do was leave the court-room early to see the defendants being marched down the corridor back to their cells. Goering looked very masterful, but he was the only one; it would have been difficult for someone like Keitel to look masterful after a military defeat. When Goering committed suicide, the rumour that was flying around among us at the time was that Frau Goering, when she visited her husband in prison, had given him the cyanide capsule as she kissed him.

When we first entered the court-room, we were given an American handout which included a seating plan and a thumbnail sketch of each of the defendants [see pp.viii–xii]. The court-room was very full: there were a lot of lawyers, and all the interpreters, and the press, and a good many visitors. And the atmosphere in court was quite a dramatic thing, you know. We don't have capital punishment now, so perhaps our trials don't have the same feel, but the Nuremberg Trial, of course, was concerned with capital punishment in a big way.

Sylvia De La Warr, visitor

I went into the court-room every day. I sat there the whole time. I saw all the evidence, heard all the speeches, and they had some really extra-ordinary films. The strange thing is that you'd think they would have destroyed some of the more terrible evidence, but they hadn't destroyed a single thing. It was awful, but tremendously gripping as the story developed. You didn't see much emotion, though occasionally a witness who was newly out of a concentration camp would get upset, remembering.

The defendants didn't seem to listen. I suppose they'd got themselves into a state where they *didn't* listen, much. I don't think they had any feeling that they'd done anything wrong, or if they had, they kept it very close to themselves. Keitel, who looked very much like an old-fashioned German soldier – I thought he sometimes looked a bit ashamed to be there among them. They were a very mixed group, of course, and some of them thought the others were very low-grade, according to *their* lights. Goering was always trying to catch the eye of the wives. The delegation sat at tables, and the wives went and sat there, just behind them – we didn't sit in the gallery. And when he saw any stray women coming in he had a sort of look to see if he couldn't get a little joke going with them.

I initially felt that Speer ought to be acquitted, because he was young – or younger – and he was obviously a much nicer man than some of the others. I think most people agreed on that. And he had stood up to Hitler quite a bit. One felt that, for getting Germany back into the comity of nations after all this was over, he might be a useful man to have around. And I was saying this to one of the lawyers, Mervyn Griffith-Jones, one day, when he showed me an exhibit which had come from the place where Speer had been working the slaves. It was a length of rubber tubing with a sort of network of wire on the outside, and sticking on the wire were bits of flesh. And from then on, I wouldn't have liked to plead his case. He couldn't have *not* known that these things were being used to beat the workers. It was very German, really, that ruthlessness in getting your job done; he was absolutely determined to get his armaments out, and if he hadn't used any wrong methods in doing it one wouldn't have blamed him – he was doing it for his country, as far as he knew. I think Mervyn Griffith-Jones was determined that I should see that they weren't just being ruthless towards Speer – that there was a reason for their feeling that he shouldn't have carried his enthusiasm as far as he did. I think they were more horrified by the cruelties than perhaps anyone is now.

Yvette Wilberforce, visitor

I was told that I would sit at the bench of the French public prosecutors, and I arrived very early so as not to miss anything. One entered the court-room through a very narrow door facing the court. The court had not yet arrived at this point, but there were young American photographers in uniform standing on a table, with their back to where the court would be sitting later on, pointing their cameras down at the prisoners, who were lined up on the benches. I hesitated in the doorway, and then I heard this voice at my elbow: 'Wollen Sie auch photographieren?' And I looked straight into Goering's face! He was grinning impudently at me. I think I may have been the last maiden he caused to blush as I hurried to my assigned place!

Then the court-room began to fill up. Madame Falco was always there; she made sketches of the defendants. She said that one got fond of those people, although one knew that they had done abominations, and I must say that the day they were to die ... I have such a horror of the thought of hanging. I went to church and said a few prayers to the Lord to forgive them their sins, which probably they had been led into by themselves and by circumstances.

One of the many unprecedented aspects of the Nuremberg Trial was the presence, in force, of the world's media, which ensured that information about the events in the court-room was transmitted to people all over the globe. Journalists filed both straight reports and more impressionistic pieces, and the proceedings were photographed and filmed. In this way it was possible for people who had never set foot in the court-room to imagine themselves there.

This book's participants vary widely as to the amount of time that they spent in the court-room, and their reactions to many of its aspects are similarly diverse. Some were involved in the trial as workers, while others were merely spectators. They were not all equally gripped by the proceedings, and among the details of what they heard different things caught their attention. They have differing views as to whether or not Hess was sane, reflecting the wider controversy aroused by his behaviour in the dock, and they are by no means unanimous in their reaction to Justice Jackson's performance during his cross-examination of Goering.

Those participants involved in interpreting (Uiberall and Steer) had an exceptional opportunity to observe the defendants. They developed a good-humoured relationship with Speer and Schacht, who used to help them covertly over tricky points of translation; and on a deeper level, they came to respect certain defendants and to realize that these defendants trusted them. Some of the lawyers also had contact with the defendants away from the court-room. The visitors sitting in the gallery, however, had a more limited impression, and in general people seem to have been most struck by Goering's dominating presence. Compared with him, the other defendants generally left little impression (and the German counsel hardly any), and to many observers it appeared incredible that such lacklustre figures could have led a movement which had left much of Europe in ruins. Exactly what had happened to the physical, social and psychological fabric of Nuremberg was plain for all to see, and in the following chapter people recall the impact it made upon them and the ways in which it impinged upon their daily lives.

4. Living in Nuremberg

The ruins of Nuremberg provoked differing reactions in those who came to attend the trial. Some were so profoundly shocked by the devastation that they never forgot it, while others felt they had seen far worse sights during the previous few years. The amount of contact which they had with the German citizens who lived and worked among the ruins varied widely, but to judge by the participants in this book nearly all of them experienced at some time or other painful, confusing and ambivalent situations which caused them much heart-searching. They felt compassion for the hardship and suffering of ordinary Nurembergers, yet events and surroundings continually reminded them that this had been, and to some extent still was, the most Nazi of Nazi cities. They had fought the war with Russia as a valued – indeed an indispensable – ally; now they saw something of how the Germans and other European peoples viewed the Russians, and began to feel apprehensive about the prospect of a Europe in which Russia would be a considerable force. With thousands of refugees, displaced persons and former concentration camp inmates to be taken care of, and ordinary citizens reduced to beggary, prostitution and lawlessness in the struggle for survival, they were confronted at every turn by an upheaval and a devastation which were more than merely physical; yet nearly all the Germans they spoke to dissociated themselves from the regime which had unleashed this catastrophe on the world. And many Allied personnel, who had learned their attitudes towards Nazism in a hard school, were bewildered and incensed by the conciliatory behaviour of some of their fellow-occupiers, behaviour which was tacitly and even openly encouraged in the climate of shifting international attitudes which marked the approach of the Cold War.

Peter Uiberall, interpreter
There were portions of Nuremberg that were flattened. Remarkably, there were some great art structures untouched: churches, fountains, much of the old castle. But large areas were rubble. The reason for that is very simple. When I first got to Nuremberg there was an air force unit also in the court-house, and they had some of their strategic bombing maps,

and I had a chance to look at them. The map of Nuremberg showed every Nazi Party office, and since this was the national headquarters of the Nazi Party, almost every other house had one of these little marks showing that it was a target. There were so many targets in Nuremberg that if they had hit every one of them with pinpoint precision they would still have reduced the inner city to rubble. At the edge of the city there were camps for displaced persons and refugees. A lot of German refugees came in from Silesia, for instance.

I was told that when the Americans first entered Nuremberg, people came out of the ground. And when *I* was there, there were still one or two hotels which were 'upside down' – that is, built down instead of up, with several storeys underground, and ventilation and everything. That was the way people had lived during the war.

Alfred Steer, administrative head, language division
The people were living in air-raid shelters. They would salvage lumber and bits of sheet metal out of the wreckage and make a lean-to against a wall that was still standing, and try to live in that little lean-to. Most of the people were women: all of the able-bodied men who had been captured in Russia and eastern Europe had been retained by the Russians for labour. A male head of a household was a rarity. So here were these hundreds and hundreds of women, with small children, living in these absolutely terrible conditions, hungry, cold. They cooked on open fires, and in a German winter, lady, out on the street, cooking on an open fire ... well, it was a very unpleasant experience. We lived constantly on top of that; driving back and forth we went past this. We adopted two or three different groups, and helped them out, but we couldn't touch it. I liked the Germans – I always had, in spite of the Nazis. And the suffering in Germany that winter of 1945-6 was intense.

Mary Burns, secretary
Right across from the Grand Hotel was one of the gates to the old walled city. They wanted us to go and see it, so we made a little excursion in there. That was pretty much of a shock. I had been in England, of course, which had been bombed, but nevertheless it was a strange experience to go into this place. There was movement, but *quiet* . The first impression seemed to be that nobody was there. Well, there *were* people there, of course. They were living in hovels underneath the debris. I remember one evening, before we had dinner, we walked over there; and at first you'd think nobody was there, and then you'd see maybe a little candle peeking out. And as you walked you'd observe somebody coming out and looking. There *were* people in the debris, and that's where they were living. I remember the quietness, as though you were in an abandoned graveyard, and in some senses it *was* a graveyard. Very strange.

Priscilla Belcher, visitor
Nuremberg was terribly damaged. In the walled city there was a church with a plane hanging in it, stuck in the roof, which they couldn't get

down. We were told it was a British plane, and they couldn't get the pilot out until they got more rubble cleared, and this was a year later. You would see people begging on the road, women pulling carts. You would see them ploughing in the fields with one emaciated cow and the woman on the other side. Every scrap was precious. They would paw over dumps and things. They were living burrowed in the ruins – in the winter it must have been brutal.

Seaghan Maynes, journalist

The conditions we lived in were palatial compared with those of the Germans. We were living in a big castle, with all our food laid on and German cooks to cook it for us. We had transport if we needed it. We had no expenses. But the Germans were experiencing a lot of deprivation. After the trial I spent some time in Hamburg and Cologne, and there was real hunger there – in fact their ration limit was, I would say, below that of any international standard nowadays. The Germans used to go out and ambush coal trains coming from the Ruhr. They would wait for them to pull up at a siding, and then youngsters would jump up on them and throw down bits of coal which their mothers and fathers would collect. They had no heat. All over the British zone this happened. They would go out from the towns into the country, and work for farmers to get a bag of potatoes or some cabbages.

In Hamburg in my office – I set up a Reuter bureau there – I had a German secretary. She was impeccable in appearance: spotless dress, and so on. One time I had been out on a story about Jewish refugees being brought back to Hamburg on a ship, working very late, and this girl was staying on at the office till all hours. She had no transport, of course – no German had any transport, they had to walk – and Hamburg was devastated. We had launched tremendous air raids on the place. So I told her I would run her home. We got into the car and drove off to a district which had been flattened. It was a mass of rubble, and a bulldozer had cleared tracks through it where we could drive. I wondered, 'Where the devil is she going?' Then she said, 'Here.' I said, 'Well, look, I'll bring you home! I can't leave you here!' And she said, 'No, this is it.' And I saw where she went: she went into a hole in the ground. Her mother and two other youngsters were there, living in this hole which had been the cellar of a house. And yet this girl appeared as though she had come out of a very nice home where the laundry had taken care of her clothes. How the devil they did it I just don't know. A packet of cigarettes was of more value to her than her weekly wage in Deutschmarks. This was the way they lived, bartering. Of course, some of the German girls, young girls with children, just had to become prostitutes, or not exactly prostitutes but 'mistresses', to put it more politely. They would shack up with a soldier to get things from army supplies – cigarettes, bars of soap, silk stockings – for barter, in order to keep their children. These were decent girls from decent families. This was one of the tragedies of war, to see the destruction of a whole social fabric through necessity, hunger, deprivation.

Eddie Worth, photographer

There was a rotten smell outside our village, which wasn't very far from Celle, where all the weapons were produced underground by slave labourers. There was a train load of these poor devils, and they were in a refrigerated van, although the refrigeration wasn't on. An air raid went on all night, so the train stopped, and in the morning when they opened the doors ninety-nine per cent of them were dead. They hastily buried them by the side of the railway line, but they didn't bury them very well, and by the time the Allies got there they were niffing a bit. I was with the British then, and the CO of the press camp was a White Russian. He had no love for the Germans, I can tell you. He decided that these blokes had to be buried properly, so he summoned the main gauleiter of the village. Up they trooped, and what were they wearing? Their gardening clothes, and all the rough clothes they could find. He took one look at them, and said, 'Do you go to your funerals dressed like this?' Silence. He said, 'Well, all go home, and put your Sunday best on, and then come back.' That was ordinary citizens, the people of the village, who said they didn't know anything about it. But the railway line ran *through* the village, so they all knew about it. And he had them all dress in their best clothes, and come back and bury them properly.

One night we were talking to the waiter fellow who looked after us, about how odd it was that we couldn't ever find a Nazi in Germany. He said, 'Oh no! It was very good when we were winning – we were all Nazis when we were winning. But when you're losing it's a different matter.' He'd never been a Nazi; he was one of the old school. But that was his point of view.

Priscilla Belcher, visitor

All through my time in Nuremberg, there was a sense of tension in the city. For example, we had a tram-car that we could ride into town on, but if we were women going together, we found ourselves being jostled and pushed, very subtly. If we walked down the street, on the sidewalk, and we saw a group of German men approaching, they would fan out, and it was a case of either charging through them or going into the gutter. If you had a man with you, an officer, this wouldn't happen. A number of our patients in the hospital were there with injuries that had occurred from being stabbed, or from being beaten and robbed. They were told never to go into the walled city after dark, but they would be lured in. There was this sense of tension, and you knew you were in enemy territory – as opposed to Heidelberg, which I visited, or Oberammergau, where we went on leave, where everything seemed to be jolly and peaceful, and they had not been damaged by the war, and you felt very comfortable. You *didn't* feel comfortable in Nuremberg, *I* didn't, and we ended up feeling that we would rather go into town by car or jeep, in groups. We did some travelling around, but we always took a male officer with us.

It wasn't wise to drive at night. They strung piano wire across the road at a turn where, if you lost control, you would drop off the road into a gorge. A friend of mine who had come up to visit me drove into a wire and was thrown over the edge and killed at night. Even in Oberammergau, which was lovely and peaceful, we were driving in a jeep from Oberammergau to Garmisch, with the top of the jeep down, and we happened to look up the hillside, and there was this boulder rolling at us. We screamed, and the driver was able to pull over the road and avoid the stone; if he hadn't, it would have dropped in his lap. We saw figures running. Also, and this happened particularly in the Nuremberg area, you'd ask directions in German, and they'd look blank; finally they'd answer you, after you'd struggled in different ways, in faultless English. It was a subtle way of getting back at you. So you knew that there was a feeling of tension in the area, which you just couldn't get around. I think it let up a bit after the main trial was over.

When the judgement was reached, we couldn't go to the court-room – there was a tank outside our hospital, and we had to stay in, because there was talk that some group of soldiers who hadn't been captured were going to try to release Goering. The GIs were making bets on how many counts the defendants would be indicted on, and on who would hang and who wouldn't. We were listening to the radio in the Red Cross office, and when we heard that Goering was indicted on all counts, and to hang, oh, they cheered! I went into a back room, and there were three Germans there: an older woman who was a widow, a young woman, and a young man. They had all claimed that they had had nothing to do with the Nazis, who were getting their just deserts. And they were weeping. That sort of astounded me. I talked to the older woman. Her husband had been in the navy at the time Hitler came to power, and they never thought much about it. They were good Catholics. But then she became upset, and wanted him to get out, but he couldn't because it was his life. 'So,' she said, 'we did insulate ourselves. I heard about concentration camps, but I couldn't believe it, and live. I heard that some priests had been taken, but I couldn't believe it. I thought that after all, von Papen and some of the others were Catholics, so surely such things couldn't happen.' She said that she wished they could only go back.

Alfred Steer, administrative head, language division
It was all a dirty experience, one of the most unsatisfactory and unpleasant experiences of my life. First of all, you're living, in reasonable comfort, in German homes that have been taken over, their owners thrown out, in a city where there is intense suffering. That's very unpleasant. Secondly, you are sitting in judgement on an era that included absolutely incomparable crimes, unimaginable suffering and so forth. That in itself is very, very bad also. Then the third thing that got to me was this: that our citizens, the Americans, did not react well. I thought the British reacted much better. Well, the British have long experience of dealing with 'lesser breeds without the law', to quote Kipling, and we

Americans have had much less experience of this, you see. And so we went over there, and the Germans could make themselves very agreeable to the boss, the head man – being obsequious, giving you all sorts of services, and so forth – and the Americans uncritically accepted it all, and let down their moral standards in a fashion that I emphatically disapproved of. For instance, they took up with live-in girlfriends, in spite of the fact that they may have been married men with wives and families in the United States. There was one instance that I got involved in that was particularly unhappy. We had an army captain, who took up with a WAAC, and they lived together. You know – they're two adults, and you can't say they mustn't do it. But he was married and had several children, and some time in early 1946 the US authorities, who could see that the occupation was going to last for a while, put through a programme bringing the families of these army personnel over to Germany. And among other things, this guy had for some reason put in to have his family brought over. The authorities had gotten his wife and children on to a ship in New York when he was notified about it and decided that he just couldn't face the situation. What he did was shoot his girlfriend that night, about two in the morning. He sat there all night with this dead woman lying across the bed, and finally at daylight he shot himself. And I was involved in getting word to New York as rapidly as possible, to get that woman off the boat, since for her to land in Bremerhaven and then find that out would be absolutely ... this kind of thing, it just makes the back of your neck crawl.

We had a WAAC captain named Sara Kruskall, who ran the personnel office for the US forces. She came to my office one day and said, 'Commander, you're going to have to find a job for —' I'll call her Jaruzelska. This was a Czech girl whom we had tested, one of those people who claimed that she could speak Polish, Czech, Hungarian, English and Russian. We'd checked her out and found that she could say 'Yes, no, it's a nice day' in each language, and that was about all, so she was practically useless as far as we were concerned. So I said, 'Sará, I don't have to put that woman to work – what's the matter with you?' She said, 'You have to do it, Al.' I said, 'Why?' And she said, 'She's the General's girlfriend.' So I said, 'Look, the General can support his own damn girlfriend. I don't see why I have to.' 'But', she said, 'the General has come up with a new ruling that all Allied personnel in Nuremberg have to be here on official purposes. They can't be side-effects or girlfriends or anything like that. Since you have the largest division, you have to find a job she can do and put her on the payroll. Now here are the printed requirements for the different classes of civil service personnel. You write up a job description that she can handle.' So I finally knuckled under to Sara, who could be one determined woman. I saw that the lowest one on the list was a CAF 1, which at that point had an annual salary of $640. I figured, 'Well, if we're going to nick the US taxpayer, let's make it for the minimum.' But after I sent off the job description to the branch office of the civil service in Frankfurt, the word came back that, according to the job description, the job was unnecessary. So the second time I pitched it a bit too strong and got her in as a CAF 2 at about $200 more annually. Then the problem became: how to use her? With a mere smattering of several languages, I figured she ought to be able to read at least the captions on file folders, so – the file room. Time passed, and one day I was going to lunch when one of the interpreters called me aside, saying, 'Al, you've got to see this!' We went down to the file room office where Jaruzelska worked. The people who were constantly coming and going, withdrawing documents and bringing them back, had to queue up outside, and two old church pews had been placed there for them. And who was sitting at the end of that bench but the General himself, who was in charge of the whole thing, with a big bouquet of flowers in his fist, waiting for Jaruzelska to be let go at noon to go to lunch! Just incredible! But how could you respect that man? He had a wife, and children in college, in the United States.

The Germans were given rations, which varied from time to time and which were heavy on potatoes and bread and very short on protein. They didn't *look* like they were starving; they didn't have drawn faces. But it was kind of a puffy look that they had, and they had no strength whatever. I was going out to a reception once, at the press camp, in my Opel, all dressed up in my white uniform. I got about half-way there, and then I had a flat tyre. To change a tyre in a white uniform was out of the question, so I saw a couple of Germans standing at the side of the road and hollered over to them would they consider changing my tyre for me if I paid them with cigarettes? They agreed. The Opel had a back part which let down, and the spare tyre was lifted up, out and over. Two Germans didn't have the strength to lift that tyre up and over that door, and I, trying to keep my uniform clean, had to do the muscular work of lifting it out. Then they were able to jack up the car and change the tyre. I don't think anybody starved to death, but the mortality rate went way up because people were undernourished. The resistance to the normal diseases which good nutrition will protect you against – they didn't have it.

Also, they were very mean to each other in ways that shocked me and depressed me. They would ride around town on these trolley-cars, and would crowd on to them even when there was no room for them and hang out the door. More than once I saw them kick somebody else off to get a better grip themselves, and the guy would fall right there in the street, in front of oncoming traffic. I'll never forget the first time I saw that. A friend of mine was driving a truck in front of me, and he was the first to get there and help the guy. None of the Germans made any effort to pick him up. Of course there was a great shortage of trolley-cars – the airforce on their raids had had instructions not to bring any ammunition home, but to use it to shoot up any form of transportation. There was a field outside Nuremberg that was full of smashed-up trolley-cars – you should have seen it.

There were a lot of displaced persons, some incredible number, and they tended to flood back to their home areas, but not completely. There were always a few left, particularly the criminal element. And many of them, of course, had been able to get hold of war weapons, particularly machine-guns and small arms. They made up bandit gangs, who would besiege an isolated German farmhouse and kill people, rape the women, steal everything in sight, and so forth. In view of what had been happening to them in those forced-labour camps, I could understand this violent desire for revenge. We were out hunting one time, in Linden, and as we drove into the village a German jumped out of the bushes and started waving wildly at us. We recognized him as one of these guys that we'd been using on our hunting trips, and he'd recognized our car. He said, 'Stop! Stop! Don't go down there! There are two cars down there full of Poles with machine-guns!' So we called out the MPs, but they didn't get them. This was how dangerous the countryside was.

Something similar happened when I went on a trip to Frankfurt. I made quite a few trips out of Nuremberg. One of the lawyers presenting the case against, let's say, the SS would get some information that there was a prisoner being held in Munich who had some information that he might be able to use, and he would ask me for an interpreter. Frequently I went myself, if it was a place I particularly wanted to see; sometimes I'd give him two interpreters, because many of these prisoners were in France, and he would need a French interpreter and a German interpreter; and frequently I'd give him a stenographer. So we'd have a little group, often including women, taking off from Nuremberg to do a specific job. We had them out doing this in various parts of France and Germany, including eastern Germany, much of the time. The army made it a regulation that all male personnel had to carry sidearms, so I was issued with a nice little .32 which I've still got upstairs. One time we were going across the mountains to Frankfurt. The main road was closed because the bridges were bombed, and we had to go by back roads. We came down a long declivity into Frankfurt, at night, and I saw a car ahead blocking the road. There shouldn't have been a car there blocking the road. I remember reaching into my coat and getting hold of my gun, and so forth. I warned everybody to be on the alert; I didn't know *what* we were going to hit. Actually, it was MPs blocking the road to warn us. There *had* been a hold-up, and we were not to go down there. So we waited there for some little time before the MPs sent word through that it was all right. But it was tricky.

There was an SS detention camp north of Nuremberg. The other members of the German armed forces were allowed to go home, but the SS were detained, because they were a criminal organization and had not yet been tried. Some genius put in a bunch of Polish DPs as camp guards. Well, there was shooting from that camp at the oddest hours, day and night – it was just over the hill from where we lived and we could hear it. One day I went out there with a couple of other guys to see what was happening. The Poles had this incredible, brutal sense of humour: they would shoot at a prisoner with the idea of just missing him. They would holler at him, 'Tanz! Tanz!', and shoot at the ground, and the guy would dance wildly. Completely wrong, but understandable, I'm afraid.

Joseph Stone, lawyer, Subsequent Proceedings

You had to have dealings with ordinary Germans. The waiter was German, the chambermaid was German, the elevator-operator was German. The Americans were lucky that they were victors in Germany and Japan – they were two citizen groups that had very strong types of government, and law and order and obedience were the number one thing there. So the Germans gave you no problem. They were ... servile, if that's the word. They made sure that they didn't antagonize you in any way. For example, I remember going up the elevator one day in the hotel where I was billeted, and the elevator-operator was almost washing his hands ... 'Mr Stone' ... you know. I got out of the elevator at my floor, and there was an old lady on her hands and knees washing the floor. He must have thought that I was out of earshot, because he began yelling at her in a *very* nasty sort of way. I didn't know what he was saying, because I didn't understand German, but I turned around and gave him a sharp look, and he immediately stopped, and smiled weakly at me. It was just nastiness. Apparently he regarded himself as a level above *her*, in whatever social caste system was in his mind, and he was acting like an SOB if there ever was one. Whether that was typical or not I don't know. If you watched them getting on the trolley-cars ... of course it was hard times, there's no question, from the German viewpoint. The trolley-cars were *loaded*. And I actually saw some people hanging on the side of the car, using their feet to kick other people who were trying to get on. Whether or not *that* was common I don't know, but I did see that. Oh, they were great with flowers and animals, they were very good with flowers and animals. The waiters were all very kind and pleasant; the woman who sold some old maps at the entrance to the dining-room of the hotel was extremely pleasant.

I can only remember one time that I got into a discussion with a German. We were in a German home – I'm not sure why, but I think it was because the woman at this home was introducing us to some artists who would do charcoal pictures of whomever wanted them done. She was married to a doctor, who was still a prisoner of war somewhere in Germany, ministering to German prisoners of war. Something started, with her bellyaching about the fact that her husband wasn't home, and a political argument ensued between her and me. I don't remember now what question I put to her, but Ralph Goodman, who was a very gentle, kindly, polite, Victorian lawyer type of person, said, 'Joe, you can't ask her that question – it's too embarrassing.' And I remember slamming the table and saying, 'Dammit, Ralph, till they learn how to answer that kind of a question this whole thing is meaningless, and that's a question the answer to which they're going to have to learn to live with!' That was about the sharpest exchange that *I* had. In my recollection she sort of smiled, with one of those looks, you know: 'This poor man, what does he want? He doesn't understand.' It was the one time I got ... upset.

Fraternization was an individual type of thing. I'm a non-fraternizer – I don't know why. Maybe I just liked English and American girls! I stayed with the staff pretty much, in terms of my own social life. I did not date any Germans. That doesn't mean that others didn't: I know some – whose names I will not mention – who spent a good deal of time with Germans. And from a single young man's point of view, back in the forties, which had a different outlook on sexual matters from now, maybe it was to their advantage. I don't really know. I'm not sure why I felt that way. I don't know that I was blaming every German youngster, or child, or woman for everything that went on. It's just that I felt comfortable with my own people, so to speak.

The GIs in Nuremberg were not the GIs who'd been through the war. They were youngsters who had come over as occupiers. And I remember that when I was on my way to Nuremberg, while we were in mid-ocean, the report came in that Goering had been convicted, as had the military people. And I remember getting into some kind of a hot argument, and becoming *persona non grata* with several military people who were very chagrined at the fact that some military personnel had been convicted. I took issue with them. At the same time I also took issue with some army officer whom I heard lecturing GIs on the boat. He was saying, 'You're going to like the German people – they're very much like us, very clean, and they believe in sanitation.' I remember saying to him that this was hardly the attitude that they ought to be taking over there, because they were going to be forgetting everything else that the German people had done.

I remember at the PX there was a big carton put out for contributions for German children: candy and so on. I was more of an activist in those days, and I went in and arranged for another carton for DP children. They weren't worrying about the DP children; it was the German children ... give them a baseball bat and a ball, and they'll all become Americans, believers in democracy. Fine, if you want to do that, but it seemed to me that the DP children were entitled to equal treatment, at least. We lawyers – and if the truth be known, I guess it was mostly the Jewish lawyers – had raised about $3,000 for DPs, and one of the lawyers was going back to the States. We gave her the money to buy stuff, and she bought it and sent it all over in my name. One of the things was a 200lb bag of coffee, which split open in the post office, and there were hundreds of pairs of shoes. We got all that stuff to the DP camps.

I also defended some DPs who were charged by the American authorities with assaulting GIs. The young occupying forces were stationed in many small towns in Germany, bored stiff with nothing to do. So they invented a little game called DP-hunting, which involved putting a friend or two off the road so they can't be seen, and then you go out and antagonize one or two DPs, to the point where, if they strike back, then your friends come out and you beat the hell out of them. On one occasion the DPs, instead of striking back, ran back to the camp, yelling, 'They're killing Jews!' Then some other DPs came out of the camp and grabbed these three GIs and held them, while they got in touch with the army. The problem was that the head of the army camp was a Jewish colonel, who made sure that nobody ever touched his boys. So he surrounded the DP camp with military vehicles and machine-guns to get back his three hostages, whom they were willing to give back, and who hadn't been hurt, really, except that one had lost his glasses and one had gotten hit once or twice. The colonel insisted that the culprits be handed over, and eventually they were. The Jewish army chaplain came up to Nuremberg looking for someone to defend them, and I was a busy little bee in those days so I volunteered. My boss had a fit, because I was in Nuremberg to try Nazis, not to be down there defending DPs, and I said I could do both. They had apparently been coerced into making written statements of admission, and I said I didn't want to hear any of that. It was a five-man American court, and they weren't going to say the American army was coercing people into making confessions. The two who described being hit in order to make them confess got convicted, and the two who kept their mouths shut about it got acquitted. We appealed on behalf of the convicted ones, and incarceration was reduced to about three months, but the thing that hurt them was that they probably couldn't get into the United States, where they wanted to go, because they had a conviction of assaulting an American GI. It was unfortunate.

John Pine, visitor

With regard to the behaviour of the Germans, there was nothing resentful at all that *I* ever saw. I should perhaps say that I was a civilian all the time that I was in the Control Commission, but the whole time that I was there prosecuting, which was for two years and a quarter, I carried a loaded revolver in my hip pocket, and used to shove it under my pillow at night. And I got so used to it that it was part of one's furniture, so to speak. But I never had any cause to use it or any thought of using it. I did it on the basis that it would be ridiculous to find oneself in a difficult position and having nothing to defend oneself with, but having done that, the occasion never arose at all. One never saw any signs of any resentment: they were so utterly cowed and bemused by what had happened to them as a nation, and they were so inclined – perhaps even a little over-inclined – to try and ingratiate themselves, helping one carry one's bags, doing this, that and the other for you, smiling sweetly at you, and so forth. In the early days particularly, one's rule was that one shouldn't fraternize with them, which I think, in a way, was a mistake, because it had to come anyway. When hostilities finished, in April/May of 1945, there *was* a good deal of fraternization, particularly between boys and pretty girls. And then the order came round that there was to be *no* fraternization, and it was during this period, I think, that the tendency was for them to try very hard to ingratiate themselves – not necessarily because of their innate love of the British, which I don't think specially existed, but because they wanted cigarettes, and it was only through cigarettes that they were going to get anything to eat, pretty well, because the currency had collapsed. They were extremely well-behaved, because they weren't prepared to risk misbehaving in case they got into trouble. They couldn't do too much for one.

They were much more frightened of the Russians than of the other Allies. They were terrified of the Russians, both the women – for obvious reasons, with what they expected in the way of brutality from the Russians – and also, the fact that Russia was very short of machinery ... they suspected what was going to happen and it did in fact happen. The Russians' first six months of the peace were taken up with getting every bit of machinery out of Germany and taking it back to Russia. And of course the Germans know the Russians a good deal better than we do, and they expected this. But they were terrified, terrified beyond measure. I don't think there was anything like the sort of good feeling between the Russians and the Germans that there was between the British and the Germans.

Dorothy Reilly, secretary
I was horrified by the state of Nuremberg. I shall never forget it. I can close my eyes and see those buildings with rooms and bath-tubs hanging half-way out ... just devastated. Most people with whom you'd care to associate had got out some way, or else they got papers so that they could come back and forth, go to Switzerland, and so on. So the ordinary Nurembergers, the working class, were the only ones left in Nuremberg. I never found sullenness in dealing with a porter or a waiter. They were strictly polite, as were the young, fresh-faced girls who waited on table in Berlin. They were probably children during the thirties. We used to go to a little town outside Nuremberg, called Furth, and that was quite a different atmosphere: it had been bombed heavily, but not nearly to the extent that the old city of Nuremberg was. We would take snapshots of them and their children, and they would smile as if life was still pretty good. Once in a while I took the trolley-car, and nobody actually gave way to me. I didn't look obviously American, because I never wore a uniform. They had a certain amount of personal pride, and *I* had no quarrel with them.

There was an interesting thing that happened to me some time after the trial. I was coming back from Acapulco on a Mexican airline, and there were two young German people sitting opposite me. They were heading for Canada, because he was not allowed in the United States; he had been a member of the Hitler Youth. I said, 'I think you have a most beautiful country,' and he said, 'When were you there?' I told him I was there in 1945 and 1946. He said, 'Was that the trials?', and I said yes. He said, 'That was all a lie, the concentration camps.' I said, 'Well, I saw the films, and Dachau was just outside of Munich. There was no way people could not realize that something untoward was going on.' But I never was able to convince him. He was perfectly delightful, but I always remember that his reaction was the same as any German's. He just didn't know, he couldn't believe it. I think he was in the regular army. The Prussians always felt themselves to be much above the Nazi crowd, and they were responsible for the failed plot to kill Hitler.

Roger Barrett, officer in charge of documents
I don't really remember the occasion, but I went to Dachau, outside Munich, when you could still smell the human flesh, and I talked to people who lived along the road where they marched the prisoners out of Dachau every morning to work in an underground aircraft factory near Munich. As the prisoners marched along, if they fainted and fell out of line because of lack of food, they were machine-gunned and left lying there. Early in the morning, when the crematoria were turned on, the electricity in the houses went down, and when the ashes from the crematoria settled, they settled on the front lawns. And these people said they really didn't know what was happening! They *convinced* themselves they didn't know what was happening. Our housekeepers, where we lived in Nuremberg, firmly believed that Hitler really didn't know what was going on, and that Hess didn't know what was going on – that Hess was an intellectual, and the rest of the Nazis were doing things without letting him know, and he was badly misled. The Germans that I'd seen before the war were all pro-Hitler, the ones my age, and the Germans I saw at the time of the trial professed ignorance, which I didn't believe. My daughter, who is a sculptress of some note, lives and works in Cologne, and we have a great many German friends through her, but I still feel a little uncomfortable with German nationals because of the experience. I probably shouldn't, but I still do.

Jean Tull, secretary
At the outset I lived in the Grand Hotel, and I can remember tarpaulins flapping over holes in the structure and the bags of water, chemically treated, in all the corridors for drinking purposes. Then I moved to a house in the suburbs, Novalisstrasse 33, with six other British girls. The daughter of the house was in attendance to keep the place clean. It must have been a humiliation for her. It was all very strained at first, and I felt sorry for her, but we got to like her extremely well. Her family were supposed to have been Nazis; of course they claimed that they had to join the Nazi party, otherwise their lives would have been made miserable. But we kept off awkward subjects with her. I did have a contretemps with a dressmaker whom we had visiting us at Novalisstrasse. She brought her boyfriend along, and he wanted cigarettes; you paid people in cigarettes in those days. He was trying to make out how the German people had suffered in the war, and I managed to recall enough German to tell him a thing or two, which I was very glad about. 'Who started the war anyway?', I finished up!

The centre of Nuremberg seemed to be all rubble, apart from the Grand Hotel and the Opera House, which were still standing. The Opera House was used as a cinema for Allied personnel, and upstairs were a dance-hall and club for American enlisted personnel. I can vividly remember a smell of death in that building. I assumed that it came from rotting bodies somewhere nearby – in the adjoining building, perhaps, or in drains. There must have been a lot of people buried in that city, under the rubble. And when we walked through the centre of the city the same smell was wafting around. But out where we lived, in the suburbs, there seemed to be very little bomb damage.

Brady Bryson, lawyer
After my work on the concentration camp case I had a little period of thorough rest and relaxation, waiting for the next development. I began to wander through the German countryside. In those days, after the war was over, there was a great deal of disorganization on the continent, especially among the German population, among all forms of government, among the military forces. Military people just seemed to arrive on their own, footloose, from all over the world, stay a while, and go. I never quite knew what they were doing, or how this came about. I fell in with a young army second lieutenant whose name was Gould, a very pleasant young man from upstate New York. He had a jeep. Whether he had it officially or not I can't say – that's the way the world was at that time, in that place. We got sufficiently friendly that he fell to inviting me to go with him in his jeep, and I didn't have anything else to do. We explored the general area at will. We would go into hostels and villages, and look at this and that, and drink a little beer, and try and find a sandwich for lunch, and see the countryside, and what not. He liked the outdoors; so did I. I recall that once we even went deer-hunting with some German buddies of his, and afterwards we had a little party and cooked our venison.

In the forest I would occasionally come across a woodcutter, who was out there doing, I suppose, what he had always done even before there was any war and probably continued to do during the war. He was still there, and he would be clearing and trimming the forest, keeping it in shape. I had no real command of German, and of course these woodcutters really wouldn't know any English, but I knew a few German words. We didn't say anything very complicated to each other, but it is extraordinary how with a few words and a certain amount of sign language you can communicate a great deal. I would say that I always found them very cordial, friendly and amiable. At that level, whatever was going on in the war struggle was apparently not resented, and I suspect that's fairly characteristic of humanity. I'm not sure at what level the resentment resides, but it doesn't begin to take in everybody. And I think many people feel, 'This is where I am in life, this is my lot' – whether it's in America, Japan, France, Russia or Germany – 'and whatever happens above me is not within my control. And so I do my best, and I don't blame anybody who's situated the way I'm situated and doing it for the same reason that I'm doing it.' I wouldn't say that I got into anything like a moral or philosophical discussion with Germans and other foreigners at that stage of my life, in view of my experience and role there. I would hear discussions of this kind among our staff, particularly among those who had a German-Jewish background, of which there were a number: they had very strong feelings about the whole war experience, and of course were bitterly anti-German. I guess what I'm saying is I don't think there was all that much partisan revulsion among the common people of the belligerent countries.

Seaghan Maynes, journalist

We had bombed the hell out of the old medieval town. But correspondents who had gone through France and Germany had seen devastation way beyond the limited bombing in Nuremberg. The Germans in Nuremberg were completely subdued, deferential. They would agree with anything you said. For example, what did the Germans think about Goering's suicide? If I asked an English-speaking German in English, he would probably say to me, 'Ah, he took the coward's way out.' But if you were in a beer-house with some Germans whom you knew, and after a few beers you asked them the same thing, they would probably reply, 'He cheated them.' In other words, he put one over on them. There was the difference. We were the victors, we were in command. We had the control, the power. These people were utterly dependent on us. You never really did get an impression of German thought unless you knew them well, and usually it took some time.

Peter Uiberall, interpreter

Ordinary Nurembergers behaved very well towards me. I have no complaint. But that doesn't qualify anything – after all, the war was lost for the Germans, and they were happy that it was over. The occupation forces were not abusing them; I did not have that impression *anywhere*. We had a lot of Germans working for us. I hired a lot. After the big trial was over we went from four languages to two, because the Subsequent Proceedings were only English–German, German–English. So we hired a lot of new people, and those with other languages went home. We had tests going on in various German cities, and those who qualified we brought to Nuremberg as translators or court interpreters. I'm quite sure they realized I was a refugee. There were quite a number of former refugees. And we could only do our work if we worked without a chip on our shoulder. There was no other way. I didn't see any abuse, in that respect, at all. We had people coming out of concentration camps, who were serving as linguists, and they did their work decently.

One of the most amazing, though somewhat gruesome, experiences was a letter of commendation that the interpreters received from a very high-ranking Nazi, for their work. It was Ohlendorff, the head of the extermination groups that killed thousands and thousands of Poles and Jews and people in the eastern areas. Ohlendorff had been tried, in the trial against the Einsatzgruppen, as they were called, and we staffed the trial as interpreters. He was sentenced to death, but got a short reprieve because he offered to testify in other trials, which he did, and in that same period of time he asked permission to offer a letter of appreciation for our interpreting. And that, I think, was the best that was ever said about interpreters. The man was sentenced to death, and in his letter he expressed his gratitude for having been given a fair opportunity to be heard, thanks to the work of the interpreters. I'm very proud of Nuremberg, of the fairness of the Nuremberg Trial; I wouldn't say the same about other trials.

I remember a German colleague of mine, an interpreter who had been a lieutenant in the German armed forces. One day he came into the office in tears. I said, 'What's wrong?' And he said, 'I cannot go on. They are talking about the Warsaw ghetto, the uprising, the massacre. I was one of the German troops who had to do this. I just can't go on.' He was released from his assignment with the interpreting branch, but was later picked up by the German defence, and he worked for them as a linguist. A very, very decent young man, who just couldn't get over the memory of what he saw and what he participated in.

Bernard Meltzer, lawyer

When I first came to Nuremberg and looked around, I said the Germans had gotten retribution. It really had taken a pasting. And I remember there were eerie sights: there would be a room with a light on in it, in a building, and the room seemed as if it were suspended in mid-air because everything around it had been blasted away. The Germans were docile. Americans, of course, had clothes; they had money; they had cigarettes. But to the best of my knowledge, *no one* was physically attacked during the trial. There was a curfew, which was largely honoured in the breach. The Germans' docility seemed to reflect the German respect for power. The war was over, and there was a new group in power. Of course they were weary and beaten, and their homes were destroyed, and so on, but none the less the lack of any attacks, any robberies, *I* found somewhat surprising. Maybe that's because I come from Chicago!

At the same time there was a curious split personality among some of the Germans, who claimed to know nothing about the Nazi abominations. 'Well, maybe there were concentration camps' ... the ones I talked to knew nothing about them or at least about the horrors that had taken place in them. And the Americans were very good, on the whole, about no fraternization; of course we had our own communities, so the usual pressures for fraternization didn't exist. We were billeted in a very nice house, and one day a woman appeared at the door – it was her house. She explained that her daughter was soon to have her fourteenth birthday, and she wanted to have a little party, and she was hoping that we could provide some chocolates from the PX. In a way this request involved a microcosm of the problem of generational responsibility and guilt. There were eight lawyers billeted in that house, so we put it to the group. Well, the first thing we did was run a counter-intelligence check, because this was a new house. It turned out that this woman – who said she had gotten a PhD at Berkeley, and was related to a very important sugar family on the west coast – was married to a doctor who was a very important cog in the local Nazi machine, otherwise they wouldn't have gotten a new house in 1939. So now we had these questions: should we provide chocolates for this fourteen-year-old girl? Does the girl really care about the chocolates? Are we providing them for this woman, who ' hadn't the slightest idea' of any of the concentration camps and was married to an active Nazi? Well, we decided to forego a collective decision here: everybody could do what he wanted to do with respect to the chocolates. And I refuse to tell you what I did!

Normally, however, my only contacts with Germans were professional, when I was interrogating them, and the contacts that you have with people who are serving you in restaurants and so on. Occasionally, I heard other Germans denying knowledge of Nazi atrocities or intimating that they had been careful not to find out. But I didn't try to pursue issues of knowledge and responsibility with them.

If you have to lose a war, I think you should lose it to Americans, because the first thing Americans want to do is fix things up, get things going. Of course, the Americans had suffered least of all the countries involved – they hadn't been invaded or bombed. And also, the conditions were so appalling in Hamburg and Berlin, and Frankfurt, and Nuremberg itself, that one's sense of outrage at the Germans was compounded with pity, simply because they really had gotten retribution – not only in losing the war, but also when you looked at their cities and their homes you saw what an impact the bombing had had. Because I didn't have much contact with Germans I'm not sure of this, but the impression I got from others was that it wasn't easy to find Nazis, and that those who admitted they were Nazis claimed that they had been forced into it by economic and professional obligations. I remember when I presented the case against Funk, the presentation was written up in the German newspapers, and I was flooded with letters saying, first, that the writer had not been a Nazi, and then, that 'My uncle went to Atlantic City at such and such a time,' and there were all kinds of names close or identical to mine – Metzler, Meltezer – and was I related to them, or did I know their kin? An American serviceperson was a lifeline then, you see, and so everybody was trying to get attached. But *I* didn't know any of these people. I remember that one burst of notoriety very well!

Ron Chapman, clerk

The day the sentencing was actually given out, there was some fear that there might be some demonstrations by the Germans. Just outside Nuremberg there was a large camp that housed a lot of what they called the 'hardened' SS members who had been taken prisoner, other than ordinary prisoners-of-war. And there *was* a rumour – though I think it was exaggerated – that there was going to be an attempt at a break-out, to rescue these defendants in the trial. In fact guards were put on the roof of the court-house; there were two tanks stationed at the entrances with their guns pointing up the main street. And the day the hangings were carried out there really was a major security operation. They imagined, I think, that there were going to be demonstrations from the German people as a whole. But it was all a damp squib. On the day of the hangings, the trams – there was a main tram-route that went straight past the court-house – were full of Germans going off to work just as if it were an ordinary day and nothing had happened. The trams just passed by and people didn't even glance at the court-house. As far as we could see there was no showing of emotion at all among the German people. In fact even in the German newspapers, it was on the front page but not in six-inch headlines or anything. And the few German people we spoke to seemed very unconcerned. There were no demonstrations or anything outside the court-house; in fact it was even quieter. I think there was that feeling, you know ... it's not very nice, whoever it is, when you're getting twelve people being hung. It was rather a shadow on that particular day.

When we first went to Nuremberg there was 'non-fraternization', but of course there *was* fraternization, even though it wasn't supposed to be allowed. I should say that seventy to eighty per cent were quite friendly and amiable, about ten or perhaps fifteen per cent just ignored you or didn't really want to get involved, and I suppose you could say that another ten per cent both ignored and disliked us. They were more the younger type, who had been brought up under the Hitler hierarchy and the SS and the Hitler Youth Movement. The older people were very friendly – I mean, we visited houses and had conversations with them much the same as in France, Belgium and Holland. I think there were a few who didn't like us but were too frightened to show it. After losing the war they couldn't afford to be too outspoken. You did find one or two with whom you felt that if you got knocked down they would be pleased rather than sorry, but on the whole, I think, the older people especially were very pleased when the war was over, as pleased as we were. They had obviously suffered, as civilians, a lot more than civilians had over here.

Patrick Cooper, airman

For the first few months after the war there was a policy of non-fraternization; I forget exactly when that was abandoned, but it was in fact broken a great deal before it was actually taken off the books, as it were. I was fortunate in that a little later on, after I'd settled down in this small town outside Nuremberg, I got to know some Germans who were academic. One was an academic family; the other was the widow and family of a diplomat; and there were one or two others. They were people of culture and intellect, and, not to put too fine a point on it, I was fortunate to get to know some people like this, people that the ordinary young GI wouldn't necessarily meet at all. So that was a stroke of luck, really, for me, and gave me an insight into another aspect of the German population, German attitudes. And these people were ambivalent in their attitudes towards Nazism, towards the whole war. Understanding the German mind at that time was beyond my capacity; I was only eighteen.

The people I knew at that period had lost a good deal. There was a lady, some years older than I was, whom I met at a concert; she wanted to learn English and I wanted to learn German, so we'd talk. She was the daughter of a professor of Hebrew and Eastern languages, I think in Munich. I knew the old boy; he was a German of the old school: the wing collars, and so on. He was right out of the nineteenth century. He was well into his seventies at that time. To me, at that age, he seemed ancient. He had been chucked out of his job, since there was no call for a professor of Hebrew after about 1933 or 1934. So *he* had lost his career. But, you see, it would be a mistake to say that people like that were rabidly anti-Nazi, or anything like that. He was a typical absent-minded professor. He spoke no English, so he and I used to have these curious conversations in a sort of pidgin English/German; I was picking up German pretty quickly. When neither one of us could find a word, we would try Latin, because I had studied Latin in high school. He was, I think, a prime example of the kind of decent, patriotic, solid, middle-class, worthy German citizen, who had been destroyed, in a way, by this horror of Nazism, and yet he was not a resistant. He just sort of took it. And that was one of the points about a lot of the people that I got to know. I was in Germany for four years, and by the time I left I had met a great many people from all walks of life, with all kinds of stories to tell about the Nazi time.

I hadn't known much about Nazism before I got to Germany. I was terribly young, and I wasn't particularly politically aware in my teens. I think I was pretty ignorant, really, when I got there. During my teens, which would be round about 1940 to 1945, I wasn't particularly aware of the persecution of the Jews – I don't think many people were, in America at that time. We heard these rumours, but nobody was prepared for the full horror of it when it all came out in 1945. So when I got to Germany I had very mixed feelings. I was a well-brought-up southern boy. I remember one of the very first Germans I actually talked to on a person-to-person basis. After being shunted about a bit, on arrival in Germany, we finally got to an air base outside Nuremberg; we were taken into the headquarters, and the commanding officer was there, and the sergeant-major, and they were sort of processing us, but treating us very kindly. And there was this quite handsome woman, reasonably well-dressed, acting as a sort of secretary, speaking impeccable English. I didn't know who she was – I mean, I knew she had a funny accent, but I didn't know, you see ... and I was responding to her questions, as she filled out the various forms, with 'Yes, ma'am,' and 'No, ma'am,' and being terribly polite, just as I would be to her counterpart in Georgia. Some of the old-timers, who'd been through the war and hadn't been sent home again, they were sort of smiling at this, because, you know, *their* attitude towards these people was quite, quite different from mine. And I think this is significant; it's important in my case to realize that I came afterwards, and I wasn't prejudiced, particularly. Even in spite of all those horrible propaganda movies that one had seen, and the way the Germans had been portrayed, I still wasn't that prejudiced, I don't think, and didn't have much animosity towards the Germans. And in any case, as I've said, I was fortunate, in due course, to get to know a different sort of German from the sort that a lot of GIs met, in the beer cellars, and the red light district, and the black market, and so on. I don't mean to say that I was the only GI who had the good fortune to meet a different class of German, but I did, and that was important for my whole time in Germany. I pretty soon began to see the complexity of it. You know, it *wasn't* just black and white. That didn't make it easy for me; indeed, it made it more difficult.

By then, the Cold War was already starting, and we were already beginning to worry about the Russians. I think that the anti-Soviet feeling began to grow up very rapidly. And of course – this is a very important point, I think, about that period – there's no doubt in *my* mind that a great many Germans contributed to that anti-Soviet feeling on the part of the Americans. Many Germans – how shall I put it? – encouraged young, gullible Americans to be anti-Soviet: they would talk about the rape of Berlin, and the various horrors that the Germans and other central European peoples had suffered at the hands of the Red Army, and of course the fact is that there *was* a great deal of that sort of thing – it's a matter of record. Another thing was that we soldiers, even non-combatants like myself, who had never heard a shot fired in anger, all of us who had military training, whether we'd fought the war or not, had the greatest respect for the German soldier. There was no doubt about that.

The trials were public, and everything was published. At that time I was learning German and couldn't yet speak it very well, so I had to rely on my contact with English-speaking Germans, and *their* assessment of these matters. Nuremberg, first of all, was a hotbed of Nazism. It was one of Hitler's favourite places – he got a better response there than almost anywhere. They built that huge stadium there; I went there two or three times, just to see the thing. So I think that a good many Nurembergers *were* Nazis, and pretty keen on the whole thing. I think, though, that the people *I* got to know ... there was obviously a great mixture of feelings, and people were ambivalent about it. I think the attitudes broke down into two or three categories. I knew people who rejected the principle that these people should be brought to trial at all. They said, 'Why? Why should these war leaders be brought to trial as war criminals? By what right can a victorious power put on trial the leaders of a nation? What is the constitutional basis of it?' There was discussion along those lines, and I remember it. There were other people who said, 'Oh yes, they *should* be brought to trial and punished for their deeds, but it should be a fair trial,' and so on. But I think that both of those categories – those who thought that they shouldn't be brought to trial and those who thought that they should be – felt that they would nevertheless get a fair trial, that it would be fair. I think that they trusted the Western Allies; they didn't trust the Soviets, but they trusted especially Britain and the United States, not so much France. They were content that the British and the Americans would be fair, and that the defence would be heard from. Even if they rejected the principle, they still thought, 'Well, it will be fair.' It's important to remember that during this whole period the ordinary German was far more concerned with getting something on the table to eat, and fuel to keep warm – the basic essentials of life were in short supply. I think that most of them were so occupied with pure, simple survival that they weren't giving a great deal of thought to all these other issues, and they were in a state of shock and demoralization anyway. So I would reckon that a great many ordinary, uneducated, working-class Germans were just concerned with survival, and trying to put their lives back together.

There was another aspect to it. The average GI or the average Tommy would just meet people at the bars or in the black market, and these people's attitude would be that whatever the soldiers wanted to hear, they would hear. So a lot of what the GIs would hear would be pretty highly suspect, and you had to 'cross-reference' it with lots of other people. And another fact was that we were all angry at each other, you know – there wasn't much trust. It was building up gently and slowly, and we were getting on terms with the Germans so it was gradually being established, but in 1945 and 1946 we were still very suspicious of each other. I was in the air force, and a great many air force soldiers wouldn't wear the air force patch, the insignia. If we went off into towns alone, it was better not to be identified as air force. But there again, though, there were very few reprisals. At the end of the war the Allies feared some kind of guerilla war, an underground resistance to be continued by the Germans against the occupation troops. There was all kinds of talk about bands of underground resisters who called themselves 'werewolves'. It didn't happen – it *had* been just talk. But still, it was a worrying factor for us.

At the time of the hangings we were mostly confined to barracks, in case there were demonstrations. And I remember that I stayed on base, and didn't go out that day. I went out the next night, with a German friend of mine, a lady who was a bit older than I was. She was a widow of a German soldier who had been killed in Russia, and she was quite a cultured woman. I make that point because it's important in the context – I mean, her attitudes were civilized. I went to meet her and a doctor friend of hers. *His* attitudes were very ambivalent; I think he was skating on very thin ice. He may have been dealing in some form or other of contraband, but I'm not sure. I met them at a Gasthaus. The only thing you could have at that time was very weak beer, which they made, or Rhine wine – the wine was good – and maybe black bread and a piece of bacon. It must be said that their basic reaction was one of revulsion and shock. They didn't really think they'd hang them – they really didn't. I think a lot of people believed right up to the very last minute that they would be reprieved. And for a few days after it happened, most of the Germans I came into contact with reacted to the executions with resentment, sullenness, anger. They thought that they shouldn't have been hanged, even though some of these people had been real anti-Nazis, in so far as one could be – I mean, resistance to the Nazis was diffuse and at a low level, because it was so dangerous. Very few people had the courage to stick their necks out during the Nazi period.

The subject of the concentration camps was often brought up, and almost all of them would say that they knew nothing about these things. Frankly I didn't believe them; I didn't believe many of them, anyway. I think that some genuinely *didn't* know; I think it depended a lot on where you lived in Germany and what you did for a living, and what your contacts were with the various parts of the state apparatus. It was perfectly possible that a sort of apolitical, ordinary, working-class person without any great curiosity could probably go through the whole of that time without knowing much about it, if indeed anything. So it was possible for some of them to say truthfully that they didn't know, particularly if they weren't living anywhere near these places. Before I was actually sent to Nuremberg I went to a replacement depot near Munich, and I was there for about ten days while they sorted us out, and this was about five miles from Dachau. And when people round *there* said they didn't know we simply didn't believe them, because we knew from what we had been told by reliable Allied sources that you could smell it.

There were one or two DP camps in the Nuremberg area, and I got to know some of the people in them. We used to try to do what we could to help them – give them little presents, whatever we could manage. They were miserable. Most of them wanted to be sent to America. Many of them didn't want to be sent back to the East at all, because they were terrified of the Russian soldiers. And many of them were still simply in a state of shock and disorganization, and malnutrition. The United Nations agency, UNRRA, was working there, trying to help these people. These inmates were pretty rigidly controlled as to their contacts with the Americans and the rest of the Allies, and many of the Jewish ones had relations in America, whom they wanted to write to. At this particular time, they could write to them but it had to go through the German post, for some reason, and that was a long, slow process. What they wanted the GIs to do was take their letters and mail them through the American military post; in those days, a letter could be posted from Germany, through the American army post office, and be in New York the next day. So one of the main things they asked us to do was post their letters for them, which we did – after all, it didn't cost *us* anything, since postage was free at that time.

Many of the camp inmates were survivors – they were all survivors, of course, but these were survivors in the sense of God knows how they had survived. They had had to use their wits and their ingenuity to survive, and who knows how much it had cost them in terms of scruples?

In the NCO club at the base where I was stationed there were several chaps from one of the DP camps working as waiters. Jobs like that were highly sought after, not for the wages but for the 'take home', in terms of food and whatever they could get. The currency was worthless, and we dealt in cigarettes, tobacco, chocolate and all kinds of consumer goods. It was a barter economy, absolutely, at that period. Among these waiters were two former pilots with the Polish air force, who had been shot down in 1939 and taken prisoner, but had somehow survived. Many of the Polish officers had simply been slaughtered, but these two had come through. They were aristocrats – upper-class, educated, officers by definition. They were always cheerful, they were survivors. They didn't want to go back to Poland: they had been afraid of the Nazis, and now they were afraid of the Russian soldiers. Another one, who had a shock of black hair and was very engaging, had a smattering of every language in central and eastern Europe. He was always buttering up the GIs to get various favours from them. He always had a funny story, and he was always after something. On the black market he could get you anything, if the price was right. He passed himself off as someone rather grand, from Poland, but the two former pilots would have nothing to do with him – they just laughed at him. I remember one night, when this scamp had been up to some trick or other, one of the Polish pilots said, 'He is not an aristocrat, he is not even a Pole. He is a *gypsy*!' With this mixture of eastern Europeans who were all milling around in Germany, there was a great deal of animosity among *them*, and a conventional southern American like myself could get himself in all kinds of muddles with these people, simply by not knowing the ground rules. It was a very curious and difficult time.

Yvette Wilberforce, visitor

It was very odd. The Germans didn't act in a hostile way. The British were billeted in houses that had been requisitioned, but the French lodged with the inhabitants, the natives. We had our messes for food, but we lived with the families, and we got on very well with them. It was extraordinary. One felt very little undercurrent of hostility. It was not at all as it was with the Germans in France, when nobody would have been seen talking to one of them – except a few people who collaborated, but they were so few. We were really hostile. We pretended not to see them; they pretended not to see us, but not in the rigid way that *we* did.

There was one thing that struck me very much. There was a hotel in Nuremberg, the Grand Hotel, where the Allies stayed and the visitors stayed. It had cabaret every night, and people turning somersaults, and so on – Germans. It was such a jolly place, and yet, those people, how could they do it? I suppose they were starving and they had to – all they could do was sing funny songs and turn pirouettes, so that was what they had to do. Once, in a mess in Berlin, there was a pianist playing "Lili Marlene", and they said to me, 'You know who he is?' 'No.' 'Oh, he's the composer of "Lili Marlene".' Now how *could* he, who had written that sensitive, patriotic, touching song, a beautiful song, come and play the piano in officers' messes for the French? Because he was hungry. I suppose so.

Bernard Meltzer, lawyer
Cigarettes were the form of currency in Nuremberg. The first time I experienced that I was appalled: it seemed an attack on the dignity of the individual German. But everybody said, 'Listen, that's what they want – they don't want your Reichsmarks.' So in a very short time that became the new form of currency, and people completely forgot how valueless the cigarette was in the United States compared with Germany.

Joseph Stone, lawyer, Subsequent Proceedings
There was one refugee working at Nuremberg, a young lady, who made sure that she was absolutely the purest thing at Nuremberg when it came to money and the 'black market'. That was a term that covered any kind of a transaction; if you took some cigarettes and swapped them for a camera, you were a black marketeer, and virtually all of us were. Everybody I knew was doing *something*, including me. I'm not going to be holier-than-thou. But this young lady didn't deal with cigarettes; she took her American money and changed it legally into German marks, and the rate was horrendous! And it became a big joke, because apparently she was the only one doing it in Nuremberg, and when she went down to the office where that had to be done, the young GI on duty didn't really know how to do it. It was always a problem for them – they didn't know where the forms were, because nobody was doing it except for her. So she was a pain in the neck to them, really, when you come down to it. Those who were involved – at least reputedly – in black marketing at Nuremberg were, I think, Czechs, not all, of course. They were the ones who were reputedly up to their eyeballs in it. The rest of us – not all – got our cameras. My brother was studying at the Pasteur Institute in Paris and needed a microscope, and I managed to get one for him. We all bought little things here and there, but there wasn't much to buy. I was there nearly two years – others were there even longer – during which time you were bound to be doing something. Of course, you'd pay in cigarettes. The currency wasn't worth anything really, although they'd have a currency reform every once in a while.

Whether or not you had people doing things for you for cigarettes I guess depends upon you as an individual. I personally did not have people doing things for me, even if they were Germans. At that time, frankly, you weren't well disposed towards the Germans. Now, my next-door neighbours are German, and I get along fine with them, but that's forty years later. One research analyst, at age twenty-two, had bought a car, and she had a chauffeur. I said, 'What the hell do you need a chauffeur for?' And she said, 'If I get home at night, he can open the gate.' She didn't want to get out of the car. 'He can wash the car, keep it clean, and if I have some errands to do, he can do them. It doesn't cost much.' Now this individual, as a refugee herself, may have felt that this was all very appropriate: they kicked us out, and ruined our lives, and the hell with them. Whether or not young men were taking advantage of young German girls I don't know; I can't answer that. I'm not passing judgement on it. I did a lot of administrative work on behalf of the staff, and one member used to come in and click his heels, needing more soap and more chocolate. I'd ask why, and he'd say his girlfriends needed it. So he was obviously active with soap and chocolate. It all tied in, it seems to me, with the feeling that, dammit, the Germans had brought it on themselves, Hitler was an animal, they'd caused the world to come to the position of war, tens of millions of people had died – anything that happened to the Germans they were asking for, and it was their own goddam fault. That was it. If I had stopped to think about it, I probably would have come up with something like that. Call it a rationalization if you want, but on the other hand, it was a very unusual time. And the Germans didn't seem to be overwhelmed by it. The ones you ran into contact with, the waiters ... they were there, they were surviving somehow or other. So that while, if you look at it in a very strict and purist way, there was a moral vacuum for many, it was not one hundred per cent. My boss's boss I'm quite sure had none of these dealings of any kind. He was a very sweet person, and I'm sure he was not alone. But I didn't feel dirty doing it. Maybe I should have. Now that you think about it, forty years later, it's hard to defend. On the other hand, look at it this way: when I bought that camera and microscope, I paid with many cartons of cigarettes. And that man said to me, 'Now I can have a roof on my house.'

Alfred Steer, administrative head, language division
President Truman had sent out a presidential broadside to all of the US government, saying that there were going to be trials, and everybody was directed to co-operate. And with this presidential directive, you see, we got all *kinds* of people. Some departments used the presidential order as an excuse to unload unusable or undesirable personnel. We got them over to Nuremberg, and what did we find out, very quickly, but that some of them were incompetent, so one of the first things I had to do was to sit down and winnow them out. I would interview them, and then we would arrange to have them sent back to the States, and charge the US taxpayer. I got down to one individual, a Jewish boy named Wally Cohn. He had been born in Germany, and his parents had fled to the States when he was a small child. His German was poor; he spoke street-corner English, but couldn't write literate English, so we couldn't use him. I called him in and said, 'Wally, I guess you know what's going to happen now.' He said, 'Commander, don't send me back! Please don't send me to Siberia!' I had put aside a room where I had collected these unusables until I could get a shipment organized to send them home, and they had dubbed the room 'Siberia'. So I said, 'Well, Wally, what can we do? We can't nick the US taxpayer to have you sitting around.' He said, 'Listen, Commander, have you got a car?' I had a terrible car, an Opel which I claimed the German army had taken to Stalingrad and back. He said, 'Let me have it for three days!' I said, 'Look, I have to drive back and forth to the court-house every day. What am I supposed to do, hitch-hike?' 'No,' he said, 'you can have my jeep.' Now he'd been in town four days, and he had organized a

jeep for himself. This was Wally Cohn. So I told him to go ahead. Well, the car came back in about three or four days, repainted, with a new motor, re-upholstered with, guess what, army blankets, and it ran like a top. And I said, 'Well, Wally, I'll tell you what – you are now special administrative assistant. Forget about going home.' He turned out to be invaluable.

We were working in the court-house, in these huge old rooms, and from every ceiling hung a single light bulb, twenty watts. It was fall, November – you know what November is like in Germany. I was supposed to keep about twenty people at work in each room, writing and reading and typing, and the illumination was absolutely impossible. Nuremberg was eighty-nine per cent destroyed, and you couldn't buy *anything*. The civilian economy was gone. So I called Wally in, and I said, 'Wally, we need reading-lamps. We've got about 200 people at work in this building, working their eyes out. I can't tell you how many reading-lamps we need, but you go get 'em and I'll tell you when to stop. I'm not going to ask you any questions. Just get me reading-lamps.' He said, 'Yes, sir,' and he looked a bit doubtful. I'm not surprised, because it was a terrible assignment. That was about nine o'clock in the morning. At noon, a British lieutenant, Second Officer Esmé Sherriff, in her willowy way – she was a most attractive young lady – came into my office, and said, 'Commander, may I speak to you?' I had laid down the law to all department heads that they were under no circumstances to leave the offices unoccupied – there must always be someone there to answer the phone. She said, 'There's something strange. You know you said that we must never leave the office unoccupied? I told the girls that they could go for lunch, and I went over to the window, and I was standing there looking out and smoking a cigarette, and when I finished and turned back, the strangest thing – all our reading-lamps were gone!' I thought, 'Oh, boy!' So I said, 'Officer Sherriff, I think I can help you. You go on back to your office, and, er, stand by.' Then I called Wally in, and said, 'Wally, the first thing you gotta learn is who is in this outfit and who isn't.' He said, 'But Commander, they're limeys! They're limeys!' I said, 'I *know* they're limeys, but this is an international organization and they are part of it. Now take 'em back, boy!'

But he turned into a tremendous strength for the division. It was a very social place, and we used to have parties. I had a nice house with a lawn. I would call Wally in and say, 'Wally, I want to give a party on Friday evening. I'm going to have about sixty people. It's nice weather, so let's have some Japanese lanterns in the garden. Clip the hedges and get everything looking nice, and put a few chairs around. Put a bar on the porch, and let's have the cook arrange a buffet supper. Get a few musicians in.' So I would come back from the Palace of Justice on Friday around five thirty or six o'clock, and there would be three or four German musicians tuning up by the piano, and the cook would be doing this and that, and everybody would be rushing around. And it would be a very nice affair. On Monday morning I'd call Wally in, and say, 'Wally, that was a darned nice party you arranged for us – what do I owe you?' And he'd say, 'Commander, you owe me 168 dollars, 425 marks, and fifteen cartons of cigarettes.' This was the way you organized a Nuremberg party.

Wally Cohn did indispensable work, but procuring scarce items in an absolutely smashed economy was necessarily close to the black market line. I warned him early on, 'Wally, a lot of people make an awful lot of money round here on this black market. I'm not telling you what you're going to do or what you're not going to do, but I'm warning you about one thing: if you go to the black market, and get caught, I won't lift a finger to help you. I'll help them throw the book at you if I can. So don't touch it, or at least don't let me know about it.' I'm sure he did, but he kept himself clean. There was one guy in town, whom I knew vaguely: he and I had lived in the same district, Drexel Hill in Philadelphia. I looked him up after the war, and he owned two luxurious apartment blocks in Drexel Hill, occupying one of the best apartments and living off the rents. The money to buy these places came from the black market in Germany. Talk about a dirty job.

I had to go to Berlin on business at one point, and one day we went out to the Wannsee, an enormous series of lakes connected by the Elbe and two or three other canals to both the North Sea and the Baltic. There was a German yacht club, with forty or fifty huge cruising yachts out of the water on props – they hadn't been used during the war. I found the caretaker, who let us in, and, gosh, there were some beautiful yachts there. I asked the fellow in German, 'Do you suppose I could buy one of these?' 'Oh yes, sir,' he said, 'the Germans can't use yachts today, and they're trying to get money.' I saw a particularly nice one about forty feet long, a sloop, and said, 'That one would kind of interest me – what do you suppose it would go for?' 'You could get it for 40,000 marks,' he said. Forty thousand marks – forty cartons of cigarettes, at black market prices! I had visions of taking a discharge in Europe and sailing that thing home. Oh, what a dream! Well, I came back to earth about a day later, and of course I didn't do it.

I found that my Opel, the one that had been to Stalingrad and back, became less and less reliable, and I finally decided to go out and get a jeep. The jeep is an open vehicle, but the GIs got together and 'winterized' some of them: they added tops and sides and doors and so forth. And some of them were quite artistic. Through Wally, I found a field about thirty miles north of town where there were about 10,000 jeeps. When the troops had been demobilized they'd simply driven these jeeps into the field, and then marched off and been flown back to the US. So I went through this field of jeeps and said, 'I'll take this one!' I drove it back to Nuremberg, and it used up all the oil on that thirty-mile trip – the motor was completely shot. But there was a character in the motor pool, a mechanic, who wanted to go and see the trial, so I arranged that for him and he put a new engine in for me. And then Wally took it on, and had some of his boys attend to it. When it came back, would you believe, in the middle of the dashboard was a cut-glass bud vase with one rose in it! Shortly thereafter the authorities started cracking down on individual vehicles. On the hood of mine was 'USA' and then a number. I decided that I didn't want to be under these regulations, so I got Wally and his magicians to change it to USN. And then, of course, it wasn't on any army or navy register, so I had a free jeep, and I went everywhere in it! Then I got a trailer for it, and went down to the South of France. My cousin Richard Fawcett, a Liberator pilot, had been killed in France, and my aunt wanted me to find his grave if at all possible. They told me, 'This is war-torn Europe – you just can't go down there. You can't get gas.' A jeep is notoriously inefficient when it comes to gas. So I loaded ninety-five gallons of gas in the trailer, and went all over southern France. And I found the grave.

There was an enormous surplus of everything military. There was another field with, I think, 500 pursuit aeroplanes, wing to wing. And they came up with the regulation that armed service personnel stationed in Europe could buy certain types of surplus military equipment that was available. One GI who had fought through the war decided that he'd always wanted to drive a tank, so he went up to the tank park and plonked down 300 bucks and bought a tank. He was having a ball, driving all over Nuremberg and the vicinity and giving his friends joy-rides in his very own Sherman tank! Well, there was quite a flap about it, because the German roads and bridges were in terrible condition; of course they hadn't been maintained throughout the entire war, and armies had fought over them back and forth. The German civilian authorities were trying desperately to keep them open, and here comes this dumb American with a six-ton tank, chewing up their roads and straining their bridges! The military government finally cracked down, and said, 'Look, boy, you can't do this.'

Life in Nuremberg was not all work. There was a great deal of social activity, and there were a good many opportunities for travel. Everybody found his or her own means of constructing an off-duty life which would counteract the strains of living in Nuremberg: some people pursued the leisure activities which approximated most closely to what they would have done at home, while others made a point of getting away from Nuremberg as often as possible. The sight of the other Allied nationals at play also had its fascinations.

Sylvia De La Warr, visitor
There was quite a bit of social life – big dinner-parties, and so on. David [Maxwell-Fyfe] was a Scot, and I remember there was a St Andrew's Night celebration. They'd had a haggis flown out, and the Russians, who came to the party, were entranced. They thought they'd never seen anything better than the haggis being piped in! And then when *we* went back to *them* – oceans of vodka! You could have drowned in vodka! There was a little container of it in front of everybody's seat, and you had to be awfully careful not to think it was a carafe of water! People sometimes went away at the weekends: for example, there was marvellous trout-fishing. The rivers had all been enormously stocked and not

fished for years. But apart from that, one began the day at about half-past eight in the morning, and got home at about half-past five; then one generally had dinner at home, and then maybe worked again. I used to potter about and read in the evenings. There was no question of going out and doing anything – at that time it was still too dangerous to go out without a guard, and I didn't have a guard. But with David being a lawyer, most of my life had been spent with him working in the evenings, and I was very used to it. We shared a house with three or four of the delegation, including Khaki Roberts and Harry Phillimore; we might get together and talk a bit in the evenings, and then I think everybody used to work, or go to bed and read, if there wasn't a party on.

I sat in the court-room every day. I enjoyed it. I used to go and sit in the Old Bailey, when David was doing those sort of cases. It's rather like a theatre – you can get awfully gripped by what's happening. But at Nuremberg it could be terribly slow, what with the simultaneous interpretation, and some of the cross-examinations were really rather boring – let's face it. And *then* one was rather longing for the break, and hoping something would happen. But there was really nothing else to do – one had to get thoroughly soaked in the trial. I went out to Nuremberg for a while, and then came home to Liverpool for a while, because we had a Liverpool constituency and the children were young. So I couldn't be in Nuremberg all the time, though I would have been, I think, if I could have. During the times when I was at home in Liverpool, I think David used occasionally to go and explore the battlefield of the Thirty Years' War; Nuremberg was on the edge of it, and some of the trenches and things were still visible, as marks. He was tremendously interested in battlefields. He gave a lecture on it to the troops who were stationed there, with maps and screens and so on. They all pretended to be frightfully enthusiastic, but I often wonder if they knew what on earth was going on!

Dorothy Reilly, secretary

Although I knew some Americans of German descent, I had never been in Europe before the war; a great many of the British staff had been. They didn't speak German, but they had friends who lived there. I can recall visiting some of the little walled-city towns like Rotenburg. Judge Biddle had the rank of a five-star general, with his own staff and his own plane. To enable us to get out into the fresh air and to get wholly away, the authorities made available a villa a couple of thousand feet up in the Bavarian Alps, called Duisberg. It was a beautiful place, and I think we spent almost every other weekend there in the early months of the trial. We did most of our travelling in 1945: we got away at Christmas-time, and went to Paris by plane with Judge Biddle. We took the train to Mulhouse, which was an army post. From there we went to Basle, Geneva, Berne and Zurich, and we came back by way of Strasbourg, which was heavily bombed. So we saw a lot of Europe. It was almost the price of one's sanity. It was not easy to live in a ruined city. It was depressing in itself to go into the court-room. Another thing about getting away was the fact that everything was so inbred. You saw the same people day after day after day, and nothing ever changed. Gossip was rife; and you know that conquering armies conquer – everything was free to the winning side.

Priscilla Belcher, visitor

Once we went to a wonderful VIP party, with a buffet supper, and the two Russian judges came and sat at our table. So we tried to talk to them a bit – why not? They weren't going to talk about the trial, but they wanted to know what it was like in England, when they heard I'd come from there. They were very pleasant, but they left without finishing their food. Thereafter there was dancing, and a gentleman in civilian clothes, with big thick glasses, came over and asked me to dance. I had civilian clothes on too. He introduced himself as Mr Razumov, and he wanted to find out all about me. Was I connected with the Tribunal, and so on. I didn't give him too much information; I thought I'd keep him guessing. So he ended up singing in my ear, out of tune, and then he said, 'Yes, ve make good music,' kissed my hand, clicked his heels and left me in the middle of the dance-floor! He was the Russian secret police man: wherever the Russian judges went, he went too, and checked out everybody who was involved. Then he invited A.G.[Steer, Priscilla's sister-in-law's brother] and me to a party at his place. He'd been in America and was very Americanized: he loved American jazz and spoke English quite well. I suspect he didn't last too long in the other regime. The Russian judges kept very much to themselves – they didn't even show up at *his* parties.

Jean Tull, secretary

The social life was tremendous fun. There was a lot of friendliness between the American and British delegations, and to a lesser extent with the French. The Russians kept themselves to themselves for the most part, but I can recall a group of them in the Marble Room of the Grand Hotel one evening who were prepared to dance and let us practise a few words of Russian. We had a long break over Christmas and New Year, 1945/6, and about six of us did a little trip into Austria. We had weekends skiing in Czechoslovakia, and house-parties at Garmisch, which was something of a playground. We had good PX rations. I can remember going to the PX and buying clothing. That was what the British girls liked so much: we hadn't seen nice clothing for a long time. I seem to recall that my first pair of nylon stockings I had in Paris, and I let out such a shriek of delight!

Mary Burns, secretary

We were all young girls in our twenties, and at that time, of course, there were no dependants of any military personnel there. So American girls were pretty popular – and this would be true of girls in the other delegations as well. In the Marble Room of the Grand Hotel, which was in operation even the first time I went over, they had a German band playing American jazz, and that's where, it seemed, everybody went, every night. You'd say, 'My, I'm sick of it,' but you found yourself back there that same night! That was all there was, really. Of course there were a lot of opportunities to have a date with whoever was around, and it was all a lot of fun. That was the mainstay of our life there – you had the court in the day and the Marble Room at night.

The delegations had their own social circles; I would call it more protocol than anything. When they needed some female 'bodies' at some of these social events, then people in subordinate positions, like myself, were asked. Since I worked in Justice Jackson's office I was a frequent guest at his home, and he entertained the other delegations, as the rest of them did. I was at a number of the British parties, which were the same thing. Everything was the same; nobody had the opportunity to be very different. So it was a routine of parties and Marble Room, Marble Room and parties. But we did have other breaks. The trial started in October, and at Christmas-time there was a recess, and many of us went to Berchtesgaden. Down there we met more of the military boys, who were very hospitable to us, and we did a lot of skiing, and I went on ice-skates a few times. So we did have that kind of diversion. But it was always the same little group, you know, wherever we went.

The Russians were pretty much on their own. I don't really recall any social contact at all, except one time when the British, I think it was, had a party, and I and other girls were invited. There was a buffet supper, and then some dancing. However, the thing that was weird about it – and I did not understand it at all – was that it was pretty tiring to dance with these big men, and I'm not a very big woman, and we were all exhausted and would go over to the bar for a drink of water, bourbon, anything! And our hosts would come up to us and whisper, 'Dance! Dance!' I didn't know till the next day what was going on, but that was when Churchill made his Fulton, Missouri speech, about how we should beware of the Iron Curtain. I didn't even know what that meant when I heard it the next day, except that, whatever it was, I paid a price! You learn the *real* story of something like that much, much later. It was a touchy evening ... the delicacy of relationships.

Joseph Stone, lawyer, Subsequent Proceedings

There was a movie-house in Nuremberg. I had some young kid of about ten or twelve sitting next to me one night, and we were seeing something about a bombing, and he suddenly began shaking all over and ran out of the movie-house. I guess he had lived through bombings. I'd never seen anything like the state of Nuremberg. It was war-torn to the nth degree. It didn't affect me, I must confess. Either I am an insensitive individual ... but in terms of the whole Hitler period, concentration camps and everything, dammit, that's what they brought on themselves. I kept referring to it as twentieth-century open-air architecture. I did not feel any remorse or twinge of conscience about it. That was their headache, they brought it on themselves, and maybe it would teach them a lesson.

Apropos of teaching them a lesson, American soldiers parade very poorly. I remember the first time I went to watch a parade – I think it was a Fourth of July parade – they must have gotten all the cooks and truck-drivers to do the parading! And to a German audience along the street where they were parading ... I thought to myself, 'Oh my God! They're going to think this is ridiculous!' They were out of step, they were straggling, and everything else. Then it occurred to me that maybe this would be a good thing, that the Germans would get the idea that a bunch of stragglers that don't know how to march so straight can beat their boys, who march straight, and that maybe the concept of militarism, with all its straight lines and everybody doing the goose-step, wasn't so damn important after all. So later on I appreciated the fact that the American soldiers paraded very poorly. Those parades were hilarious, *I* thought. You never found Telford Taylor around at those parades, I'm told. Of course, Tel wasn't really a military man. Somehow or other, any military chore that would have had him leading a parade or anything, he was off out of the city on official business somewhere. Tel might deny that, and I have no way of proving it, but that's what I remember. I think it was Sandy Hardy, a young lawyer and former football-player for Boston College, a big, hulking guy ... Sandy was not afraid of anything in this world, and he used to say to Taylor, 'What kind of a general are you? Look – you got a tear in your shirt here. You oughta clean that up! Why don't you go down and say hello to the boys that are on your staff? They want to be able to write home and tell their mothers that they met the General.'

Taylor was not a military man, but he was a fantastic individual. He played tennis beautifully, he played bridge beautifully, he danced on the dance-floor beautifully, he wrote magnificently, he was extremely hand-some and six foot two or whatever – an unusual individual. I remember that he and his wife, and two other couples, were travelling somewhere in Germany, and over Berlin something went wrong with the plane and everybody was ordered to bail out. Benjamin Ferencz, one of the lawyers, who is quite a small man, tried to push the door open with his shoulder, but couldn't manage to shift it; then Telford Taylor leaned over and pushed it open with his hand, and Ferencz fell out. He pulled on the ripcord of his parachute, and got the most awful shock when the ring came off in his hand. Nobody had told him that it was *supposed* to do this! Mrs Taylor, who was five months pregnant, landed on a roof and then fell off, but she and the baby were both fine. Taylor was slightly injured: he landed on a railway track, I think. Anyway, that was the version *I* heard, as I remember it!

I'd had a lot of chest pains, so I went to the doctor. It was fairly well known that it was not hard to get into the American hospital; the difficulty was getting back out of it! They didn't like to let their patients out, for some reason. The wife of another attorney told me about a German doctor, so I went up to see him and took my research assistant Ellen Levy with me. He couldn't quite grasp her relationship to me, and he finally apparently decided that she was some girl whom I'd gone out with, who'd become pregnant, and that she needed some kind of medical treatment. We got over that one, and finally it must have dawned on him what the relationship was, because he immediately said she couldn't stay in the room – obviously, because she wasn't my wife, she wasn't my girlfriend; she was an assistant. So she had to leave, leaving me to try my pidgin German with this doctor, who immediately tried to establish his credentials by asking me if I knew some doctor with a very Jewish name who lived in the Bronx, because he was a good friend of his. They were all trying to emphasize how friendly they had been with Jews, prior to this recent unpleasantness. I said the Bronx was a big place, and I didn't know Dr Cohen, or Dr Levi, or Dr Schwartz, or whoever he was asking about. Finally he decided I just needed a rest, and there was nothing wrong with me, I was overworked, etcetera. I asked the person who'd put me on to him, 'What kind of a fee do I pay this man?', and she said, 'You just give him a pound of coffee.' I said, 'I can't give a doctor a pound of coffee!', but she said, 'Oh yes, you can – it's a very good fee.' It turned out he was a gynaecologist; he probably hadn't looked at a man in twenty or thirty years! And it suddenly dawned on me that I had been the only male in that waiting-room; there were a lot of women there. It hadn't dawned on my child-like innocence at the time!

Alfred Steer, administrative head, language division

When we were in Nuremberg, one of the things we loved to do was go hunting at weekends. During the war Hitler had this stupid idea that hunting was pleasure and should therefore be forbidden, and of course the deer multiplied and ate the farmers' crops, and the farmers were driven crazy trying to raise enough to feed themselves. So when the Americans came, what did the military government do but abolish and confiscate all arms in the hands of the Germans, including hunting weapons. So who was going to keep the deer population under control? The German foresters would invite us out, hoping that we would shoot a few deer in their woods. They let us have the deer, of course. We loved it, because we had difficulty keeping our mess going at the house where we were staying: there were only six of us, and the army didn't want to supply a mess for only six. We had continual trouble with some character who was deep in the black market on the side, trying to get him to allocate us enough food. So we used to say to each other, 'Now go take a ride in the country and be sure to hit at least a few chickens!' I had good friends among the Germans, for instance the forester in the little village where we went hunting. He was a grand guy. We'd all sit round the table at the inn after the hunt was over, and have something to eat and some beer.

Years of living under Goebbels's propaganda machine had taught the Germans not to believe anything they read in the papers. Therefore they wouldn't believe anything put out by the military government either. Instead they would go around to the GI billets and mess halls and pay the GIs fantastic sums for a black market copy of *Stars and Stripes*. It's a lousy sheet and always has been – it's perfectly useless. It was particularly ridiculous because one of the newspapers put out by the military government was *Die Neue Zeitung*, and was edited by A.R. Rosenberg, employee and later editor of the *New York Times*. At that point he was an army major. He took over *Die Neue Zeitung* and turned it into an absolutely world-class newspaper, and here were these Germans turning up their noses at it and slipping GIs something on the side to get them *Stars and Stripes*! I thought it was just ridiculous. I used to go out of my way to get hold of *Die Neue Zeitung* – it was the best newspaper I could find in Europe, better even than Swiss newspapers. I couldn't get London newspapers.

Eddie Worth, photographer
I didn't really have any kind of social life in Nuremberg. It was such a dead city. Some of the reporters would just go to the court, come back, and go straight upstairs and booze. But *I* used to go out and walk. I'm very fond of walking, and I know every inch round Stein now. Also, in the grounds of the castle where we stayed were massive greenhouses, big enough to drive a tractor inside, and as I'm fond of gardening I used to walk round them. The people who worked there were very nice to me; I actually helped them, as there were lots of things, seeds and so on, that they couldn't get, and I used to write to my wife to send them. So that was very interesting for me, but the others, I'm afraid, were wasting their time. After all, if you're being paid, why not take advantage of it all?

I lived for ten months without spending a penny of my own money on the PX ration. I don't smoke, and I certainly didn't drink hard stuff the way they did, so I used to give it to the old man who looked after us; and in exchange he supplied me with everything: all my laundry was done, and so on. I've thought since that this bloke must have been a millionaire by the end of the Nuremberg Trials, because he got a carton of cigarettes from me regularly, and they used to sell them to each other *separately*. Another thing they used to do was dry the coffee after the Americans had used it, and then sell it again.

Daniel Margolies, lawyer
I didn't really have much contact with ordinary Germans. Colonel Gill was the administrative officer, and he was the bridge champion of the state of Maryland. And he had gone through the IBM cards – in those days before the computer they had some card system that they used – and he had gotten every bridge player or columnist in the army to attend the trial in some capacity. Anyway, we had a small continuous bridge game going on for weeks, of a quality that I've never known before or since: I mean, we had real bridge experts. That took up a lot of time, and if you spend a lot of time playing bridge you don't really have a chance to go out and mingle with the local population.

Ron Chapman, clerk

The Russians were billeted at one end of Nuremberg, well away from the Americans, the French and us. We never had any contact whatsoever with the Russians, other than in the court-house during the day. You seldom saw them in Nuremberg during the evening, whereas we used to have dances occasionally in a big cafe in Zirndorf, the French would have dances occasionally, the Americans were always having dances. And we all intermingled, but we were more or less contained in the Zirndorf-Erlangen side of Nuremberg. The Russians were right on the other side. I always had the feeling that they were really on their own as regards the trial.

In the cafeteria where we used to have midday lunch, it wasn't self-service, but you took a tray and went along, and the German chefs served you, then you came along to the end of the counter where there was a pile of sliced bread. You took one or two slices of bread, and then you went and found a table. You sat with anybody – there was no rank or class distinction whatsoever. I went there one day for lunch, and the only table with seats was where our captain was sitting, and a Russian colonel. So I sat down beside them. This Russian colonel must have had ten slices of bread with his lunch; he must have taken as much as he could grab. He threw his knife and fork to one side, and took his spoon, and literally shovelled the food into his mouth. He lowered his mouth till it was almost level with the table, and he'd take a slice of bread, screw it up and put it straight in his mouth. After about three minutes, the captain, who was sitting next to me, put his knife and fork down and folded his arms, saying, 'Chapman, I can't eat with that pig at our table!' I'm pretty certain the Russian didn't understand English, because he carried on without the slightest pause. You had the feeling that a lot of them hadn't seen white bread for years; it was amazing to watch them eat. I think a lot of them had been brought up in very rural districts. And when they went into the PX to buy their weekly rations, they would buy up everything they could get their hands on. It would be six tins of boot polish, six tubes of toothpaste, ink, the sort of stuff that you would normally buy just when you required it. They would buy up stuff that wasn't rationed. Cigarettes and sweets were rationed, and you got so much each week, but certain incidentals such as soap weren't rationed. They would buy it up by the bucketful, and I honestly think they had never seen some of the stuff before. If you were behind two of them in the queue it was really fascinating how they'd take the toothpaste and smell it, squeeze it, lick it. It was really something new to them. It used to amaze the American servers behind the counter.

Mounting the guard outside the court-house each day was quite an event. The four nations took it in turns, with the Russians one day, the French the next, and so on. For our mounting of the guard, they used to send down a special unit from the British sector every month, then they'd go back and another lot would come. You had the Coldstreams, the Grenadiers, the Irish, the Scots, you had the Lincolnshire Regiment. And when the Scots Guards mounted guard, it was quite something to watch. They were led into the courtyard by a lone piper, and when they fixed bayonets the whole of the court-house staff, the civilian staff – French, Russians, and so on – would all be staring out of the window, taking it in, really fascinated. It was as if they were mounting the guard at Buckingham Palace, and when the Scots Guards put on a show they really did: there was a flash on command as their bayonets came out and their white faces lit up. When the French did it, they'd have their little spurs on and their uniforms all over the place – nobody was watching *them*. And when the Americans did it, they'd be slouching and chewing gum all the time.

Once the hangings were over we were posted back to the British sector, to the Force Training Brigade of the Royal Army Service Corps, as clerical instructors, much to our chagrin. Going back up to the British sector from Nuremberg was quite hard for us. We had lived in the American style, which was much better than the British soldier's lot. I never put my army boots on for fourteen months. In fact we weren't allowed to wear boots in the court-house – we just wore civilian shoes. When we went back up north and I found my boots in the bottom of my kit-bag, I think they were covered in cobwebs, near enough. It was hard going back to the British beds, bunks, with their two blankets and no sheets. It was a rude awakening and it really did show up the difference in living standards between the British and American forces. We felt envious of their uniforms, their food, their PX rations, everything.

As this chapter shows, life in Nuremberg is a subject on which almost all of the participants have much to say, because there was much to think about. It is important to depict what they saw and heard as fully as possible, otherwise it might seem that the trial could have been taking place anywhere – in the Old Bailey, perhaps, or in any American county court-house. Of course this was not the case: in its physical context, as in so many other respects, the Nuremberg Trial was without real precedent, and although the participants vary in the degree to which they were exposed to – or went in search of – the realities of Nuremberg, none of them could ignore the extraordinary setting of this event. The fact that, for many people, a nation was symbolically on trial ensured that living in the midst of this nation was likely to be a somewhat heightened experience, but some were almost overwhelmed by the kind of commentary on the trial which life in Nuremberg was furnishing every day. The momentous moral issues being aired in the trial could not be left behind when one emerged from the court-room into the street at the end of the day – everywhere one saw them being acted out, or their results illustrated.

One of the great questions was that of whether ordinary German citizens had been aware of the atrocities taking place in the concentration camps. The people recorded here encountered a more or less complete denial of knowledge from members of the German population, which shocked and depressed them since they were unable to

believe it; occasionally, however, chinks in the armour became visible,
and Patrick Cooper in particular provides detailed and fascinating
observations in which he charts the particular ambivalences of his
German acquaintances.

The three vignettes which close this chapter are each illustrative of
the dark side of life in Nuremberg. John Pine describes the time he
visited Belsen concentration camp, something that many visitors to
post-war Germany did. It was, after all, one of the reasons why they
were all there. Ron Chapman's account of the dramatic shooting
incident at the Grand Hotel is a reminder of the difficulties of
presenting a united front against the Nazis, even after their defeat,
when there were potentially explosive antipathies between certain
members of the prosecuting nations. The people of Nuremberg,
particularly in Priscilla Belcher's recollection, were by no means
universally reconciled to their situation, and there were homeless and
often lawless people of other nationalities to reckon with. Al Steer
describes the huge ammunition dump outside Nuremberg and the
Allies' efforts to get rid of it by blowing it up harmlessly, bit by bit, until
the day it 'got away from them' and obliterated, among other things,
the Allied team and their POW German colleagues who had been
working together to render it safe. In view of the atmosphere in post-
war Nuremberg, it is ironic to record this literal attempt at defusion
which went so disastrously wrong.

John Pine, visitor
During the time that I was prosecuting, I paid three visits out of my area in
Hanover. One was to Belsen, during the Belsen Trials. We didn't stay
long there, but I have the most vivid memory of Ilse Koch standing up in
court. She was giving evidence. As I remember her she was a magnificent
figure of Aryan womanhood, standing erect in her black leather
jackboots giving evidence, not the least bit frightened or anything. She
was the one who had cut off live persons' skin to make lampshades. How
she could have done it I don't know.

We had a good look around Belsen, and as I'm saying this now, if I shut
my eyes and think about it I can still recall in my nostrils the stench of the
human flesh that was still about. There were masses of what were
obviously human bones, there were the crematoria, there was a vast
amount of ash. And then one saw the sleeping – and indeed, living –
quarters of the inmates of the camp. They were sort of bunks, with very
little head room indeed, and to my recollection there were three, four and
even five bunks one on top of the other. And there were all the signs of the
human excreta which had dropped down from bunk to bunk. Looking at
it, it really made one feel ... it revolted one, and yet it made one feel so
humble, that they could have all gone through that, and some of them
even survived, how ghastly the whole thing was, and at the same time one
had the smell in one's nostrils, and one could see where all these heaps of
naked dead bodies had been piled up one on top of the other like a whole

lot of dead animals' carcases. It was a very humbling experience to be in there; what it would have been like to have spent days in there, as lots of people did do who were working there, I don't know. I don't think we spent more than two or three hours there: a most interesting experience, but one can't but say that one was extremely glad to get away from there – and yet I can still see it all so vividly before me.

Ron Chapman, clerk
While we were at Zirndorf we used occasionally to have a truck take us into Nuremberg for the evening. A friend and I went in one night, and we went to the ice-skating rink. Our driver had arranged to pick us up at the Grand Hotel, which is a really luscious hotel now, and in those days was used purely for high-ranking officers of the Allied troops, a lot of whom were working on the trials. We'd arranged to meet him there at about ten o'clock. It was snowing, a cold night. When we got to the Grand Hotel he hadn't turned up, and we were standing outside, and there were two Americans always on guard at the door there, two military police with their armbands, restricting whoever went into the hotel. These two Americans saw us standing outside waiting in the snow, and said, 'You can come and stand in here.' So we went into the foyer, and they got talking to us, and we were still waiting for the truck. Then suddenly, without any warning at all, the two glass doors flung open, and a little Russian in uniform – he must have been about forty-five at least – came staggering in, holding his throat and making a horrible gurgling noise. He just collapsed at our feet, and these two American military police were looking absolutely flabbergasted. One of them bent down over this chap who was gurgling, and said, 'This guy's been shot!' And we could see blood coming out of his chest. So the other American went flying into the hotel to call an officer, and an American medical officer came out, and a Russian civilian came out who was something to do with the trial. And *he* got down on the floor, putting his ear right against this Russian's mouth and asking questions, trying to hear what this poor chap was saying. The medical officer was down on the other side, saying, 'Get this guy to hospital, quick!' This officer asked us what we'd seen, and luckily the two military police said, 'They don't know anything – they were standing here with us when he came in.' That let us off the hook. Next thing we knew our truck arrived, and we crept in the back and went to Zirndorf.

A few days later, in the American *Stars and Stripes*, which was their army paper, there was a report of this. Apparently they'd arrested an American soldier for shooting him. The story went that this Russian was a chauffeur driving for one of the high-ranking Russian officers who stayed at the hotel, and he was just round the corner with his car, waiting, when this American came along and asked for a lift. I don't think the Russian understood him, and he said no, and the American just shot him. Pulled out a gun and shot him. He died in hospital; he was dead in about twelve hours. I said to my friend Smith, 'I'm glad we weren't outside!' Whether the American was drunk, or went berserk ... but you found that the majority of Americans really hated these 'Russkies', as they called them. They didn't get on at all.

Alfred Steer, administrative head, language division

Close to Nuremberg to the north-east was an old Nazi ammunition dump, with thousands of tons of ammunition of all types, stored in bunkers. Some explosives could be chemically reclaimed and recycled for useful purposes, such as fertilizer, but vast stores of explosives still remained. Explosives deteriorate with age, becoming more unstable and liable to accidental detonation, so it was decided to blow up the stuff in small increments. Small shells and other small bits were set off almost constantly, as they did not constitute a threat. Tuesdays and Thursdays, as I recall, were set aside for the large blow-offs. On those days everyone in Nuremberg was supposed to open their windows at twelve noon and leave them open for an hour, during which time the large explosions would be set off. Window glass was in very short supply, and open windows would not be shattered by the detonations.

I became curious about this. I had always liked big bangs, and since I had at my disposal a fine source of bribing material, namely passes to the court-room, I had them give me a VIP tour of the ammunition dump. I found there two US navy gunners' mates, about four army sergeants, and maybe fifteen German prisoners of war, all of them ammunition specialists of some sort. They worked in complete harmony as professionals and were proud of their job, which was a necessary and, of course, a dangerous one. The dump consisted of many bunkers, each full of explosives, spaced carefully through a wooded area. They showed me the empty bunker which was about to be blown up with the bi-weekly shot. It was maybe a hundred feet long and thirty feet wide, on a concrete slab, with arched steel walls and ceiling, and huge steel doors and door-frames at each end. The whole thing, except the doors, was heaped with earth, and at one corner were some 500lb bombs and some shells – they looked quite unimpressive in that huge bunker. Then I was led some 200 yards away, down into a ditch with an overhanging protective roof of some sort, and they let her blow. The shock shook me like a terrier shakes a rat. At Saipan the navy battleships had fired 14-inch guns from astern over my head on to the beach, and it was the same feeling. After the debris had stopped falling, we ventured out. The bunker, except for about half of the concrete slab, was completely gone, most surprisingly including the huge steel doors and frames.

Well, one spring afternoon in 1946 it got away from them. When I returned home from the court-house to my street, Bulowstrasse, which was on a hill facing east, a whole segment of the horizon seemed to be on fire, with geysers of flame shooting up here and there and an occasional tracer shell carving an arc against the sky. There was a steady roar, punctuated by louder explosions. And my friend Sigmund Roth was getting out-of-control drunk. He had landed on Omaha Beach a corporal, and had fought all the way across Europe, ending up in Prague as a captain, with every promotion a battlefield promotion. He had a chestful of medals. 'That's just how the front looked, Al,' he said, 'and that's how it sounded.' Then he would get mad, shouting at no one in particular that he'd fought his war, and by God, no one was going to get him to go into another front like that. He grabbed an antique brass candelabra that happened to be on a nearby table and twisted it in half – he was an ox of a man – then threw the pieces out of the window, said window being shut at the time. Then he'd shut up, and we'd see tears streaming down his face; von Zastrow and Uiberall had come home by this time, and were just as puzzled as I was as to what to do with him. Then he'd start shouting again that next time, by God, the young guys could fight the war – he'd done his job. We tried to get him to stop drinking. No success. We tried to get coffee into him, food into him; we tried to get him upstairs to bed. Nothing worked. Finally we poured liquor into him until he collapsed.

The next day the ammunition dump more or less burned itself out. They never did find out who made the mistake, and just what the mistake was. Several of the American–German explosives team had simply vanished, doubtless vaporized by one explosion or another, we learned later. When truckloads of GIs were being concentrated on the area to fight the fire, one German peasant had reportedly shouted to the GIs in a passing truck, 'Was gibt's?,' which means 'What's up?' Some GI had not only learned a few words of German, but he also possessed a wry sense of humour. He shouted back, 'Die Russen kommen!' ['The Russians are coming!'] Within minutes that village self-evacuated, out on to the road, headed west, away from the Russians. There were horse-drawn wagons piled high with movable goods, with grandma on top, seated on a feather bed, holding a rope tied to a cow following on behind. A few more minutes, then the same with the next village, and then, quickly, all the villages far and wide. In short order all the roads were hopelessly jammed. They didn't put out that fire – they couldn't get to it for the traffic jams. It burned itself out.

5. Law, morality, experience: summing up

Hume Boggis-Rolfe, visitor

I thought then and think now that it was inevitable that there should be war crimes trials. I wouldn't at all have agreed with the idea of shooting them out of hand. The proof of the pudding is in the eating, and the fact that some were not condemned to death is proof, for me, that it was right to hold a trial. I thought it was as well run as it could be, and that there were people there who were highly competent, as they had to be. It was a very difficult business, with so many witnesses and so much paperwork – as there is in any big enquiry – and it required people of considerable ability to do it. As for the idea of trials in the present day, personally I don't very much like it. I don't like the idea of someone getting off scot free, possibly lying in order to get British nationality, but I'm not too happy about people being prosecuted many years after the event. There is the extraordinary difficulty of getting reliable evidence more than forty years after the event, of merely *identifying* somebody: some people change very much as they get older, others hardly at all. It isn't that some don't deserve it, but I'm not too happy about the necessity of retrospective legislation to make it possible. I don't know *what* the answer to that is.

Andy Wheeler, lawyer

It was a great thing for me, the biggest trial I'd ever engaged in. I guess we were all aware, at the time of Vietnam, that we were probably doing some of the things we'd accused them of doing. It did depend upon who won. But I'm convinced that something had to be done, and that we did it as well as it could be done, with the combination of the court being so fair and the prosecution sticking to what they had decided.

As for trying people nowadays, I think it's being overdone somewhat. It's hard to feel really strongly about these fellows so long afterwards, when most of them have been living a peaceful life for years, and of course the Americans did give special attention to bringing back to America some people who were obvious candidates for a judgement against them, just because they could help America with their scientific knowledge and so on. That didn't come out at first, but it looked pretty bad afterwards when it did come out. I guess that's the way war is. As regards something like the Demjanjuk trial, I think it's very risky to do that so long afterwards. Witnesses are so hard to find, and it's so hard for them to remember truthfully what *did* happen. So they take a chance in starting it at all. But with some of the worst ones, it's pretty hard to say that they should not be prosecuted.

Daniel Margolies, lawyer

The trial got rather tiresome after a while. You know, there were an awful lot of defendants, and a lot of evidence. But I thought that the significance of it ... you see, after World War One – and this is part of the justification for it – there was a great debate in the United States as to who were the aggressors in World War One. The United States has a large German population, and there was a large isolationist movement which on the whole regarded our involvement in World War One as the result of a conspiracy between Mr Wilson and some of his friends in England. And if you look back on World War One they were all pretty nice people, really – the Germans behaved relatively well. There were all these stories of atrocities they'd committed in Belgium and so on, but I think the evidence is fairly clear that they didn't do a lot of what they were alleged to have done. It was not good against evil in the way that it really was in World War Two. I mean, it's hard to find anybody who doesn't feel that fighting the Nazis was a good thing. I understand there *is* a doubt – I mean, there *are* neo-Nazis, and there *are* people saying that concentration camps were merely health camps where you sent people to reduce, and things like that. But I don't think very many people take that seriously. So I think the record is fairly clear, and I think that even the German lawyers felt that, on the whole, they were given about as good a break as they could be. I have a feeling that if the British ran similar war crimes trials in the future they would run them fairly. I'm not clear that this would apply to all countries across the board. Lawrence was an extraordinarily impressive judge – I mean, if God was going to create a really impartial judge then Lawrence was it. He was the personification of a great judge. The other judges were somewhat paler by comparison, but he was a very strong personality. He was quite wide awake and alert throughout the whole proceedings – much more so than I was. I was there mostly because I was Dodd's assistant, and I was in at the trial a good deal.

I can understand people's scepticism about the trial. And there's no doubt that if you take people out and shoot them you save a lot of time, and you certainly get a lot more satisfaction than keeping Mr Hess around for umpteen years. On the other hand, you don't really know what happened. You do not have a solid historical record, and you might well make martyrs of those killed in this fashion.

Having been drafted at the age of thirty-four, by the time the trial was over I was thirty-six. I figured I ought to do the job and finish the Peace Treaty. You see, the Americans among other things had the so-called 'economic case', which was Schacht and others, which we lost, by the way. But we did in the process learn quite a bit about the German economy. So I was offered a job in the State Department to work with the German section on drafting the Peace Treaty. Well, after the conference broke up in London in 1947 or whenever it was, over the currency issue, and we each decided to cultivate our own zone, as you might say, you couldn't have a Peace Treaty with *pieces* of Germany, and even when we sewed three pieces together and got what's now called West Germany we still had Berlin sort of floating around. So we have a document with the Germans which is in lieu of a Peace Treaty, and which I worked on. We have a Japanese Peace Treaty, and an Italian Peace Treaty, and an Austrian Peace Treaty, but we don't have a German Peace Treaty – we never did get one. And I never did leave the State Department; I decided I would stay there until I retired. To that extent, it changed the direction of my life. If it hadn't been for the Nuremberg Trial I might have gone back and become a lawyer. Who knows?

Patrick Cooper, airman

I think the first thing I would say about that whole thing was the total unreality of it, to rather ignorant, provincial troops. I had come from Georgia. Nuremberg was flattened by the war; the horror of the destruction was overwhelming. I think the impact of the destruction of Germany – the towns, the cities – by the bombing, the impact of that upon us replacement troops, young troops who hadn't actually fought through the whole campaign, in Europe and so on, was greater than it was on the combat troops. They'd gone through it, and they were a lot angrier than we were anyway, because they'd been fighting; whereas we were replacement troops coming in at the end of hostilities, or in my case several months after hostilities ceased.

We arrived in the midst of this unbelievable destruction ... you've seen photographs of what Germany was like, the major cities, the impact of the bombing. The demoralization of the people, and the starvation – they were hungry. And not just the indigenous population: Germany was full of people wandering about, people who'd been released from various camps, people who'd been brought into Germany from other parts of central and eastern Europe. Some of these were trying to get home; others were fleeing, wanting to get away from the Red Army, particularly those from eastern Europe who were not sympathetic to the Soviets, and felt that if they fell into the hands of the Red Army they would be sent to God knows where – and many of them were. And so the whole atmosphere in Nuremberg at that time was one of demoralization, fear, hunger, a kind of helplessness. I've never recovered from it – I mean, I don't think one could. The aftermath of a war must be worse than the war itself, because while the war is going on you're engaged in it, your energies and attention are engaged, but afterwards there is this horrible demoralization. It had an enormous impact on me, and everybody I knew; my mates felt much the same as I did. I remember funny things that happened, but it was really a demoralizing time for us. We rapidly came under the influence of it, and I think that by late 1946 I probably needed counselling or psychiatric help to handle it all. And what happened to the GIs at this time, what with the devastated state of Germany and the moral ambiguities around them, was that a great many of them drank too much, they threw themselves into very dubious associations – the black market, and so on – and of course the squalor of the sex for cigarettes thing was one of the worst aspects of the whole thing. I'm glad to say that I didn't have much to do with that myself, except once or twice early on ... it was inevitable, really. We all did it. We were kids. But I did form one or two relationships with German girls that were not on that basis. A lot of soldiers went haywire at that time because they were three thousand miles from home and in a position where you were the master – I mean, you *were*. And we were still technically at war until some time in 1946. Venereal disease was a dreadful problem at this time. I think that the early years of the occupation of Germany were pretty horrific, for the occupiers as well as the occupied. It began to get better around 1948 – they allowed the dependants of officers and soldiers to come over, and began to build a kind of little America in West Germany. And in the British zone they were to some extent doing the same kind of thing, but not on the same lavish scale.

We were conscious of the trial going on all the time – it was a kind of constant presence. Every day, five days a week, for month after month, there was this drama being unfolded in the Palace of Justice. Among the Americans and British, what you thought about the trial very much depended on what kind of war you'd had, or whether you had relations who had suffered, if you were Jewish or Jewish-American. It all very much depended on what your own personal background was. That's why it's important to give you some idea of who and what I was at that period: a very young, pretty ignorant, provincial American, a long way from home, and suddenly most of the accustomed signposts had disappeared. It was a time of great confusion, and I was trying at a very early age to deal with very complex issues, and make up my mind where I stood. In fact one didn't think about it all the time; you were going about your business. So a lot of this is retrospective stuff, thinking about what you were at that time. And I must say that my own attitude was a bit ambivalent. I wasn't too keen on it, to be honest, once I'd thought it through. I had trouble with the constitutionality of it, once I really began to think about it. These men were criminals, they'd committed criminal acts, so why not a criminal trial, rather than a sort of political trial, with charges of crimes against humanity and so on, which is a very vague concept? Also, I am a southerner, and we'd had a bit of this in the American south, after the American Civil War. Various officials were brought to trial, for so-called 'war crimes', such as being in charge of the notorious Andersonville prison camp in Georgia, and one or two others. So that was an interesting sidelight for a southerner. So I think that a lot of us, once we really began to think deep on it, had trouble with the constitutionality and legitimacy of it, and I think a great many Germans did, obviously.

Nowadays, I think it seems a bit pointless to bring an eighty-year-old, semi-senile man to trial for something that happened forty-five years ago. One wonders what good it can possibly do. I think that it goes all the way back to the very beginning of the whole thing. If you accept that a conquering power has a constitutional power to bring people to trial, then I suppose you say, 'Right, once you've started, you go on doing it until you get them all.' So I think you have to make up your mind first of all whether you think you should have done it in the first place, and I'm still ambivalent about it even after all this time. I mean, suppose the shoe was on the other foot: suppose the Allies had lost the war, and they'd come in and hanged Churchill, and Truman. They could have made a case. So I have to say that I still have my doubts. And another thing is that the whole thing has been coloured by novels and movies about trying to track down top Nazis – books like *The Odessa File*. A lot of that stuff is highly suspect, in my view. To glamorize it confuses the issue even further.

Dorothy Reilly, secretary
I always felt that the trials ought to be held. When I first went to Berlin and saw the damage, I hadn't seen the damage in England. It wasn't a really active hatred that I had for the Germans, but I certainly had no use for the Nazi Party. I suppose if I hadn't been such a reader all my life I wouldn't have found the trial so interesting, but I *was* interested in history, so I took it very seriously. That was why, when I got away, my freedom was even more precious. How marvellous it was to go to Switzerland, and have non-army food, sleep in linen sheets. Oh, it was heaven. And everything so beautiful – every building, every house.

I regard it, in retrospect, as one of the most challenging, useful and exciting experiences of my life, from the standpoint of a real stride to maturity, to the lifelong friends that I made there. The only disappointing thing was that after the Nuremberg experience I wanted to go into the Foreign Service, but I knew that, being female, I could never reach higher than fourth secretary of an embassy, because women were not then assigned to higher posts. But in the first few years afterwards it was a great boon to my working career. I was asked to go to Belgrade, but I refused that one, because I thought that after the closed life in Nuremberg, anything behind the Iron Curtain I couldn't take right then. Another time I might have. So instead I went to Turkey. Then, many years later, I discovered that having worked for a judge was a great asset – in other words I could command a higher salary when I went to work for the court here, some time in the late sixties.

Seaghan Maynes, journalist
The trial, to me, was a showpiece. It wasn't a juridical process; it was a revenge trial. This is my own opinion, and I think it was shared by a lot of other correspondents. It doesn't say that they shouldn't have been held, because the purpose was to show crime followed by punishment, as an

example to the others. But the legal process was very suspect. They made a charge to fit a crime, *after* the crime had been committed. In that atmosphere, as distinct from now, I can see good reasons for having the trial, because public opinion all over the world had been convinced that an example must be made. But take the case against Schacht. If Germany had occupied Britain, would our Minister of Transport, or somebody, be on trial for his life? Should Ribbentrop, the German Foreign Minister, have been executed? He was a diplomat; he didn't take part in any killing. I had little niggling doubts about these things at the time. 'What did *he* do to deserve death? After all, his country was at war.' In hindsight, I can say that the winner calls the shots and fixes the charges, and the vanquished haven't as much of a chance as they should have. I wouldn't have missed it, but I wouldn't want to see it again. It wasn't a neutral court. If, forty years afterwards, you haven't been able to bring a man to justice, there's no point in trying to do it to some senile old man. What defence could *he* put up? Who can *he* call? They're all dead, or unwilling to testify. At the time, yes – bring them forward, make them answer the charges.

But I've seen so many trials where the defendants were obviously not guilty – particularly the military people. I covered the trial of the German general Kurt Student in the British zone. He was brought up on charges of using prisoners as a defence screen on the island of Crete, when the Germans invaded; also they had bombed Red Cross hospitals and killed prisoners, and used prisoners to launch attacks on the Allies. It was obvious he was going to be sentenced to death, we thought. There was nobody to deny these things. The trial was half-way through, and the prosecution case had nearly ended, when a brigadier-general, a New Zealander, came up to Charlie Wighton of the *Daily Express*, and me, while we were having a beer in the bar. He said, 'You're newspapermen covering this trial? I'm here to give evidence.' I said, 'You're a bit late! The prosecution case is nearly finished.' He said, 'Oh no, I'm coming to give evidence for the defence. I was there in Crete, commanding the New Zealand troops. The Germans *didn't* use our prisoners as a screen – they were trying to get them out of the way of the battle. And the bombing of the military hospital, that was when we were attacking on the beaches. There were military and medical tents beyond the beach area, and some bombs dropped on them, but it's very doubtful if they were properly marked with the red cross because the whole thing was in a state of chaos at the time.' This chap gave evidence for Student, and Student was sentenced to something like ten years and was out in about two. He had to be given *some* punishment, because he was a German general. But if that brigadier hadn't appeared, Student would have been hanged, because everybody believed him guilty and there was nobody to say he wasn't. It's awfully difficult, in a war situation or the aftermath of a war, to deliver justice. I think Nuremberg failed in that. And its principal objective, to make sure that nothing like that happens again – that hasn't worked. Look at all the other little wars going on. Look at South America, Palestine, the Lebanon.

If you look closely at any war you end up very cynical. You can't help it.
Because war itself is unjust. You are forced to the conclusion that might is
right. The winner decides the question of what is right and wrong. I
started my newspaper career in Belfast, in Northern Ireland. As a young
reporter, I saw so-called 'justice' there. One third of the population had
no rights, couldn't get a job, couldn't get a house – and this was under the
British government, not the Russians. The police were an arm of
government, an armed militia, not a civil power operating for the civilian
population. I saw people on one side caught in possession of a revolver,
or charged with murder, and found not guilty; and people on the other
side found in possession of a bullet getting four years in prison. As a court
reporter I covered all this. I saw the elementary principles of justice
denied in my own country, before I went off to Nuremberg or anywhere
else. So Nuremberg wasn't a cultural shock to me.

I've often thought about whether there would ever be another trial like
it, an international court of justice following a war. I don't think we'll ever
see that. We'll probably have little trials in little countries, where the
winners take it out on the losers, but an international trial on the scale of
Nuremberg I don't think will ever happen. If there is an international
conflict, the next one will be so devastating that who will decide who is
guilty of what? In fact, most of us will be specks of radioactive dust.

Peter Uiberall, interpreter

You hear a lot about this nonsense of 'victors' justice'. That is wrong from
many points of view. I would just say that my German colleagues – and
we had quite a number of Germans working as interpreters, especially in
the Subsequent Proceedings – have often told me that they appreciated
the Nuremberg Trial as the only possibility to separate the sheep from the
goats, that a war crimes trial removed from the sixty-five million Germans
the collective guilt that otherwise would have automatically been placed
on them. It was the possibility of demonstrating to the world, in a fair and
decent fashion, who was responsible, who did these acts, how it was
possible that many people did not know the details. Without the trials, I
believe that many people in the rest of the world would consider every
German guilty of what went on in the concentration camps, without
giving any consideration to the fact that millions of Germans did not
know what was going on *in* the camps at all. They knew that something
awful was happening to their Jewish neighbours, against which most of
them were unable to do anything, but the details of what went on in the
camps I think would have revolted the majority of the German people.
And the Nazi leadership made very sure that these details did not become
known. An American I knew, who had studied in Germany before the
war, told me that his landlady had said that Buchenwald was 'a camp for
political prisoners and crazy people'. Now, if you accept the latter
explanation, you're not overly concerned about hearing cries and shouts
and screaming. This is not really an apology, but to some very small

degree it is understandable that the people did not really find out what was going on.

I'm sure the trials were necessary. And for the Germans they were important, although many of them don't realize this now because they're too young. At the time the trials were going on, there were all kinds of rumours – for instance, that the trials were held in secret. Nonsense! There was a room on the ground floor of the court-house, where you could go and get a pass to attend the trial. Anyone could do that, except somebody the police were after, so of course some of the Nazis didn't want to do that. But the pass was available, and people came from all over: Rita Hayworth, the movie actress, was in the court-room one day. A lot of people, from all walks of life, came to Nuremberg to see what was going on; it was by no means held in secret. It was also broadcast every evening, in summary, on the radio, so that people in Germany could hear what was going on in the court-room during the day. Of course the executions were not public, but there were official representatives present.

For me, it certainly was the most important thing that I feel I have ever done. I went to Nuremberg through sheer coincidence; it was a good break. I came in right at the beginning, when they were setting up the interpreting system, and this was very fascinating and challenging. After the penultimate Subsequent Trial we went home, and I had the interesting job of 'phasing out' the language division: talking to everybody, learning what their plans were, scheduling them so that nobody who wanted to go home or stay longer had a complaint; there were over 300 employees.

It's interesting now, when I talk to children, and when they look at me I see in their eyes the thought, 'Aha! A living fossil!' Because it is so long since then. I found it very rewarding, in a spiritual sense, to be taking part. Not in the way of seeing that revenge is taken ... of course not. Looking at Goering, especially on that occasion when I had to translate the judge's remarks to him, it didn't look like the same man. He had absolutely no power; he was a miserable figure. He had lost a lot of weight, and was in a uniform that was much too big for him, without any rank insignia whatsoever – it looked like sackcloth. He was standing there wretched and miserable. It did not reach the same person who committed all those crimes. If you ran into an old, old man, half-blind, sitting at a kerbstone and begging, and somebody said to you, 'This is Adolf Hitler,' what would you say? It's difficult. So with people like Demjanjuk, you can't reach them. He'll die anyway. Of course his trial should take place, it has to, because, you see, every trial of a person responsible for such crimes in a sense helps those who are *not* guilty. For the Germans I think it was very important that it was pointed out in the Nuremberg Trial, very clearly, by witness after witness after witness, *who* was doing *what*, and who was not. There is no room for vengeance, there is no room for real justice in the world. You cannot revive the six million who were murdered; you cannot even do justice by reaching everybody who has committed a crime. What does that do? The thing to do is to learn what happened, and to make sure that it doesn't happen again, ever. That's much more important.

After World War One Germany fell into a deep and lasting depression, with no hope for improvement in sight, and while that was general – as was the plague, which affected Christians and Jews alike – it was a time when a lot of people were looking for somebody to blame it on. And the best people to blame for one's own misfortune are always the others, people who are different in some recognizable way, and preferably people in a minority, who cannot defend themselves. I've never gotten hysterical about anti-Semitism as such – it's a question of the actions it causes. Also, I believe that the German government was weak in permitting Hitler's armed hoodlums to rise and eventually take power. When the national government abdicates in time of crisis, and cedes its power and law-enforcement functions to organized mobs, then it is possible for Holocausts to occur, anywhere and at any time. It is all to do with the attitude that freedom can be taken instead of given. Germany before Hitler had reached a point where so-called freedom was taken by armed mobs, freedom not only to do well for themselves but to terrorize and brutalize others. That is the kind of freedom that cannot be permitted – that's why we have governments, to prevent this sort of thing from happening. Now, you'll find a lot of people who talk about imperial governments, when what they really mean is the responsibility for maintaining law and order. *Somebody* has to have this, and we hope that it is always a government *of* the people and *for* the people.

Priscilla Belcher, visitor
I was a missionary's daughter, and my work had been personnel. I'd grown up working with people, helping people. But I had these mixed feelings about the Germans in Nuremberg. I'd see little old ladies scrounging among the bricks and I'd feel sorry for them, and then I'd feel angry when I saw someone like Clara, who had suffered intensely from medical experiments and was crippled. You really felt torn. That's why I never wanted to go back, although I eventually did.

I think my Nuremberg experience did have an impact on me in a number of ways. It left me with – I hate to say it – some prejudices, which my recent visit did not wipe out. It also left me with sympathy for those who were the victims, not only of Nazism but of the aftermath and the reassignment of countries. It led me to look into history more to try to understand why and how it could have happened. A whole nation couldn't have all been blind or rotten? I still haven't the answer. I have kept up my interest in European affairs and political movements as a result. It reinforced my feelings about war and prejudice and I supported the Human Rights Movement and the Anti-Vietnam War Movement. When I got back I worked as a personnel director in a large Jewish hospital in Boston, where I had the opportunity to work with some of the survivors and help find employment for the Hungarian and Latvian refugees who came over later. It was very rewarding. I also found myself at odds with the church I grew up in. The congregation seemed more concerned with their own needs than with those of the people who survived Nazi captivity. I had seen the Unitarian Service Committee at work in Europe, and I changed to a local Unitarian church.

I have very mixed feelings about having war crimes trials today. One part of me says, 'It's over with. Let's remain alert and aware of it, so that it won't happen again, but let's go forward and forget it.' And the other part of me says, 'Those sons of guns! Getting away with all of this and probably living it up!' And I can understand that if I or members of my family had been subjected to what some people were subjected to, *I* sure would want vengeance. Maybe I shouldn't say that, but I would feel very strongly. I leave it to the people who were most involved.

I knew several of the guards who stood in the court-room, and they used to tell me about the remarks that were made among the defendants. One of them told me that sometimes it was very difficult, because you got to know the men, and then to go into court and hear what they did ... I guess I said to him, 'Well, you can tell your children about this when you go home,' and he said, 'I'm not sure I want to, but on the other hand, I keep saying to myself, "This is history. You're living history."'

Anna Cameron, secretary
I think my Nuremberg experience made me a much more understanding person. And it made me feel at one with the whole world. Before, I would think, 'Well, the Germans are this way, the Danes are that way, the English are that way,' but when you live, and work, and see people all the time you find out that they love their families, and they do their best for their homes and their country, and they're just like we are, in their own way. You sit in your own little town, and you think, 'Oh, *those* people out there' ... I never can think of anybody in the world as being that way any more, especially because I've had the opportunity to live in the Far East also. This world is just made up of human beings, and maybe if everyone had a chance to get around we'd lose that 'us against them' attitude, because it isn't necessary. It's so sad when you see the situation between the Palestinians and the Israelis now. They're very much alike, in many ways – very well-educated, and all they want is a homeland.

When I read about war crimes trials today, I myself think, enough of this. The war's over. Maybe I'm wrong, but then I'm not Jewish, and I haven't lost my relatives and all of my people. So I probably would have a different attitude. I'm sure that those Jewish people who lost everything that ever mattered to them want to see every last person who ever hurt their families brought to trial. This fellow Demjanjuk, how could he have lived here so long, and such a normal life? But I guess that if you don't get in trouble, and you mind your own business and don't cause any excitement, you can get away with it.

Joseph Stone, lawyer, Subsequent Proceedings

There seemed to be several people there whose whole life after that was still Nuremberg, in terms of their thinking, their giving of talks, their letters to the editor. For all of us, I think it was an important part of our lives. It was a highly unusual legal situation in which I had the opportunity to be a participant, and I'm not likely to run into that kind of situation again. I'd like to believe that it was part of history, and that it was important to history. After World War One there was some feeble attempt at war crimes trials, but the thing petered out into a fiasco. Nuremberg in the 1940s did not peter out into a fiasco. There is now a historical record. The number of documents, the number of hours, the testimony that was given, the depositions that were taken from the leaders of the German government, German military, German medical, German judicial … It's a historical record that just can't be denied, at this point, a historical record that was fairly and honestly obtained. So I feel happy, proud, pleased, that I had that opportunity.

I would like to believe that I was pretty well formed morally by the time I got over there, and I'm not aware offhand that it affected me in a moral sense. I think, and I don't say this too flippantly, that if it taught you anything it taught you that you'd better not lose a war once you're in one. Losers don't fare that well. But of course, the Germans were fortunate that it was the Americans who were trying them, because the Americans are very benign occupiers. There was an old gag there, that the British and French got all the industry and the Americans got the scenery. Bavaria was a very picturesque place, but there wasn't anything worthwhile there.

You know, victor's justice, if you analyse it, applies day to day, not just in a war situation. The State of New York is a powerful institution, which sends out – through the police and others – people to apprehend criminals, and then it tries them. That's victor's justice also. Criminals who are tried are always tried because somebody stronger than they are has gotten hold of them and has determined whether or not they met certain standards of civilized living. So from that viewpoint, the world, as a place to live, had in effect set certain standards. These are in the Kellogg-Briand Pact, that outlawed war, and the Geneva Pact. Murder is murder, no matter how you perform it. Every civilized country has some kind of justice that applies to a person who commits murder, or robbery, which is what the Aryanization programme of the Nazis was. The things they were being tried for were essentially crimes that every civilized nation has recognized, and they either knew or should have known that somewhere along the line, maybe they'd have to answer for them to those people who were strong enough to apprehend them in the name of civilized practices. So I don't buy this victor's justice thing – it's a superficial way of looking at it.

Waging aggressive war was something that was implicitly outlawed by the Kellogg-Briand Pact, which stated that war should not be resorted to as a vehicle for settling international disputes. I suppose that there was nothing known as crimes against humanity; maybe they were pushing it, along those lines. But then, if they *didn't* try these people, what was the alternative? Was it just to let them go scot free, and never be tried? I suppose any civilized person would have to conclude that war is an abomination. Certainly the poor youngsters who fight the wars that the older people agree ought to be fought ... it can't very well be defended as a concept. It's unfortunate that we have in the world people like Hitler, who leave you no alternative but to either wage war or not survive. And the law of survival is number one. So you get involved in this type of activity, and hopefully Nuremberg becomes another step towards building up some kind of an international awareness and agreement, a movement towards ultimate peace, because the world of law has been in some way helpfully developed another step forward. I think it was.

The trials after World War One fell by the wayside; this was a more highly developed procedure, that finally worked. The lawyers on the staff at the Subsequent Trials were very well-meaning, hard-working, dedi-cated. I don't have the feeling that they were vindictive. I don't know what else you can expect. If you criticize Nuremberg, you've got to come up with something positive. What was the alternative? What could have been done better? At least there are people in this world today who ought to be aware that, if they're going to get involved in activities of this kind, maybe some day they're going to have to pay the piper. And to that extent I think it was a very positive thing. There are also people already who are claiming that these Nazi abominations never occurred, that the Holocaust is a myth engendered by Zionist activists, etcetera. How do you fight people like that? How do you move on, unless you have some kind of a step like Nuremberg? To me, Nuremberg said primarily that people in responsible positions are going to be responsible for their activities, and if they're taking actions that are criminal under any civilized concept then they're going to have to pay for it.

With regard to war criminals today, I believe that they ought to go after them. I think it's appropriate. At this point, most of them are on the threshold of dying, but at least it has a value of keeping an awareness of what went on, and gives the lie to these people who are claiming that it's all a myth. Also, there's no reason why they should have had a good life for the rest of their lives afterward. I haven't attended any of those trials, so I don't know how fair they are, and a lot of time has passed, so it's conceivable that some mistakes have been made. On the other hand it's equally conceivable that every one of them has been properly tried and convicted. I see no reason why these people should just go scot free and everybody forget it. It's just something that the world shouldn't forget. Demjanjuk swears that they've got the wrong man, but apparently a lot of people identified him. If you simply accepted his word because he swears he's not the man, there'd be very few criminals being disciplined. It's hard, any criminal trial is hard, if you're a relatively soft-hearted person. But the world was faced with a situation it had never faced before. I don't say there had never been atrocities in wars, going back, but by and large, my feeling is that if a guy was involved in something like that he ought to be tried. That leaves open the question of how you convict. The American government apparently was sloppy in how it handled all of these Nazis – a lot of them slipped through, and got to South America. So from that viewpoint a lot of them got away with it. Unfortunately I don't know what you can do about them. I guess we have to play it out, the whole business. We're getting towards the end – another ten years at the most, and almost everybody who was primarily involved will be gone. And then hopefully the world will try to remember, but the world's memory is kind of short, I suspect. Maybe books like this are important ... I don't know.

Paul Graven, prison guard officer
It was a very good duty, you might say. I learned a lot of things, and met interesting people. It taught me a lot about getting along with people. It taught me about what is and isn't important. It taught me how bad the war really was. A lot of people in the military, on both sides, hadn't known much about the concentration camps. Having been in the service, having been shot at and having shot at them, I was glad to see the trial come about, although there were some legal entities that I did not understand. And I'd seen Buchenwald and Dachau, after only three or four months in combat, so I was quite bitter about the whole thing. I was very glad they were bringing the defendants to trial, and I think it was a good idea and that legally they justified what they did. Of course, in any military operation you are taking commands from the one above you, and they brought it out in the trial that these were the leaders, the ones giving the commands and responsible for it all. So I think it was justified. With the hangings ... you felt kind of sorry that they had to come to that end, but on the whole I think they deserved what they got, and I still think that. And if they find any more, I think they should bring them to trial.

Yvette Wilberforce, visitor
I thought the trial was extremely well conducted. Top people, wise people, with no axe to grind. They let some of them go who were really, in effect, murderers. There is no doubt in my mind that the Tribunal was very justly set and did the right thing. To go on pursuing them now, as they are doing in various countries in the world, seems to be more a question of vengeance, but this was not vengeance – this was very necessary punishment, and the disposal of *them*, because they couldn't be let loose.

Alfred Steer, administrative head, language division
I have said that this was a dirty job: one of the reasons that I had reservations about it was because there were reservations on the legal side. Objections were made that it was *ex post facto* law, and victors' justice, and we in Nuremberg used to ask ourselves to what extent these objections were justified. We finally worked out among ourselves this rationale: to be sure, it was *ex post facto* law, in other words there had been no international body which had passed a law before the war that it

was illegal to plot a war, and so on. But every legal system that ever existed in the world, from ancient times down to modern, is constantly updating its definition of a crime by precedent, and this is a sort of incremental way of doing *ex post facto* law. It can be justified from that point of view. And also, the victors sitting in judgement over the vanquished of course stinks, but on the other hand, if we, the Allies, did not judge this incredible series of crimes, who would? Not their own government, certainly. The only government that existed in Germany – and this was true for several years thereafter – was the Allied military government. There wasn't any German government – it had completely collapsed. Therefore we felt we had justification from that point of view also.

Then we had another view which we thought was a partial answer, namely that the crimes were so unparalleled that something had to be done, and done now, while the evidence was still available and people's memories were still reasonably current. I don't think the world was ready then for that kind of attitude; I don't think it was widely accepted. When I finally came home I was asked to make a number of speeches on this sort of thing, and I found over and over again that people were not really quite willing to accept this. But I think it was good, and I have noticed several results of the Nuremberg Trial, the most striking one being that the principle is now firmly established on the US side, and I think in many other countries as well, that an army officer is *not* required blindly to obey the orders of his superior regardless – he has a personal responsibility to check that it is a proper order, and if it isn't he is required, by moral and actual law, to disobey that order. Now that came out in Nuremberg quite clearly. The SS and the SA and all those criminal organizations invariably used the defence, 'I'm not at fault, I was ordered to do it.'

Was it a fair trial? We asked ourselves that at the end, before the actual verdict came out, and we agreed among ourselves that, if there was anything wrong with the verdict about to come out, we were afraid it would be too lenient. These defendants had shown without any question of a doubt that they were guilty of all possible crimes, and that whatever they got they richly deserved. And when the actual verdicts came out we felt they were a little on the lenient side – there should have been a few more executed.

Hitler gave an order that the commandos who had been captured in the Dieppe raid – they were mostly Canadians – were to be executed. And Jodl had transferred that order over his own signature. This constituted documentary proof of his guilt, and he accepted it. I had to admire him. I remember when I was serving in the Pacific, we were trying to take a mountain which had a lot of caves, and the Japanese troops kept sending women and children out of the caves, and when the Americans came out to take them prisoner the Japanese would open fire from their hiding-places. The Americans radioed the message back to headquarters, 'We don't want to kill women and children but what shall we do?' No answer.

They sent this message four times, and finally the answer came through, 'Save Marine lives.' Nobody at headquarters was going to go on record, you see, as giving these orders, but there was no question what the Marines had to do. That's the heat of battle. It's something else. But to take a man prisoner, so that he's at your mercy, march him off to a camp and then some days later execute him – that's murder.

The trial was a landmark in my life, most emphatically. We have something here in western Europe and the United States which is absolutely *einmalig*, a one-time thing, namely Western civilization. What we had in the Nazi experience was an abnormality, an excrescence on the body of Western civilization, looked at as a whole over time. It was like a cancer. What World War Two meant to me, still means to me, was this incredible effort, which involved the whole world and in which the British of course played a brilliant role, to underline the fact that this way – the Nazi way, the fascist way – Western civilization must not go. This way lies destruction and death; this is lethal, this is mortal. And we risked our lives to prove that and to stop it, and we eventually did. Therefore what Nuremberg means to me, and meant to me really from the very beginning, was that I was a part of writing the final verdict, crossing the t's and dotting the i's, writing a final record which hopefully following generations will be wise enough to accept and understand. It's always been a great satisfaction to me. But career-wise, no: it was a blind alley, a detour. I would have been much better off if I'd got out as soon as possible, come back and got a job. When I came back at the beginning of 1947, everybody was already home and all the jobs were full. I decided to go back into the academic world, and I found to my annoyance that after being gone seven years you can't pick up. I had to go back to the beginning and start all over again. But the satisfaction of having been involved in this unparalleled effort outweighs, and helps me forget, those dirty, disagreeable, shameful aspects of it.

I think we should pursue war criminals today. My feeling is, if they haven't been found already, yes, definitely. There's a statute of limitation on everything except murder. This Demjanjuk that the Israelis recently tried – if that *is* the man that they say he is, fine. But I'm kind of doubtful; it seems to me it's been an awful long time, and they should have done this long ago. I'm somewhat doubtful as to whether it isn't emotional semi-hysteria in Israel rather than provable historical and legal fact. But I don't know. As for Waldheim, I'm perfectly certain that there were many men in his position, who compromised their morals and character, and half-way co-operated with the Nazis. And then when the war was over they said, 'Oh no, I had nothing to do with it.' Was Waldheim one? I don't know. I wouldn't be at all surprised.

At Nuremberg we were fascinated by what was taking place in the court-room. We tried to escape from it, but we couldn't help discussing it. In the bar in the evening, we kept coming back to things in Nazi Germany. We said it couldn't happen to us. But a few days after I got back to Philadelphia, I was sitting in the subway looking at the faces on the other side of the carriage, and it suddenly hit me like a ton of bricks that there was no lack of faces as brutal, as depraved, as those in the dock at Nuremberg. In Nazi Germany the dregs of society were allowed to assume power. But every society has its dregs, and if we let them take over we will be paid in the same coin. It was a great shock to me, and a humbling realization. It sums it up for me. I'm deathly afraid of charismatic leaders, such as Hitler, and Reagan, and particularly if those leaders use the dregs of society, as Hitler did with the SA, the SS and the Gestapo, as political tools to gain or maintain power.

Annabel Stover, secretary

It was all a very marvellous experience that I think I was more than lucky to have had. I come from a very small town in the mid-west, in North Dakota, and to have had the opportunity to have these experiences ... I just feel like I was in the right spot at the right time. I thought it was the right thing to do, and I still feel that way. But I think that nowadays the time to try people has passed, and we should just forget about them. I think that if they have lived an ordinary kind of exemplary life since that period in their lives, then we should let bygones be bygones. I don't see any reason to continue. They're old people now, in their seventies or eighties I'm sure. I thought it was so ridiculous that they kept Hess in Spandau prison all those many years. It was a most ridiculous thing, but because the Russians wouldn't permit us to let him go, we had to keep him there. Think of all the money that it cost, all those years.

Mary Burns, secretary

I suspect it played a big role in my life. I was devoted to Justice Jackson, as an individual and for the way he handled the trial. I would say he was one of the people whom I've known in my life whom I admire the most, professionally and as a human being. So it played a big role because of that, but also because of the experience of living in Germany, seeing Germany. England probably remains my favourite place, for other reasons, but to have done this and been a part of it at that young age ... it played a very big role. When I went back to Minnesota I was not happy there, and I think that probably the answer to that was that experience. I realized that it was not satisfying me at all. I think that had an awful lot to do with being in Nuremberg, the people I met, the friends I made.

I always felt that it was right to hold the trial, and I always wished that I had more legal education, or understanding of people who have made objections to that trial. Technically I wouldn't have been able to answer the question of whether it was right or wrong; in my mind it was all right, and still is. I know that with advancing age you get stuck with your ideas, but I suspect that some scholar couldn't change my mind now. I felt it was right, and I felt it was well done. In today's world, with all the bureaucracy, you would *never* get a trial set up by four countries, of a fifth country, and the recruitment of all these very learned people to come in, and accomplish this, and announce their decision, in a year. Today it would go on for ten years over the technicality of where to put the chairs. I think it's marvellous, because I'm pretty disgusted with life today.

I think that Demjanjuk is kind of a sad case. Here's an old man, dying, he's spent forty years in this country, living a modest life and working. Unfortunately I'm afraid I don't think that's right, I really don't. Looking for Barbie and some of the others, probably it's all right, but in the long run I think there are a lot of other problems that need attention. I think that's more important than going back, and going back. I have some rather strong feelings, you see: I spent some time in the Lebanon.

Eddie Worth, photographer

I think the whole idea of having the trial was to show the world that we weren't the same as them, the Nazis. They used to take people out and shoot them, without a fair trial, but we gave these fellows ten months of fair trial, and after that they had no excuse whatsoever if they were strung up. I think we should have had a trial, and I'm very pleased that we did. With every passing day, as this evidence came out, I was more convinced that the world should know about it. If they'd shot the people straight off, nobody would have known.

With trials today, the thing that annoys me is why they didn't sort them out earlier, especially the doctors who were in the concentration camps. They knew about them, but they did nothing about them at the end of the war. Indeed, some were invited to America – scientists, too. If things had been the other way round, those blokes would have been against the wall.

It was a milestone in my life. I wouldn't have missed it for all the tea in China. And hearing the hard luck stories of the defendants, about how they were poor persecuted Germans, was hilarious. I had a wonderful time.

Roger Barrett, officer in charge of documents

One of the most rewarding parts of the experience, for me, was to form firm and lasting friendships with a great many lawyers from all parts of the United States and from all kinds of backgrounds, which broadened my perspective about the practice of law and about our country, and about people, in a way which was most fortuitous for me. Afterwards Justice Jackson asked his son Bill and me to write the eight-volume history of the trial for the State and War Departments and the OSS, which was a great experience. But after I got back into private practice, except for social contact with those people I sort of lost touch with them. We did have two big reunions in Washington, one before Justice Jackson died and one five or six years ago. And a number of us keep in touch. But we don't think very often about the trial. When there are parallels in contemporary living, we think about it, and it comes back in strange ways. My wife was one of the founders, and I'm senior officer, of our contemporary art museum here in Chicago, and a week ago we opened the first American showing of the French artist Boltanski, one of the most remarkable artists in the world today, the underlying motivation for whose art is the Holocaust. There are no direct references to it, no pictures of it, but it's the philosophical underpinning for his art. To walk through that art exhibit, and then to talk to him about his feelings – he was a Polish Jew in France – brought back Nuremberg, and it happens periodically with things I read or people I meet, but unfortunately, or fortunately, those things go out of your mind.

In spite of the arguments that I read and used to hear and used to participate in, about *ex post facto* law and the legality of the trial, and the technical nuances, most of the defendants, in my opinion, could have been convicted on uncontroverted evidence in our local criminal court in Illinois, for murder – their complicity was so great. There were one or two who weren't that directly involved with orders to kill people. Hess is one who comes to mind. I'm not saying he's innocent, but I don't believe Hess could have been convicted for murder in county Illinois. Before the judgment was rendered, those of us who worked on the trial made our own bets on who was going to be convicted and acquitted. We knew generally who should be and who shouldn't be, and we agreed with their decisions.

The indictments had several counts, and the count that is most susceptible of this charge is the waging of aggressive war. The argument was that there had never been enacted law making the waging of aggressive war a crime, and to prosecute people afterwards was an *ex post facto* conviction. There were two answers to that: one is that there were pre-existing treaties between the countries from which you can spell out a principle of written, established positive law. That's fully documented in the literature about the trial, and you can argue both sides of that. And the second is contained in an interesting position that Justice Jackson took, which was that the common law grows by deciding individual cases. We'll assume that at one time a certain kind of conduct was not a violation of law; and then it came before a court and the court decided that it *was* a violation of law. By incorporating natural law into case law, that's the way case law grows, and the American and British systems are based on cases. Every time a new principle of law is applied in our cases here, you could make the charge that it's a new principle and it's never been adopted by a court before. Jackson's view was that at some time this is a crime, and why not start now, and this is a development of the common law. I have a hard time with the lawyers in my office, defending the count on aggressive war from a technical point of view, but as I say, since most of the defendants would have received the same punishment under other counts it doesn't bother me. And many of the people who participated in the trial will defend all of the counts on the basis of pre-existing written treaties which they can piece together. I haven't engaged in that scholarship and I don't take a position on it.

If the world order had turned out the way we thought it was going to at that time, and if the Russians had acted the way we assumed they would – as a country, not at the trial – this would have been a remarkable stepping-stone to the development of a world order because it provided for individual responsibility for violation of international principles. In other words, if a citizen of one country can be prosecuted by outside sovereignties for what he does, that's a necessary stepping-stone to having a world order. And we were very optimistic about other international organizations which could be developed as a result of this and some of the other principles of the trial. As the world turned out, the legal significance to date has not been great. I suppose you primarily read, hear or think about it in connection with other instances of atrocities in subsequent conflicts. I think the most significant result of the trial was the documenting of what was done for all time, and I think it was one of the most significant events of the century, probably. We have professors in Illinois who stoutly maintain that these things didn't happen, and a hundred years from now there will probably be even more people who believe they didn't happen. But the record is there, and there's never going to be any question. I think that's the most significant consequence of the trial.

Working at the trial gave me the self-confidence in my profession to deal with brilliant lawyers from around the world. And it completely changed my perspective. I had never spent much time outside of an area between Chicago, Illinois and a suburb twenty miles away where I was born and where I still live now, and when I first got to London to work on the case I knew pitifully little about the Nazis or what had been going on, other than the part of the war I'd been fighting. I had been to the Olympics in 1936 and seen Hitler, and I had mountain-climbed in Austria; my mother was born in Austria. I had seen good sides of the Nazis, who made the trains run, but I really hadn't thought about the serious problems of the world. Really, I probably would have been, conceptually and in most ways, an isolationist for the rest of my life. And having had this exposure, I have a feeling of responsibility for what happens, or for learning about and trying to do what I can about what happens in other parts of the world, other than my own little corner.

Bernard Meltzer, lawyer
The trial has had its detractors; it had detractors at the time. The novelty of the trial was, of course, the formulation of the crime of aggressive war, and that formulation prompted the *ex post facto* charge, that the Charter was legislation after the event, and so on. And there are answers to that charge, although I don't know that they're satisfactory. Incidentally, some people who at first were moved by that criticism subsequently changed their minds. The first answer is that the condemnation of retroactive legislation was designed to avoid the risk that conduct that was not morally culpable at the time it took place should retroactively be condemned. The trial did not involve that risk. Given all the strictures about aggressive war, the Kellogg-Briand Pact and related documents, and given the foreseeable consequences of war with modern weapons, one could scarcely say that those who started an aggressive war were unaware of the immorality of their conduct. The other answer – and this

is one of the answers that Jackson gave in his opening statement, I believe
– is that the international legal system, to the extent that we have one, is a
primitive one: it's like the old common law system. There's no super-
legislature; it grows by embracing the changed and changing values and
sentiments of a community. And given the Kellogg-Briand Pact and
related declarations, a condemnation of aggressive war reflected what
were then the prevailing mores of a community. Now obviously we could
argue about that premise. Beyond that, there's another answer that I
think the French gave, and that is that in the old days war was a
justification for what would otherwise be violations of the domestic law
against murder, so that if a German soldier killed a French one it was not
murder, because war was a justifiable exercise; but after the Kellogg-
Briand Pact one could scarcely say that aggressive war was a justifiable
exercise. And finally, as Jackson said, aggressive war was, of course, the
incubator of violation of the *rules* of war and the escalating cruelties and
atrocities of modern warfare. There's nothing novel about the rules of
war; and to condemn a violation of the rules of war while leaving the
matrix, the source, of the evil untouched was a futility.

Now there are all kinds of problems. One problem is that while it was
easy to determine that the Germans had been guilty of aggression, the
question of when war is aggressive is an incredibly difficult one, and as far
as I know no definition has been formulated although there have been
various attempts. But the final difficulty of Nuremberg is of course that
only the victor can apply the law; the victor becomes the master of truth
as well as of those he defeated. Nuremberg's formulation of aggressive
war as an international crime did not invent that inequality. Long before
Nuremberg, the victor applied a unilateral standard, for example, in
dealing with traditional war crimes, violations of the Geneva Conven-
tions. None the less, the final irony of Nuremberg is that the Russians,
because they were the victors, notwithstanding their aggression in
Poland, could hold the Germans accountable for aggressive war.

There are other aspects of the *ex post facto* problem that the Tribunal
was able to avoid by redefining crimes against humanity. When crimes
against humanity were first defined, I think people had in mind what
symbolized the Nazi regime, and that is the concentration camps and the
persecution, degradation and murder of Jews, but the Tribunal recognized the jurisprudential problems involved in holding pre-war acts
against German citizens in Germany to be international crimes. It
bypassed those problems by folding acts alleged to be crimes against
humanity into 'war crimes', offences against the laws of war, or into the
crime of waging aggressive war.

A basic strategic decision was made that the trials should be essentially
documentary, because German witnesses might be unreliable, for several
reasons: they might be viewed as currying favour with the occupying
authorities, or they might try to upset the apple-cart and settle scores by
embarrassing the victors. So although there *was* oral testimony, it was
generally testimony that authenticated a document or explained a

document. The trial was quite long without getting involved in individual instances: if we had brought in victims, there would have been the question of their reliability, the question of when you cut it off, the question of rebuttal, and so on and so on – these were difficulties that were avoided. Obviously, except for documents such as the 'Todesbücher' the use of documents illustrating general patterns rather than individual instances deprived the judges and the world audience of some of the flesh-and-blood experience of victims, and that was a cost that people were aware of. It was a cost that seemed worth absorbing, because even on an abstract basis the story told and preserved by the trial was a very powerful one – we had films of the people who were liberated from the concentration camps, and you could see that they were basically bones, half-starved, and so on. There was enough in the trial, I think, to grab the emotions of the spectators, and to record for history the savagery and the inhumanity of the Nazi regime.

I think the Russian participation in the trial was a great moral and political victory for the Russians, because after all they had been guilty of aggression in Poland, not to speak of their having unleashed the war through the Russo-German Pact of 1939. But after Poland, *and* Finland, to be represented in the tribunal was a great victory for them. In addition, I think they may have seen another political dividend, and that is that in a closed society such as Russia, every war that the Russians might start could be presented to their people as a defensive war rather than a war of aggression, whereas democracies, or open societies, have a much more limited capacity to bamboozle their people. I was conscious of that difference at the time of Suez, with the British irresolution there, as well as at the time of the Bay of Pigs. Now whether the symbol of Nuremberg had any restraining effect on those two occasions I don't know; they seemed to me to have involved incredibly bad planning. Maybe there was a kind of reservation about the use of force that might have been linked in some way to the idea of Nuremberg.

I'm not an expert on Russian procedure, but my recollection is that the Russians tend to put all of their evidence in the indictment, and in cases with any political overtones the indictment is equivalent to a conviction. The American and presumably the British situation is quite different, so that the Russians were puzzled by that aspect of procedure. Because the Russians tend to have all their evidence collected and digested before the trial, cross-examination was a mystery to them. Comparing their and the British–American use of it illustrates the difference between using a sledgehammer, which was the Russians' technique, and using a scalpel, which was Sir David Maxwell-Fyfe's technique! In fact the French weren't very good at cross-examination either. The Americans and the British were used to it, and with some variations in skill, both staffs used it with considerable effect. My recollection is that the French and the Russians were playing a game that was new to them, the French because in their trials the judge does much more of the work, and the Russians because they thought that by the time you got to the trial stage it should be just a matter of determining sentences. And even that ... I think the Russians thought that all the Nuremberg defendants should have been executed.

One of the questions that confronted the people deciding whether to have a trial was what the alternative was. The people of eastern Europe were anxious to claw, to punish, to torment the Nazis, and one of them said to me, 'Hanging is too good. Their bodies should be chopped up slowly and gradually.' I can't prove this, but I think the trial served as a kind of lightning-rod, a catharsis, that saved a lot of bloodletting, some of which, I'm sure, would have victimized the wrong people. It was a containment. I don't know whether people thought of it that way originally, but I think that was one of the consequences of it. And the question is, what to do with these people? We could have lined them up and shot them, in part because of their naked aggression. That course would not have avoided the *ex post facto* charge, incidentally. More important, we would have made mistakes, and now people, instead of talking about *ex post facto*, would be talking about a denial of due process and lynch law.

What effect the holding of the trial might have on the conduct of future leaders in a war situation, it is very difficult to say. In the context of Nuremberg, I think the more important consideration was unconditional surrender. It's enormously difficult to speculate about motives there. I remember when I was up in Berchtesgaden, I thought of Hitler's having that place, and command of Germany, and a good chunk of Czechoslovakia, and I said, 'Well, why wasn't all that *enough* for this madman?' I wondered also how the Germans could have given him political power and tolerated his abominable abuses of it. Since *I* did not understand the motivations for the kind of outrages that he committed and Germany condoned, it's very hard for me to say, 'Well, let us assume that Hitler and his henchmen are persons with rational expectations, and judge the impact of the possibility of a war crimes trial on their holding out to the death.' The prospect of war crimes trials was known to the Japanese when they surrendered, and they had a kamikaze tradition. So it's very hard to tell. None the less one would expect that the possibility of trials *might* increase resistance; on the other hand, if – either symbolically, or because of the fear of losing a war – the trials had a deterrent effect, then we might not have the war in the first place. So I suppose that the problem is essentially no different from the problem of capital punishment. If someone knows that if he's caught he's going to be executed, and if he cares about life – after defeat – he might resist; on the other hand, if, as some people – not without difficulties – argue, capital punishment has a deterrent effect, then murders might be avoided in the first place. So it's very tricky to know which factor would preponderate in a given situation.

As for the question of the trial's effect on international conduct, it may have restrained other conflicts, or generated irresolution, though I'm not saying irresolution is all to the good. Some recent conflicts have the attributes of civil wars. I doubt that any of the architects of the Nuremberg Trial thought that it would exorcize war – though I've never talked to them about it, my hunch is that they thought that in some ways the idea of Nuremberg, the condemnation of aggressive war, would enter the culture and affect the conduct of some communities, at least at the margin. But obviously compliance has not exactly been perfect; whether we would have had *more* wars otherwise is an interesting but unanswerable question. I think that if, as time goes on, there are all sorts of wars without any tribunal or any kind of international condemnation, you would expect the force of Nuremberg to diminish. None the less, for whatever reasons – and I think Nuremberg is *not* a major reason; I think the nuclear deterrent is more important – we've avoided a really great war for a much longer period than we did after World War One.

I am very troubled by the pursuit of war criminals today, for some of the reasons I've already mentioned. I think that when you have events that take place over continents, the problems of proof are enormously difficult even if the trials take place quickly. And now, after forty to almost fifty years, I am troubled by problems of identification, problems of the kind that are linked to the notion of repose, of closing the books – the statute of limitation. However, one has to recognize that if one's entire family had been destroyed in the Holocaust, or if one thought that we had tracked down an individual whose complicity and barbarities personified a system of unsurpassed evil and horror, one might feel differently. Such feelings are not necessarily limited to those whose family and friends were exterminated. Others also might feel that the crimes of Nazism and its executioners were so horrible that there should be not only relentless investigations but also relentless prosecution without a statute of limitation. That is not my own view of it, but I can understand how others steadfastly hold to it.

With Kurt Waldheim, the difficulties are compounded – not only by his past, but by his present position. He lied about his past because it was connected with atrocities that should never have occurred. His lies and what they brought him may be more important than his wartime complicity as a junior officer. As I put it in a piece I wrote in 1947, we should, I believe, draw a distinction between privates, sergeants and lieutenants on the one hand, and the top echelons, the master architects of a system – the Hitlers, the Goerings – on the other. But Waldheim's lies helped him get the secretary-generalship of the UN, which in the end had the same fundamental purpose as the condemnation of the crime of aggressive war at Nuremberg, so there's a terrible irony at work in Waldheim's case.

It's awfully hard to know how various accidents of time and place shape up as being important influences in your life. I made lots of good friends there, and Nuremberg was an exciting experience – it called into play all kinds of skills and arts that lawyers try to develop. It involved one in the legal and moral dilemmas arising from the winding up of one of the greatest, if not the greatest, moral tragedies that our history has had to confront. It pushed one into thinking about the nature of law, standards of personal responsibility and the prerequisites for a legal system; it encouraged people to think about how primitive and fragile our institutions of international law were, and still are, and how they might be strengthened. In a variety of ways it thus helped, as Felix Frankfurter put it, to fertilize one's thinking about large issues in law. Beyond that, I don't know whether the kinds of issues I dealt with at Nuremberg – and at the State Department, before I left for the service – made me rethink the idea of being a practising lawyer; at least it made me hospitable to the idea of having a shot at being a law teacher, which had never been on my agenda. But *if* Nuremberg had any influence on that choice, then in that sense, at least, it helped shape the way I spent virtually the rest of my professional life, in a career that I found quite congenial. I suppose Nuremberg also reminded me of how difficult it is to believe and grasp crimes that are directed not at particular individuals but at millions of people. In a way it's almost easier to understand a single murder, or ten murders, than the murder of millions.

I was pretty sure of how I felt about the Nazis before I was involved in the trial – I grew up listening to Hitler's fulminations on the radio, and I saw and heard some American proponents of fascism and bigotry when I was an adolescent. Father Coughlin, a priest up in Detroit, was sounding such themes on the radio. There were domestic hate groups, who mimicked the Nazis in dress as well as in 'ideology'. Beyond that, I suppose I might have felt a special outrage because I'm Jewish, although I didn't see any difference based on religion in the reaction to the evidence or to professional commitments at Nuremberg. In fact, the prosecution found something called 'Hitler's Last Will', which doled out offices to those of his immediate entourage, and it fell to my group to make a recommendation about offering that piece of paper into evidence. Our group said no: we didn't have a sufficient basis for validating the genuineness of the so-called will. If passion had distorted judgement, we might have said, 'Well, this would be a good way of getting the people to whom the will had allotted good jobs. Let the court worry about its authenticity.' So that's one decision that was quite cool and professional, and the same thing was true of other things such as the decision as to who should prosecute Schacht. I was quite conscious of the need to subordinate one's personal predilections to the professional job that had to be done. I suppose that the sort of evidence I was dealing with might have brought some kind of intensification to what I felt. You have to remember that with the concentration camp atrocities, the Holocaust, the evidence dribbled out, and *I* can't pinpoint the time, before I got to Nuremberg, when I realized the enormity of the Nazi savagery. I have no doubt that as I saw the photos of the victims, as I talked to some of them and immersed myself in this case, there was some intensification of the repugnance I felt for the Nazi system and the defendants who had leadership roles in it.

Ron Chapman, clerk

I think, having seen some of the people who came out of the concentration camps, living through the war and hearing about all these happenings ... I think *some* people felt that, although they were put on trial and it lasted a year, they were treated fairly leniently, considering the indictments against them, crimes against humanity. Shooting prisoners-of-war, and things like that, were so repulsive, that some people felt – I won't say *I* felt – that they should just have been stood up against a wall and shot, or hung, rather than spend all this money on a twelve-month trial. As for people being tried today, I think maybe they should be tried for what they did, but I should be very reluctant to say what I felt the sentence should be now. I think it's mainly Israel, the Jewish nation, that still feels that they have a right to try anybody who was actually involved in the deaths of thousands of people. I can understand that.

Going into the army at seventeen and a half, I was really – I suppose, looking back – very young. And I do feel that at that age I looked on it as an adventure more than as a necessity of war. At that age, to dodge the doodlebugs in London after a night out on the town was more of a game than thinking about the actual results. It's very difficult to explain, but looking back now, I think that if the war had happened at this time in my life, I would have very different feelings from what I had then. It was such a different way of life, an exciting way of life, after being brought up in quite a good, stern way by my parents. I attended church sometimes six times on a Sunday: I would go to eight o'clock communion, ten o'clock Sunday school, eleven o'clock matins, three o'clock afternoon bible class, six-thirty in the evening evensong, and very often a Christian Venture Service that they held at eight o'clock. My mother was very church-going, my brother was a church organist, and I was brought up fairly strictly. And I think it was leaving home, and being able to do more or less what you wanted in the evenings ... And going overseas – it's very difficult to explain, but I think the average British soldier behaved very differently overseas from the way he did at home; in fact, I would say that a lot of them behaved worse overseas than they did at home. Going to France, and never having been abroad in my life, it was a big adventure and excitement, the different way of life. Like landing in Normandy in the province of Calvados, and tasting calvados on my second night in France, at seventeen years three quarters. It was something I'd never have been allowed to do in England. There was nobody to say, 'You mustn't do this, you mustn't taste calvados, you mustn't go out with loose girls,' and that sort of thing. You had a sort of freedom, and I suppose you could say you let your hair down and did lots of things that you would never have done back home, even in the army back home. You see, a lot of people did make a fuss of you when you arrived there. In France, Belgium and Holland you were the liberators, and in Germany, although you were the conquerors, there was always somebody willing to take you in and give you a meal. There's a different feeling, when you get overseas and out of your own environment. There are different customs that you want to try:

champagne, Paris, the night-life. It came back very quickly, the night-life in Paris – not like it is now, but things suddenly appeared, the night-clubs opened, the late shows opened, and it was soon Paris again. To go in there at eighteen was quite an eye-opener, I can assure you! In our unit there were about four of us of eighteen or so, and most of the other chaps were twenty-five or twenty-six and had served in the First or Eighth Army in the Middle East, and were really mature. And we wanted to behave like them, so we went out with them and behaved above our age, really. I remember getting letters from my mother telling me what not to do, but it was too late – I'd already done it! This is what happened, because you were away from home, you were in the army, you felt grown up. And you grew up quick.

It was an anti-climax, coming home from the war. We wanted to come home, after four years, but after we'd been home six months we wondered if we *really* wanted to be home. I think what they should have done was given us six or even twelve months' leave and then said, 'If you want to come back, come back,' instead of demobilization and then finish, or else having to sign up for seven or twelve years. We did have our hard times, sleeping under lorries and being very cold and hungry. But I think the good times outweighed the bad times, and when you look back you always think of the good times you had with your mates in the army. You laugh about the bad times, although they weren't laughable at the time. Looking back I think you can say, 'We had an experience at our age which was denied to a lot of other people.'

Brady Bryson, lawyer

The Schacht case, on which I worked, was the subject of some controversy. I shared the view that it would have been definitely wrong to have simply dismissed the case, as Murray Gurfein might have done. I really didn't know his entire position on the question, although he may have thought the evidence was weak. If so, I don't know the criteria he was judging the evidence against. And of course, I also didn't experience the later developments in that case, and it is my recollection that the time did come when Schacht testified, and was examined by defence counsel and cross-examined by someone on the American staff. So I can't judge the whole record, since I didn't participate in or see the whole record. At the time I left, I felt it was certainly worth trying. I felt there was a reasonable basis, from what I could see, for the court to conclude that Schacht in fact was an active participant in the determination to overrun Europe and capture the territories that the Germans felt, ethnically or economically, were a proper part of their world; that this was going to be done by military force – it was being prepared for and would at some time be done; and that he supported it until the time he ceased to be active. Now this doesn't say that he knew precisely that the actual sequence of events would be unleashed at the moment it was, or that he could even foresee whether and when it would happen. But I felt that he was in favour of it, and that he was doing what he could to make the necessary preparations. Now that's a bit like saying that, if four people conspire to commit a crime, but they haven't decided just what bank they're going to rob or when they're going to rob it, yet they know they're going to rob a bank and they're doing all those things they need to do – gathering information, assembling tools, collecting pistols and disguises – if they are active in all that, but they haven't firmed their plan up to the point of being ready for execution, and then one of them drops out, then at that point the other three are in control, and they attempt the robbery of a bank, and they're apprehended, should the other one who had been a member of the group up to a point be considered a criminal? I'm not enough of a criminal lawyer – because that really wasn't my field – to know whether at that point you have four criminals or three criminals. I rather think you have four. Perhaps the one who dropped out would be charged with a lesser crime: probably being an accomplice, or an accessory before the fact, as the phrase goes in American law. He still would have to share the guilt, in a lesser way, and would be a criminal.

I think that analysis is not unrealistic, applied to Schacht; it depends on how much you believe his defence. And of course his defence was that, as soon as he realized where the Nazis were going, he discreetly went in the other direction and tried to get out of it all, that he was ultimately out of any governmental position of importance before the war started in 1939, and that he remained merely a minister without portfolio until his resignation from that in the early forties. He claimed that, while he had that portfolio, it was a mere formality: he wasn't active. It was his way of easing himself out without an open break.

My analysis of the evidence I saw was that a rather bitter rivalry had developed between Goering and Schacht. As I recall, there was evidence that Goering wasn't satisfied with the amount of finance that Schacht was assembling for rearmament, and that it was Schacht's responsibility to provide those funds from the resources of the German financial system. He was very ingenious in this – he really knew his finance, including his international trade, he knew his economics, he knew his banking. He is credited with having done a remarkable job of providing funds. Germany was pretty destitute, nevertheless he came up with the money to do a great deal for the German military, in the way of buying and making equipment and getting themselves ready for serious war. But Goering, who had a large hand on the military side, where his whole interest lay, didn't feel that he was getting enough, and he was pressurizing Schacht to go further and come up with more, and Schacht was afraid of breaking the economy. He was willing to push it as far as his economist's judgement felt it could be safely pushed, but he was afraid he would really destroy the effort if he broke the economy. There was a basic policy among these conspirators to wage aggressive war, and Schacht was right at the centre of it. But he apparently was fighting Goering over the question of finance – and our evidence indicated that Goering won out, and that's why Schacht fell into disfavour, and was downgraded and demoted and gradually eased out – and this enabled him to argue that he was personally unsuccessful in heading the war off; that he was really trying to do that; that there was a limit to what he could say or do, because he knew the force of their conviction; and that he thought he might be more effective in slowing them down than in simply confronting them and saying, 'You can't do this – I'm going to expose it, I'm not going to support it.' He would simply have had his head chopped off. So he could work with the materials and dream up a defence that was not totally ridiculous.

Now, we are talking about a criminal charge. Of course, in America, the burden of proof in charging and trying a criminal is beyond a reasonable doubt. Maybe Gurfein, used to prosecutions in America operating under that rule, and knowing the very large burden that a prosecutor carries in America, because he *was* a prosecutor, sensed that this wouldn't carry water in an American court, and felt, 'What are we doing trying to convict a man that we couldn't convict under our own legal system?' He may well have had ideas like that. So it was that kind of a close case.

Schacht was acquitted in the end, but I got some interesting information later, from people who came back from Nuremberg. There were four member nations, and you needed three votes for a conviction. A tie vote would not convict. The Russians voted for conviction, the others for acquittal. Their judge filed a dissenting opinion, which I have read, and to this day I feel that it was a better-written opinion than the others. I feel it is very forceful and well put together. It argued that there was adequate evidence for a conviction, considering the seriousness of all of this, and the deep participation over a period of years by Schacht in the Hitler movement, and his close working relations with all the major leaders as the Nazi Party rose. He was a member of the party from the beginning, and had supported Hitler when he came to power. So he wasn't an economist and banker who had been asked to help the government out by arranging some financing and using his talents that way; he was a person who had been identified with Nazism from way back, and at a high level. I think the Russian opinion brings this out quite persuasively. I think that was the only dissenting opinion filed in the whole proceeding, which, if true, shows how strongly the Russians felt about the case that was made against Dr Schacht.

Now, you hear rumours. I heard rumours in America, when there were people around still talking about various aspects of Nuremberg. I can't attribute this rumour to any particular person, but it was repeated to me several times, because it was known that I'd been active in the Schacht case. What *I* heard was that Schacht had very strong banking acquaintanceships and banking friends, and had participated with them in international banking, especially in Britain and to some extent in America, although not in such a widespread way. I think Schacht knew all the major bankers in London. He came to America on at least one occasion, and I recall seeing a photograph of him on a visit to America, with President Roosevelt, side by side. He was accepted as a person of very considerable importance in Germany, and received by the President, by people in the State Department, and by bankers. Whether he had strong personal friends in the banking fraternity in America I don't really know, but I think his friends were primarily British. And I was told that they protested privately, and did what they could to try to get favourable consideration for him by the court, behind the scenes.

Now if that happened, that might be considered, at least in America, an improper kind of thing. I'm not trying to come in on that – I don't even know that it happened. Nevertheless I was told that the British were very strongly for acquitting Schacht, and that they had lined up the French to vote with them. The Americans were said to be for conviction but were very uneasy about voting on the record with the Russians and against the British and French, especially since Schacht would nevertheless be let off because of the tie vote. So the Americans joined the British and the French, and Schacht was acquitted over the strong dissent of the Russians. Perhaps the very strength of the dissent made the Americans more comfortable, for the Russian opinion puts Schacht's performance, on the record, in a light quite different from his own interpretation. Some scholars, at least, may well go with the Russians on the point. My guess is that there was some dealing about all this with banker intervention and that it was a nip-and-tuck thing, one condition of the final compromise being that the Russians would file a very detailed and forceful dissenting opinion which would go as part of the historical record against Schacht, and his banker friends would have to tolerate it. However, I don't regard Schacht's acquittal as being of great importance, because enough has happened to focus attention on what should be the responsibility of people like him, even if they do only what he said he did, which is the more vital question. I think most people would regard Schacht's case as having been a sort of grey case that doesn't amount to a significant precedent.

At least until this century American participation in major international warfare was rather limited, and we were sort of neophytes about the whole thing. We came into World War One late, the first major external war we had participated in, and we weren't in there terribly long. Even in World War Two we came in rather late, and afterwards we suddenly tried to – and did – take a big hand in world affairs, because we were very strong economically, we hadn't suffered the damage. We wound up with the military might of the moment; we had the atomic bombs, and we had a lot of other things. So suddenly we began to take a role of a global character, a geopolitical role. However, the British had done this for centuries. Their wars were fought, and won, and lost, or compromised, and at one time they were on one side, now they were France's ally, now they were France's enemy. This went on for three hundred years. The British allied themselves with everybody at one time or another. They allied themselves with Russia at times, yet they fought the Crimean War. They allied themselves with the Prussians at times, yet they fought World War One. They fought Napoleon, they fought France in North America, but they allied themselves with France in World Wars One and Two. So they knew that you live by your international network, your economic network, that is spread around the world. This was the whole heart of the British system of success, prosperity and power. And they knew that this network was supported, when required, by military strength: you had to be prepared to use whatever was needed, and on the whole, if you were British, you should always oppose the strongest power in Europe. It didn't make any difference who it was; at one time it might be this one, and then that one, and then this one again, and you guided yourselves accordingly. But afterwards, if you wanted to remain prosperous and stay in business, and continue to have influence and your commercial, financial and mercantile connections, you couldn't be too vindictive, particularly about bankers. I believe the British really viewed Schacht as a man of their own ilk. I'm not saying that he was, because there was this other side of his history which was deeply buried in the Nazi Party, in the roots of fascism. Maybe, to the British, he could persuasively say that over time fascism repelled him: 'When I came to know how evil it was, that's when you saw me put my hat on and go.' So it will always be an enigma. And I don't think it's terribly important whether he was convicted or acquitted.

Subsequently, I did not stay close to the Nuremberg episode, although I considered it a remarkably interesting and insightful experience for a person of my age and background, and for some years I kept looking back on it as really quite an adventure, as it was. But I did notice that most people who had at least a reasonably important role in the Nuremberg thing kept showing up in the newspapers, and some of them began writing magazine articles and books, or appearing at legal gatherings and talking about the subject. They made something of a little career out of Nuremberg. I began to think of them as sort of Nuremberg careerists, if you please, which I think was unfriendly and wrong. I thought they had a sense that 'This is the most important thing that ever happened or will happen to me – I'd better make the most out of it.' And they were becoming sought after, in a small way at least, and living on it. On the other hand, in those years, and for some years after, I was a *very* busy young lawyer. I had no time, really, for any of this. Maybe I didn't see it as all that important to me, where I was in life and where I was trying to go. So I put in an occasional encounter with a Nuremberg person, or I'd read something about a Nuremberg person, but I put in all the intervening years essentially losing track of the whole thing.

When I was there, I had no great philosophical convictions about the whole thing. I was there, and, as is my custom, tried to do a good job on whatever I was asked to do. It's almost a given in American law that a lawyer doesn't really identify himself with the cause. He is a professional; everybody is entitled to be represented; lawyers are needed on both sides of every controversy; and if it falls to your lot to be on one side, that's the side you work for. I suppose if I had been asked to defend Schacht, I would have done just as much for him as I tried to do against him. None of that comes out of philosophical conviction; it's just out of the notion that that's what a good lawyer does. So at that time I didn't come away thinking that the trials were of *tremendous* importance as a matter of geopolitics, international morals or public ethics. I felt that a lot of bad things had gone on in that particular war which needed to be exposed in detail, fully, and I think I was pleased and satisfied that I was a participant in an effort that made the first major use of the media to bring home to the people of the world what goes on behind the scenes in a world war – what the participants do, what their purposes are, the lengths to which they will go. A more vivid grasp of what war is, I think, I hope, proceeded from this exercise. But I don't doubt that much of that has worn off, and other generations have come and gone. Also, I guess all of us have come to know how destructive that war was. But this has been characteristic of all wars in all centuries. So the notion that this horrendous behaviour has been in any way reduced, mitigated, by that trial ... I don't think it has had any permanent effect at all.

In fact, the Americans came right back after it. They were the people, you know, who fought the big First War to end all wars, who gave off the public notion, by organizing the United Nations, that they had fought the Second War to maintain peace in the world, and who appeared to demobilize. But they really did very little: they demobilized personnel on active duty, because they didn't have any need for them, people wanted to get back to their lives, and it was expensive to keep them on duty. And they scrapped and mothballed a certain amount of surplus equipment – Liberty ships and planes and so on. But they didn't stop for one instant their feverish work on nuclear weapons. They went right on. That bomb they delivered to Hiroshima was just a rudimentary atomic bomb; and only as the result of the most immense, continued effort, the spending of a great amount of money, and the use of the brains and talent of a huge number of scientists, were they able to move on to the fusion bomb, the hydrogen bomb, and to develop the rocketry that would deliver that bomb accurately a thousand or more miles away. That's not the behaviour of a nation at peace, really, or which is dominated and motivated by a passion for peace. That displays a passion to be strong and to be ready, to move around all in the world who get in the way. Now I'm not just criticizing my own country, because I know the Russians are doing the same thing, maybe with a somewhat different motivation. They didn't emerge very strong from World War Two. They lost twenty-six million people, suffered great physical damage, rocked their economy to its foundation, and had no atomic bombs. Maybe they couldn't sleep nights if they didn't try to catch up with America. Nobody knows how many people were killed altogether in World War Two, including the Japanese who perished in the American bombings; the whole world experienced it, in one form or another. Yet everybody has rearmed to the extent of their ability to do so, and wars have gone on and on.

So we live in a very dangerous, vicious, wicked world, and this trial hasn't done anything at all to turn off the tap of human energy that nourishes war. It's still running. We're kidding ourselves if we say that the trial made the world a safer place; I don't think the world is one whit safer now than it was at the conclusion of World War Two. I think that the emergence of the Big Brain, whatever its source, among the hominids was a marvellous development. Nevertheless it was fatally flawed, because it brought together immense intellectual resources and the commitment to violence that rules much of the animal kingdom. This combination is unbeatably bad, and small efforts like the Nuremberg Trial are woefully inadequate to break it up.

John Pine, visitor

I was born in 1913, so I was brought up to a whole lot of claptrap about the origins of the First World War, and what had happened. The origins that *I* was taught were entirely different from what I now believe to have been the origins of that war. I was brought up to believe that every Belgian woman, particularly nuns – why nuns, I don't know – had her breasts cut off by the advancing hordes of German barbarians. Well, I don't believe it ever happened, and I don't believe the people who told me ever thought that it happened, or shouldn't have thought, anyway. And then there was all that nonsense, from 1916 onwards, about fighting for a country fit for heroes to return to. There was never anything done about that at all; they had no intention of putting it into practice, a country fit for heroes to live in; and I think generally the whole conduct of the war was quite pathetic, in relation to the usage of manpower. Those generals, Foch and Haig and so on, sitting back in their châteaux with their champagne, and four- and five-course dinners, and so forth, saying, 'Yes, put another ten brigades in tomorrow, and we'll see if we can advance another fifty yards,' or 'Yes, the casualties are high at the moment, but with the warmer weather coming they may be less high' – I mean, the disregard for human welfare was amazing. The First World War was a *terrible* disgrace ... how man could have done it to man, how we could have done it to ourselves, behaved like that to our own armies ...

Then, during the thirties, I *thought* I knew quite a lot about what was going on in Germany. I remember my mother saying, 'Oh well, dear, don't always be worrying about the war,' and that sort of thing. And when Czechoslovakia was occupied, I had a friend, older than myself, a man of some substance – he was a member of Lloyds – and education, and going up in the train from Gerrards Cross to Marylebone, he opened a paper and said, 'Where *is* this place Cheekoslovakia? What's it got to do with *us*?' This was 1938. I said, 'For God's sake, don't you realize what's going to happen?' And that was rather the attitude of people.

I didn't think a great deal about the trial at the time, because one took it for granted. One knew it was going to be; one had known for months and months that all these people were going to be tried for their war crimes. That was at a time when I had no idea that *I* was going to be involved in it, but it seemed the normal thing to do. What else *could* you do but try them? The alternative would have been to string them up with piano wire, as they probably would have done in Russia or Germany, or just put them up against a wall as they were caught and shoot them – finished, declared outlaw, bang! Well, what was the right thing to do? Surely if we *had* put them up against a wall, or the piano wire, should we have improved very much on the Nazi methods that we'd been spending five years in defeating? So it seemed to me the proper thing to do, and the only thing to do. And I was most impressed, myself, by what I saw of the Nuremberg Trial, and what I've heard of the lesser trials at Nuremberg, and also the workings of the military government courts, and I thought everybody, by and large, did an extremely good job of which we could be proud. In saying that, I don't see that, to have saved our self-respect, we could have done anything else than what we did do: we did the right thing. Can you imagine the Nazis having a Nuremberg Trial lasting nearly a year? Can you imagine them trying all those other people, patiently, and so forth? We did our best, and by and large I think we did a jolly good job.

I think it is entirely right to go on with war crimes trials. I mean, the question of 'going on' with them can't be going on for very much longer, because everybody's getting so old. The question of people like Barbie ... what else *can* you do but bring him to justice? What *is* justice? It's too difficult a word to define. But it would be a negation of justice not to do anything about it. Can you imagine the memory of the thousands of Jews and people who were put to death in the most barbaric conditions, and you don't even take the trouble to bring the fellow to justice? What a reflection upon our memory, that we can't be bothered to do this. No, I think it must go on; it'll gradually sort of wear itself out in the effluxion of time – it must do. But *not* to do it would, I think, be very wrong indeed.

There's just one thought that I have about Hess. Now, I've never heard such nonsense ... and with my experience of life, I hope I don't myself come into the category of the less people know about things, the more they shout ... I've heard so many people say, 'It's a disgrace about Hess – he should have been let go for humanitarian reasons,' and so forth. And they know *nothing* about the subject at all. As I understood it at the time, when it came to Hess's turn to be sentenced, the English, the French and the Americans could distinguish his case, particularly as he'd been nutting around in Abergavenny, from the others, and so they wanted to sentence him to life imprisonment. The Russians said, 'Not likely! You string him up the same as the others.' A lot of argument went on, and the Russian judge eventually gave way; but he gave way on the understanding: 'Right – if he's going to be sentenced to life imprisonment, that means imprisonment for life, and no nonsense about it.' And that's why the Russians wouldn't give way. Well, I mean, it was a negation of what was agreed, everybody shouting that he should be let go for humanitarian reasons.

Jean Tull, secretary

I always thought that it was right to hold the trial. And as for my own experience, I wouldn't have done without it. I count myself very lucky to have been youthful during the Second World War. I think young people today have missed a lot. It was horrible, in many ways, but it brought out marvellous characteristics in everyone as well. I think we do need something like that, nowadays – you know, people were pulling together much more.

Sylvia De La Warr, visitor

David [Maxwell-Fyfe] was tremendously determined to have the trial, so that it would stand up to history, so that what came out in the evidence would be totally proved. There were hundreds of thousands of documents, and he was frightfully careful: he would only bring something to trial when he'd got it *totally* proved by their own documents. He was very adamant that nothing should come up which wasn't foolproof, so they couldn't question it. He was only an amateur historian, but he did feel, in reading history, that you so often got people who were apologists later on, making it seem as though it hadn't happened, and he was very, very keen to do this trial properly and then to follow it up by building bridges again. And afterwards he did a lot of work towards getting the Germans back into Europe, and working with them. That was always his ultimate aim. He did feel that there should be some kind of retribution for people who knew that they were doing terrible acts, but he was a tremendously un-vindictive man – it was extraordinary, in a way, that he should have got his name linked with that trial, because he was the most humane person you could possibly have. But he was a very *interested* lawyer, very interested in cross-examination and the way you could do it. And I think on the whole he enjoyed the cross-examination he did there, although it was perhaps the hardest work he ever did in his life. I think he found Goering quite a handful. The whole thing was a very difficult and intricate job. But I think he felt that it was worth doing, and he kept up friendships for years afterwards – with our people, of course, but also with some of the German counsel. Looking back, it seems to me that the friendships that were formed, between the members of different delegations, must have been a good thing in themselves.

Whitney Harris, lawyer

The main legal objection to the entire proceedings was with respect to the crime of waging aggressive war. No person had ever been charged with that crime before, so how could these men be brought to trial when there was no statute in being at the time of their aggression? The Charter of the Tribunal was adopted in 1945, and it declared that waging aggressive war was a crime under international law, but that is after the fact. Therefore the argument was constantly and strenuously made by the German defence that when Hitler and his associates invaded Poland there was no statute in being which declared that waging aggressive war was a crime for which an individual leader could be personally punished. There were non-aggression pacts, but historically, violation of a non-aggression pact means that the *state* is responsible. This was their argument, and it was the most difficult one that we had to overcome. The position on the prosecutors' side was that international law does grow out of custom and out of international decisions and agreements of one kind or another, that there isn't any international legislative body which can sit down and write a law. There were many international agreements – which were not necessarily worldwide in scope, but related to one part of the world or another – which declared that the waging of aggressive war was a crime. The Kellogg-Briand Pact, to which Germany was a signatory, was a very powerful and strong declaration against the waging of aggressive war. We were the first ones to test it.

The statute of limitation applies in most societies, against most crimes, but in my view the crimes of these Nazis were so evil and so pervasive that I firmly believe that whenever an individual can be found now, and if the evidence is sufficient, they should be brought to trial. I strongly support the prosecution of these people. What sort of sentence they should receive is another question. The problem with the death sentence is this: that even though, after all these many years, the evidence may be sufficient to convince the judges that the individual did commit these crimes, we know that memories are faulty, and that after all these years one might not be sure of a particular identification. And I would think that there should be great caution in executing such a person.

I think most of us who were active participants in the trial have been extremely disappointed with the lack of real attention given to the trial in respect to the waging of aggressive war. On the whole I think we must say that the decision of the court in declaring aggressive war an international crime has not been particularly effective in the post-war period. On the other hand, the decision with respect to crimes against humanity has been more accepted. I can only hope that we do have the precedent now, that the waging of aggressive war is an international crime, and even if it's ignored in particular instances the precedent is still there. And if it comes before a tribunal in the future, I haven't any doubt that the tribunal will follow the Nuremberg precedent. The great problem is always, of course, getting the leader of the state, the aggressor, before a competent tribunal. How do you do this? I don't think anyone really felt that the Nuremberg decision itself was going to bring an end to war in the world, but the fact that there *was* this trial, that these principles *have* been enunciated by a competent tribunal, and that penalties *have* been placed upon those who were found to have been aggressors, in one major war at least, cannot help but have an ultimate salutary effect on international law.

I was in Nuremberg the night of the executions; I was going to represent Justice Jackson at the executions. But the military authorities informed me that since none of the other prosecutors had asked for people to represent them at the executions, it would be inappropriate for me to represent Justice Jackson. And I accepted that. At the time I was considerably younger than I am now, and while I wasn't broken up by it I was a little disappointed. It was a tremendous historical event, and I thought I would like to be able to say, 'Yes, I was there.' Now, forty years later, I'm very thankful I was *not* permitted to – I'm glad I don't have that in my mind. As a matter of fact I was close friends with a newsman who was allowed to be there, so I did get all the information anyway.

If you look at Justice Jackson's foreword to my book *Tyranny on Trial*, you will see that he says, 'His manuscript teaches me that the hard months of Nuremberg were well spent, in the most important, enduring and constructive work of my life.' That's Robert H. Jackson, who was after all an Associate Justice on the Supreme Court of the United States and former Attorney-General of the United States, and a very big and important man in our country. Now I'm not anything like Justice Jackson, but I would have to say that the period that I spent in Nuremberg was probably the most significant period of *my* life. As an experience, of course, it obviously was – much more so than the war itself. I think it *was* constructive: I've tried to do what little bit I can to keep the achievements of Nuremberg alive.

For a long time, though, after I wrote the book, which came out in 1954, I was tired of it, and I tried to put it all out of my mind. I had the worst part of the whole case. Right at the very beginning of the case, I was trying to find out what happened, and we didn't know about these atrocities, we really didn't know much about them at all. I'd heard that the British had a potential witness by the name of Otto Ohlendorff, who had been in the RHSA [Reich Security Main Office] of which my defendant, Kaltenbrunner, was the head. So I asked the British if, when they had finished with him, they could send him down to Nuremberg so that he could be interrogated. I wanted to find out more about the structure of RHSA, what these officers were and what they did. I started out like any lawyer does: 'Where were you born?,' and so forth. It turned out that during 1941, I think it was, he had been the Commandant of Einsatzgruppen D. So my next question was, 'How many men, women and children did you kill?' He said, 'Ninety thousand.' And once he had made that confession he told us the entire story about the killing of the Jews in the East. That had a tremendous effect on me personally; it was much more significant than the episode several months later when Rudolf Hoess told me how many people he had killed. This was my first exposure. So I can say without any hesitation that Nuremberg was the top part of my life as regards my legal career, but when I finished my book I had had enough of it and for many years I tried to put the whole Nuremberg thing out of my mind. I didn't want to think about these things any more. Now I don't mind.

Most lawyers involved in murder trials are dealing with the killing of one person. Occasionally someone is brought to trial after he has run amok and killed many people. Whitney Harris, interrogating the German security official Otto Ohlendorff in Nuremberg, asked him how many men, women and children he had killed, and the reply was 'Ninety thousand.' For all the participants in this book, as they performed their duties in Nuremberg, the trial demonstrated a capacity to draw on their skills in a precise, concrete – and often challenging and exhilarating – way, and yet to be in another sense almost beyond their comprehension, such was the enormity of the things it revealed and the problems it raised. Whitney Harris, collecting his evidence from Ohlendorff, Peter Uiberall, translating in the interpreter's box, Priscilla Belcher, nursing children the like of which she had never seen before, and many others were all doing an ordinary job in circumstances so extraordinary as to be unforgettable.

'It's no exaggeration', wrote 'Genet' in The New Yorker *of 15 March 1946, 'to say that the Nuremberg courthouse is the scene of the Nazis' last big battle,' and although it is impossible to know to what extent the defendants, either individually or collectively, intended it to be a battle for hearts and minds (it seems that Goering, at least, may have done so), they cannot be said to have completely lost that battle, in view of the controversy that still attaches to the concept of the trial today. Quite apart from the objections that have been raised over points of law, there have been questions directed at the very basis of the trial and the Allies' justification for holding it. 'If you look closely at any war you end up very cynical. You can't help it ... The winner decides the question of what is right and wrong,' says Seaghan Maynes, and several other participants would point to Russia's role in the Nuremberg Trial as an uncomfortable example of this – a victorious, prosecuting nation which had in all likelihood committed some atrocities of its own.*

Such moral ambiguities were not the only problems undermining the trial. Peter Uiberall, describing the occasion when Lord Lawrence delivered a harsh lecture to Goering and he, a former refugee, was called upon to translate it into German, notes that it was in some senses a futile exercise: 'It did not reach the same person who committed all those crimes.' Goering committed suicide before his execution and was never 'reached'; and, although doubt has been cast on controversial claims that the man held in Spandau prison for decades was not in fact Rudolf Hess, the other leading Nazis – Hitler, Himmler, Goebbels, Bormann – all managed to escape direct punishment at Allied hands.

Most if not all of this book's participants, therefore, would probably acknowledge that the Nuremberg Trial had its share of unsatisfactory and frustrating aspects, and the lawyers in particular have mixed (and mainly gloomy) feelings about its effects on subsequent international conduct. At the same time many participants draw attention to specific achievements of that trial which even its detractors would allow. Firstly, it put the material permanently on record, a source of great satisfaction to people who were at Nuremberg now that events such as the Holocaust are being questioned in some quarters. Many of those who were at the trial attest to the scrupulous efforts of lawyers, interpreters and the like to do their work fairly and take no account of any personal grudges. The trial also revealed the capacity of large numbers of people from different countries and backgrounds to work together with overall success, an achievement which was perceived at the time and which the ensuing years have done nothing to diminish.

It seems clear from what the participants say, however, that the primary importance of the Nuremberg Trial was – and is – symbolic; and they emphasize several aspects of this. Firstly, it appeared to many people that, in the ruins of Europe at the end of the war, the trial was a vital containment of overwhelming feelings of grief and anger: it imposed an official, ceremonial form on events as the tasks of taking stock and rebuilding began, and people who could see and read about the Nazi leaders in the dock felt less need to exact their own forms of payment from those who had made them suffer. This is not to say that such incidents did not occur: there are many illustrations in this book of the general atmosphere of lawlessness and revenge which prevailed at the time, and they emphasize how necessary it was to provide the restraint of the trial in order to prevent worse happenings. Despite the testimony of Priscilla Belcher and others, which shows some German resentment simmering away just below the surface, there seems little reason to doubt that, had all restraints been lifted, the violence would have proceeded almost entirely in one direction and would probably have been indiscriminate.

Other symbolic effects of the trial are less clear cut, and open to different forms of interpretation. Peter Uiberall, a man with a good deal of experience of Nazi behaviour, is emphatic in his view that one of the most important and humane aspects of the trial was the way in which it established and recorded who was responsible for what, thus freeing a great many German people from the burden of guilt by association. This co-exists with a view held by some others, and perhaps formed as they tried to discuss the concentration camps with the Germans, that in view of the limited scale of resistance in Nazi Germany most German people were in some sense guilty by association, and Germany was in effect a nation symbolically on trial. Thus some widely differing symbolic meanings were taken out of the trial according to people's views and experience.

It is possible that the trial has had other symbolic effects which cannot be measured. Several participants contend that the idea of Nuremberg has entered the culture and continues to affect international behaviour – that even where it is disregarded or disagreed with, it is known about and it forms part of the debate. This may not seem

much to those who originally had high hopes of its possible consequences. They learned early on that nobody could force Goering to
repent or apologize, and that the most they could hope for was to deter
future Goerings; the question of whether the trial achieved this,
however, is a highly subjective one which provides few certainties to
cling to.

On a personal level, by contrast, the participants in this book are in
little doubt about the trial's effects on their lives. Many of them speak
of great professional satisfaction, admirably summed up by Bernard
Meltzer: 'Nuremberg was an exciting experience – it called into play all
kinds of skills and arts that lawyers try to develop. It involved one in
the legal and moral dilemmas arising from the winding up of one of the
greatest, if not the greatest, moral tragedies that our history has had to
confront. It pushed one into thinking about the nature of law,
standards of personal responsibility and the prerequisites for a legal
system; it encouraged people to think about how primitive and fragile
our institutions of law were, and still are, and how they might be
strengthened.' Work apart, many found that the social life shared by
four nations and the opportunities for travel and observation, not to
mention the feelings attached to being part of an immense operation,
combined to make it an intensely exciting time. The people who felt
that their Nuremberg experience had a profoundly negative effect on
their lives, that in some way it marked them for ever, are equally
emphatic on the subject.

In view of such differences of opinion and recollection, it is
impossible to end this book with any kind of collective statement.
Instead, the handful of participants who have returned to Germany
and Nuremberg since the late 1940s recall what particularly struck
them about the country and the city that they had known in such
different circumstances. Nobody involved in the Nuremberg Trial
wanted time to stand still in Nuremberg, or in Germany. All their
efforts, in the broad sense, were directed towards working through the
past and ushering in a future for Germany as well as for her
conquerors. The comments in the epilogue which follows – whether
wry, amused, poignant, large-minded, or simply happy – come from
people who were brought face to face with the future for which they
had helped to prepare.

Epilogue: going back

Alfred Steer, administrative head, language division

I didn't go back until 1963. I couldn't believe my eyes, the way they had built that place up. I had to look for evidence of the war. Those Germans really had done a job. I noticed that in several German cities the city fathers used the opportunity to rebuild in more logical, attractive and effective ways: they would cut a street through where there hadn't been one before, and so on. I've been back several times. I was exchange professor at the University of Erlangen, which is only a few kilometres north of Nuremberg.

Mary Burns, secretary

I went back to Nuremberg in 1956, with a friend. But it had all been completely rebuilt and I couldn't find my way around any more. The Grand Hotel had been all done up and it was now a darned elegant place to stay, and we weren't allowed into the Palace of Justice. In the end, to my humiliation, I had to suggest that we take a bus tour of the city. We had an English-speaking guide, and he could probably tell that my friend and I were Americans. And as we were going round the old city, he said, 'You Americans paid for this twice, first when you destroyed it and then again when you rebuilt it.' I was so mad. I'm still mad when I talk about it. I could have thrown him off the bus and hit him. He was taunting us, although the way I felt at the time, 'taunting' is too mild a word – it's cleaning up the act. I thought it was insulting. And that was the only anti-German reaction I can ever remember having. When I was living there I never had any feeling of antipathy, of being the military occupiers, at all.

Peter Uiberall, interpreter

I didn't know my way around, it was so different – completely built up and restored. It affected me in a sort of a positive sense, going back. That that terribly destroyed place could come back like that ... not in a bad way. Nurembergers are very much aware of the Holocaust, much more so, perhaps, than people in some other parts of Germany. They never forget it. They have an inscription on the door of the court-room that reminds them of the trial. They have a lot of memorabilia of that time.

Joseph Stone, lawyer, Subsequent Proceedings

I got back to Germany somewhere around 1972. Actually we were in France, but I said to my wife, 'Let's go to Germany for a few days. I'd like to go back to Nuremberg and see what happened, physically.' The town was rebuilt. The interesting thing was that the first thing they started to rebuild, back in the forties, during the period of the trial, was the wall. They needed housing desperately but they were putting up the wall, which I suppose from the German viewpoint was the logical thing to do because it was part of the old tradition. By the early seventies Nuremberg had been rebuilt. The inner city had been clobbered with bombs, and was just one mass of rubble. All of this was gone, all of these houses had been put back, somewhat in the shape and style in which they had been. The interiors were just magnificent, I'm told.

I stayed at the Grand Hotel, where I had been billeted for a year and three-quarters. When I was there in the forties, the Germans behind the desk were very, very co-operative: if there was anything you wanted, you got it. When I went there in the seventies, the first thing I had was an argument with the guy behind the counter, because he was charging me more than I had been advised by the American Automobile Association, that had handled my travel arrangements, and I was putting up a fuss about it. It wasn't that much more, but it was no reason for him to be charging me. And he was very nasty about the whole thing, which struck me as funny because, you know, twenty-five years earlier ... role-reversal. One of the waiters in the restaurant had been there during the trials, and I stopped him to talk. What was interesting to me was that he spoke with such great nostalgia about that period. 'Ah,' he said, 'those were the good old days.' And there was a reason for it. We were leaving cigarettes as tips. For a dinner, two cigarettes was the tip, for lunch, maybe one cigarette, which seems kind of silly today – even then, it seemed silly. But in terms of the number of cigarettes that a waiter would get ... by the end of the month he was making many times what the ordinary German was making. Not only that: this particular waiter had apparently been utilized quite a bit when the Americans, French, British, Czechs, whoever – I guess primarily the Americans – were giving parties. Whatever was left over he could take home, so while the Germans were having a rough time of it he was having a great time of it, making more money and having more food than he knew what to do with. So he regarded that as the good old days, and I thought that was kind of cute.

Brady Bryson, lawyer

I went back to Nuremberg about three or four years ago – the first time I had been there since 1946. I found myself in that part of the world, in Munich, and I took a car and went down to have a look at it. The courtroom is not easy to find or get into; it's not something that's publicized at Nuremberg, or that tourists go through regularly. But it is preserved, and if you go to the Palace of Justice and make inquiries, and are patient, someone will unlock a door and let you in. So I did this. While it was essentially laid out and physically set up as I recalled it, the most surprising discovery was how small it was. It seemed to me like a very minor court-room, and I had in my mind – having been young and somewhat excited – that it had been a very impressive, majestic kind of court-room, where the legal institutions of the Western world were gathered to hold a momentous, historic trial. And they were. But it was a small room, no bigger than the average trial court-room in America, of which there are hundreds all over the country.

Priscilla Belcher, visitor
I finally went back to Nuremberg in 1982. They had built it up and restored it remarkably, and done a really amazing job. The guide was talking about all they had done in repairing the damage, and she started to talk about how the Allies blew up the city for no reason, when the war was almost over, and destroyed this ancient place. Some of the Americans were saying, 'Well, wasn't that *awful* of them?', you know, and I said, 'Wait a minute. I remember seeing pamphlets that had been dropped by the British, telling them to get out, or else they would bomb it, and apparently they didn't get out. I think they got two warnings.' The guide sort of gulped, and then she said, 'Well, the war was practically over and they had no reason to.' And there happened to be a man in the group who said angrily, 'I beg to differ with you. I was fighting for my life on the outskirts of Nuremberg, *after* that time.' She never said a word. She never apologized. She hardly looked at me or him again during our tour. I still found this defensiveness among some of the Germans when I was back there. And I remember talking to somebody else, who said, 'Look what you did to Cologne, firebombing those innocent people,' and I said, 'Well, look what *you* did to Coventry, and Rotterdam!' When I was there in 1946, they couldn't really have done anything except try to defend themselves, because some of them were only just beginning to learn the depths of what had gone on and facing the uncertain future. They were more worried about the Russians than anything. We had an ammunition dump that blew up, and the Germans all thought the Russians were coming. There was pandemonium as they tried to evacuate every little town, and some of the patients who'd been under bombing before were jumping out of their beds and getting under them.

But to go back in 1982, and find Germany going full tilt and blooming, was amazing. Returning to Nuremberg was very eerie – I couldn't make sense out of it. And to have this propaganda, which nobody asked for, thrown at us by the guide; in Munich, as well, the guide did something of that nature. It was a strange experience, and I often almost wondered if I really were there.

Patrick Cooper, airman
I went back to the States, and went to university, and lived in New York for a few years, doing various jobs in advertising and what not. Then I married an English girl and came over to live in London. We travel on the

continent quite frequently and go back to the States from time to time, but I didn't go back to Germany until 1987. I went to a part of Germany where I was happy. After I'd been in Germany about two and a half years I was moved from Nuremberg to Wiesbaden. You wouldn't believe two towns could be so different. Nuremberg was very German, and Wiesbaden was cosmopolitan, international, with a totally different atmosphere. And by 1948 or 1949 things were beginning to improve, and Wiesbaden was a very pleasant place to be. I have the happiest memories of Wiesbaden, quite, quite different from those of Nuremberg. So I went back there, and it was marvellous. I was confronting myself. I didn't look up any of the people I'd known – they were probably all gone anyway. I spent three or four days just wandering around the town, the places I used to know.

Bernard Meltzer, lawyer
I haven't been back to Germany. I've thought of going back to Nuremberg, of taking my wife there and showing her what's happened, but – and I don't know whether my memory of Nazism, or what the trial exposed, or something else was material – it was just that other places seemed more appealing to me. Maybe one day I'll have a look. Who knows?

Suggested further reading

Many books and articles have been written on the subject of the Nuremberg Trial. The following is a selection of works which may interest the readers of this book. For those wishing to follow the actual trial as it unfolded in the court-room, the transcripts, known as *Trial of the Major War Criminals before the International Military Tribunal, Nuremberg, 14 November 1945–1 October 1946*, were published in 42 volumes (Nuremberg, 1947–9). Roger Barrett, together with William E. Jackson (Justice Jackson's son), edited *Nazi Conspiracy and Aggression* (8 vols., Washington, 1946–8), a collection of the documentary evidence used in the prosecution case. Bradley Smith's *The Road to Nuremberg* (London, 1981) charts the setting up of the trial, from initial idea to final preparations; the same author's *Reaching Judgment at Nuremberg* (New York and London, 1977), Robert Conot's *Judgment at Nuremberg* (London, 1983) and Ann and John Tusa's *The Nuremberg Trial* (London, 1983) all provide full and valuable accounts of the trial itself. Whitney Harris, a participant in this book, wrote *Tyranny on Trial* (Dallas, 1954), and another study by a lawyer who was at Nuremberg is Telford Taylor's *Nuremberg and Vietnam* (New York, 1970); there are also numerous articles in legal journals, including two by participants in this book, Bernard Meltzer's 'A Note on Some Aspects of the Nuremberg Debate', *Chicago Law Review*, 14 (1947), pp. 455–69, and Leonard Wheeler's 'Why the Nuremberg Trials are Still Going On', *Bulletin of the Boston Bar Association*, 17.5 (1946), pp. 97–105. Recent writing in this field includes Geoffrey Best's *Humanity in Warfare: The Modern History of the International Law Of Armed Conflict* (London, 1980), and his Stenton Lecture, *Nuremberg and After: The Continuing History of War Crimes and Crimes against Humanity* (University of Reading, 1984).

Personal records of the trial include *A Train of Powder* (London, 1984) by the writer Rebecca West; Airey Neave's *Nuremberg: A Personal Record of the Trial of the Major Nazi War Criminals in 1945–6* (Sevenoaks, 1980); *The Infamous of Nuremberg* (London, 1969), published in America as *I Was the Nuremberg Jailer* (New York, 1968), by (Colonel) Burton Andrus, who was in charge of the prison where the defendants were held; and *Nuremberg Diary* (London, 1948) by G.M.

Gilbert, the prison psychologist. A work of fiction that is very resonant in this context is David Lodge's *Out of the Shelter* (Harmondsworth, 1986), a novel based on his own experience as a teenager visiting post-war occupied Germany. And a book which has sparked off much controversy in Germany is Niklas Frank's *Der Vater: eine Abrechnung* (Munich, n.d. [*c*.1988]), which amounts to a denunciation of his father, Hans Frank.

Finally, there is much of interest in William J. Bosch's *Judgment on Nuremberg: American Attitudes towards the Major German War-Crime Trials* (Chapel Hill, 1970), and in the journalism of the period, which ranges from straight reporting in the major British, American and European newspapers to impressionistic pieces such as the series of occasional articles which appeared in the *New Yorker* during 1946.

The Subsequent Proceedings

* Some sentences commuted.
† One defendant separated by illness.
‡ One defendant committed suicide.

name of case	Dates held (from opening of case to judgements rendered)	No. of defendants	Death sentence	Life imprisonment	25 years	20 years	15 years	Sentence of under 15 years; forfeiture of property; credit given for time in prison and released	Acquitted	Nature of case
Medical case	21 Nov. 1946 – 19, 20 Aug. 1947	23	7	5	–	2	1	1	7	Senior Nazi doctors; people who set up concentration camp experiments.
Milch case	2 Jan. 1947 – 16, 17 April 1947	1	–	1	–	–	–	–	–	Participation in forced labour programme; medical experiments at Dachau.
Justice case	5 May 1947 – 3, 4 Dec. 1947	14	–	4	–	–	–	6	4	People who held top legal posts under the Nazi regime.
SS, Pohl, case*	8 April 1947 – 3 Nov. 1947	18	4	3	1	1	–	6	3	Pohl and other SS officials, responsible for administering various camps, mines and factories.
Flick case	21 April 1947 – 22 Dec. 1947	6	–	–	–	–	–	3	3	Industrialist and his principal associates, who worked closely with the Nazi regime.
Farben case	27 Aug. 1947 – 29, 30 July 1948	23	–	–	–	–	–	13	10	Officials of Farben-industrie A.G., a large chemicals manufacturer which worked closely with the Nazi regime.
Hostages case	15 July 1947 – 19 Feb. 1948	12	–	2	–	2	1	–	2	Military personnel charged with various war crimes.
RuSHA case	20 Oct. 1947 – 10 March 1948	14	–	1	2	1	3	6	1	Officials of RuSHA (acronym of a German title), a programme concerned with the forced Germanization, evacuation or extermination of nationals of occupied countries.
Einsatzgruppen case	20 Oct. 1947 – 8, 9, 10 April 1948	24	15	2	–	3	–	4†	–	Units responsible for mass murders.
Krupp case	8 Dec. 1947 – 31 July 1948	12	–	–	–	–	–	11	1	Industrialist and his principal associates, who worked closely with the Nazi regime.
Ministries case	6 Jan. 1948 – 14 April 1949	21	–	–	1	2	3	13	2	Wide range of influential personnel including bankers, government ministers and SS leaders.
High Command case	5 Feb. 1948 – 27 Oct. 1948	14	–	2	–	3	2	4‡	2	Military personnel charged with various war crimes.

Index

In view of the large number of people who make fleeting appearances in this book, some measure of selectivity has been used in the compilation of the index. Likewise, entries for organizations and themes are confined to those of major importance.

16X   (keep)   PDP
26/08/05   L

THE
SCARBOROUGH
PUBLIC LIBRARY
BOARD